M&E BECbooks

Practical Business Education
Book 1

M&E BECbooks

Practical Business Education

An integrated approach

Book 1

R.D. Anstis

S.H.E. Fishlock

C.E. Stafford

MACDONALD AND EVANS

MACDONALD & EVANS LTD.
Estover, Plymouth PL6 7PZ

First published 1978

ISBN 0 7121 2336 9

Printed in Great Britain by
Hollen Street Press Ltd,
Slough

Preface

This combined textbook and workbook has been specifically designed to meet the demands of the Business Education Council's General Level core modules through a structured, integrated approach whilst, at the same time, permitting students to prepare for the individual examinations required by BEC at that level.

The central theme, the World of Work, Module 3, provides the "pivot" around which the other two modules (Business Calculations, Module 2 and People and Communications, Module 1) are structured. The information is presented in such a way as to provide ample opportunities for student-based work, and to allow for the development of local themes from a sound factual basis. Every effort has been made to keep the student aware of the broader issues involved and of the practical relevance of the subject to everyday life.

The step-by-step approach adopted in Business Calculations is designed to enable the student to use the worked examples as a basis for the completion of Tasks and Exercises. At no stage are calculators specifically mentioned: indeed, the use of calculators is discouraged until the basic concepts of numeracy are mastered. Then, and only then, should calculators be used for assignments.

Similarly, the graduated stages in People and Communications enable students to develop those basic skills which are essential if they are to achieve the level of competence necessary for functioning effectively as employees. Great emphasis is placed on the basic communication skills, and it has been a deliberate policy to avoid over-simplification of language and terminology, so that the student will become used to communicating in terms drawn from the context of working situations.

The Units of *Practical Business Education* contain the essential factual information, supported by graduated tasks and assignments at each stage, most of which are designed to integrate and reinforce the core of information in the "pivot" module while enabling the student to recognise and appreciate the underlying interdependence of traditional subject areas. As the student progresses through both books, more and more emphasis is placed on the practical application of knowledge and skills to realistic, work-orientated assignments. Course objectives are achieved through modular and cross-modular exercises, many of which will prove suitable for in-course assessment, or as a starting point for cross-modular assignments.

Lecturers will note an apparent disparity between the level of work in Section I and that in Sections II and III of many early units. This is unavoidable because of the need to impart the basic skills of numeracy and literacy whilst aiming to achieve the specified objectives of the pivot module. As a result, there is a deliberate fluctuation in the level of work and comprehension required of the student, so that he/she will not only perform practical tasks to demonstrate and reinforce basic concepts, but also be able to appreciate the wider application of such skills to more complex situations.

Practical Business Education is also eminently suitable for basic clerical and commercial courses in both secondary schools and colleges of further education.

TO THE STUDENT

In order to help you gain most advantage from this book, it has been designed as a combined workbook and textbook. As a result you will find yourself faced with three different types of written work.

TASKS are an integral part of the text and answers should be written in the spaces provided.

EXERCISES are not designed to be completed within the book, but should be presented as normal written work. It is essential that this is stored carefully for future reference.

CROSS-MODULAR EXERCISES are similar to, but more complex than other work, because they involve aspects of a number of different subject areas. These should also be stored carefully as they will form a useful reference bank.

September 1978

R.D.A.

S.H.E.F.

C.E.S.

Contents

UNIT 1

Achievement Checklist
When you have completed this unit you should have a knowledge of:

- **The type and purpose of the different organisations in the public and private sectors;**
- **The basic rules of number, i.e. addition, subtraction, division, multiplication;**
- **One method of storing your course work to make reference and retrieval easier;**
- **The functions, arrangement and use of a dictionary;**
- **The functions of different words in a sentence, i.e. the parts of speech.**

SECTION I

BUSINESS ORGANISATIONS

The United Kingdom has what is called a mixed economy. Basically this means that some of the organisations that produce goods and/or services are owned by the state, whilst others are owned by members of the public in a private capacity. In a few, but increasing number of cases, the organisation itself is owned partly by the state and partly by individuals.

Within this mixture there is a variety of organisations of different shapes and sizes. Some are very large and wealthy, whilst others are small and struggle to survive. On the other hand, some very large organisations experience difficulties on continuing in business, whilst some small businesses are prosperous and flourishing.

In the private sector of the economy, firms must make a net profit in order to survive. That is, a firm must at least cover all its running costs or it will be forced into debt and, sooner or later, have to close down. (There are many emotional and emotive arguments about profits, but they are, or perhaps should be, about *how* profits are used rather than whether or not they should be made.) In most cases businesses will try to make more profit than the bare minimum to provide some reward for the owner(s), for it is the owner(s) who subscribed the money (*capital*) which enabled the business to be started. In addition the firm may wish to "plough back" profits to provide for new plant and equipment and/or for expansion.

The different types of organisations in the private sector which are primarily concerned with profit-making are:

(*a*) the sole proprietor;
(*b*) the partnership;
(*c*) the private limited company;
(*d*) the public limited company.

Usually the impetus for starting a business in the first place is to increase the wealth of the owner(s). However some owners, particularly sole proprietors and partners, could make more money by working for others, and probably enjoy shorter working hours as well, but they prefer the prestige and independence of being self-employed.

The type of organisation is often pre-determined by the size of the proposed enterprise and the number of principals involved. If only one person is starting the business then it will be a sole proprietorship (or sole trader as it is often known). If more than one owner is involved then the choice will be between a partnership and a private limited company, as the formation of a public limited company is, in effect, reserved for larger established businesses. In some cases the size and nature of the intended business will restrict the choice of type of organisation. For example, sole proprietors are more common in certain trades, such as farming and retailing, because:

(*a*) traditionally they have been small-scale enterprises;
(*b*) they can be started with relatively small amounts of money;
(*c*) their physical location and/or lack of size means that they are neither worth taking over as they are, nor do they provide serious competition for the larger firms.

Furthermore, it is fairly obvious that if someone decides to set up in business on their own, say as a newsagent or an electrician, then the only type of organisation that would be appropriate would be a sole proprietorship. Similarly if two people decide to start a business (for whatever purpose) then the appropriate type might be a partnership, particularly if the owners are combining skill and capital or youth and age rather than equal amounts of capital. In both of these kinds of businesses the proprietors are cast very much in the mould of the classic entrepeneur – providing all the finance (capital), having full control, taking all the risks, receiving all the profits and bearing any losses.

The private limited company is usually formed by the proprietors of a small family business, so that ownership can be spread amongst a larger number of people with the resulting possibilities of obtaining greater amounts of capital – usually for expansion. At the same time control can be retained by the original owners by restricting the ownership and transfer of shares (i.e. units of ownership).

It is often this quest for more capital for expansion that provides the stimulus for the formation of a public limited company. As the name implies, ownership is extended to the public at large so that those who have surplus funds can buy shares in the company.

If, as is hoped, the company uses the increased capital effectively, then the shareholders (or owners) will receive a share of the profits made. In theory all business organisation activities are pursued primarily for the benefit of the owners, but in the case of the public limited company this may not always be true. In the really big companies ownership is often spread over many thousands of shareholders, and as they cannot all be involved in the day-to-day running of the business they elect representatives (directors) to look after their interests. As the directors may be the nominees of large institutional shareholders, their interests may not correspond exactly with those of the shareholder with only a small stake in the company and whose views may not carry much weight. Furthermore, the directors themselves must depend to a large extent on the advice they receive from the managers of the business, who are full-time employees, and that advice may be influenced by the management's views of what is best for them rather than what is best for the owners. For example, management salaries are usually set amounts that do not vary much, if at all, in response to the level of profits made by the company. Therefore, it can happen that as long as the owners are satisfied with the company's performance, the management has little incentive, other than increased status and prestige, to improve profitability. However, the management will not want the company to do badly as this will present a threat to their position, and thus an element of expansion might seem desirable to ensure job security – particularly if owners can be persuaded that it is also in their own interests. Expansion may take place for two reasons: first, the firm may try to avoid recessions in a particular industry by *diversification* into other industries, e.g. a tobacco company may expand by buying a food or drinks company; secondly, the firm may try to achieve greater security by becoming more dominant within its own industry (if it should achieve total dominance it would be known as a *monopoly*). In this case, one of the major arguments for the organisation becoming bigger is that it will achieve *economies of scale* by spreading its increased costs over a proportionately larger number of units of production and/or sales.

There are other kinds of organisations in the private sector which are usually classified as being "non-profit making". This does not mean that they do not make profits at all (for they must cover their costs) but that they have been formed for purposes other than making profits for owners. Such organisations are:

(*a*) co-operative societies,
(*b*) building societies,
(*c*) friendly societies,
(*d*) sports and social clubs.

The first co-operative society was founded by the Rochdale Pioneers (a group of twenty-eight weavers) in 1844 with the purpose of providing good quality household goods and necessities (particularly food) at reasonable prices at a time when, by modern standards, economic and social conditions were particularly harsh for working people. The aim was, and is, to return any profit made in excess of running costs to the customers in proportion to the value of their purchases.

The Industrial Revolution raised living standards for many, particularly those such as engineers and artisans who had the skills needed to manufacture and maintain the new machines. Many of these people earned relatively high wages and they wished to use some of their new-found wealth to buy houses to gain the security of tenure rented accommodation could not offer. Building societies were formed in response to this demand. Groups of people joined together and agreed to save a certain sum of money each week. When sufficient was available it was used to build a house which was then "raffled" amongst the members of the society. The holder of the lucky ticket "won" the completed house. The winner continued as a member of the society until all the other members had a house, and then the society was wound up. Such societies were known as terminating societies, whereas their modern equivalents are known as permanent societies. The permanent society pays interest on the money deposited with it, and then lends the money to people (as mortgages) so that they can buy their own house. The borrower pays a higher rate of interest than is paid to the depositor, and the difference between the two covers the administration expenses of the society.

Many friendly societies (or clubs, as they were often known) were formed in the days when people who were unemployed or too ill to work received no money, and had to rely on charity (often from those very little better off than themselves) or the work-house if they and their families were not to starve. Members paid small sums each week into the "club" and then received money according to certain stated scales if they were unemployed or ill, or payments were made to their next of kin if they died. The advent of the welfare state largely eliminated the need for these societies, but some survive.

There are many thousands of clubs around the country which have been formed for social and sporting purposes. Whilst, in the main, they rely on members' subscriptions for their revenue, an increasing number of them provide bar and refreshment facilities and gambling machines which make a profit. Such organisations are not really trading concerns, and any profits they do make are used to further the aims of the club.

You have seen that there are many different types of organisation in the private sector of the economy which are used to serve different purposes. In the state-controlled sector, however, there is one main type of business organisation – the public corporation.

State control – through the public corporation – over parts of the economy has come about for a number of reasons: some industries such as gas and electricity are "natural monopolies" (this means that it is common sense to have only one supplier – we do not need or want five electricity cables or six gas mains, each from a different supplier, to meet our demands; one of each is not only sufficient but also cheaper); others are socially and strategically important (transport); and still others have been taken over to avoid large-scale unemployment or to preserve old and time-honoured institutions which may be considered worth saving "in the national interest" (Rolls-Royce (1971) Ltd). Opponents of nationalisation sometimes argue that state control has been established for purely political reasons.

Public corporations are usually established by an Act of Parliament to "nationalise" an industry and thereby create, in most cases, a government monopoly, e.g. the National Coal Board, British Rail, the British Gas Corporation, the Post Office. The provisions of each Act vary somewhat to reflect the needs of individual industries, but in general all the corporations are ultimately responsible to the people of the country, i.e. the owners, through their representatives in the House of Commons.

NOTE: Not all government economic activity is controlled by public corporations. Some state-provided services are controlled directly by government departments, e.g. education, health, and the armed forces. In certain circumstances some services can be operated in conjunction with local authorities, who may also provide other services according to local needs.

TASK ONE

(i) What is a "mixed economy"? ______________________

____

(ii) What is the name given to the money used to start a business? ______________________

____

(iii) State one reason why a partnership might be converted into a private limited company. ______________________

____

(iv) Who are the owners of a public limited company? ______________________

____

(v) List *all* the different types of organisation in the private sector. ______________________

____

(vi) State two reasons why a large company may wish to expand. ____________

____

____

(vii) Why are co-operative societies classified as non-profit making organisations?

____

(viii) What is a mortgage? ____________

____

(ix) Explain, with four examples, what is meant by the term "natural monopoly".

____

____

____

(x) What is a public corporation? ____________

____

SECTION II

BASIC OPERATIONS WITH NUMBERS

Any business, no matter how large, intends to conduct its affairs in such a way as to make a profit. To achieve this the business must sell its goods at a price which will cover not only the cost of the goods but also any additional charges. Where the income from sales exceeds the cost of goods sold the result is a *gross profit*; where the cost of goods exceeds income from sales the result is a *gross loss* (the "goods" sold may be "services"). For example:

A wholesaler buys and sells 1,000 units.
Purchases: 1,000 units at £23 – cost £23,000
Sales : 1,000 units at £34 – income £34,000
∴ gross profit will be £34,000 less £23,000
Total gross profit = £11,000

$$\text{Gross profit per unit} = \frac{\text{£}11{,}000}{1{,}000} = \text{£}11$$

However the business must cover other expenses such as wages and salaries, rent and rates, heating, lighting and many more. This must be taken into account when considering the profit made by the business. The gross profit less expenses and overheads gives the *net profit* for the business. Again if expenses exceed the gross profit the result will be a *net loss*.

Suppose, for example, in the case above the operating expenses amount to £2,000, then the net profit can be found as follows:

Gross profit	£11,000
Operating expenses	2,000
Net profit	£ 9,000

Net profit per unit = $\frac{£9,000}{1,000}$ = £9

In order to find the gross profit and net profit in total and per unit it was necessary to use fundamental arithmetic processes – *addition, subtraction, multiplication* and *division.*

ADDITION

For the successful completion of these processes there is one basic principle that must be borne in mind. This is that each digit in a number has its own special place; for example the digit 7 in the numbers 70 and 7 is totally different and if we add them the result is 77 not 14. This error can be easily made with large numbers when they are added together. An orderly arrangement in columns, with each digit in its appropriate place lined up under and above digits of the same magnitude, is essential. For example:

Add together the following numbers: 1,368, 283, 420

The incorrect way:	The correct way:
1,368	1,368
283	283
+ 420	+ 420
16,930	2,071

The 2 in 420 represents 20 not 2 alone; it must therefore be aligned with the 6 in 1,368 and the 8 in 283.

TASK ONE

Add the following:

(i) 285 + 473 + 829

(ii) 1,805 + 172 + 408

(iii) 3,452 + 4,836 + 5,497

(iv) 425 + 709 + 200 + 382

(v) 15,321 + 6,849 + 1,127 + 9,076

EXERCISE

Add together the following:

(*a*) 742, 9, 306
(*b*) 589, 698, 4,086
(*c*) 1,001, 230, 3,607
(*d*) 1,076, 716, 849, 2,967
(*e*) 1,546, 2,713, 818, 624
(*f*) 597, 747, 4,816, 5,937, 12,967

SUBTRACTION

The same fundamental rule must also be followed when one number is subtracted from another. For example:

(*a*) Subtract 613 from 829

The 3 must be aligned with the 9, the 1 with the 2 and 6 with 8.

The incorrect way:	The correct way:
8 29	829
− 61 3	− 613
1926	216

In this example subtraction is easy since a small digit is subtracted from a larger digit in each case. Problems arise when a large digit is subtracted from a smaller digit. This is best seen through an example:

(*b*) Subtract 368 from 754

```
  754
- 368
  386
```

Step 1. The 8 cannot be subtracted from the 4, in which case 1 is taken from the next higher digit and placed with the 4 giving 14. Now 14 − 8 is 6.

Step 2. The 1 is then taken from the next higher, changing the 5 to 4.

Step 3. The 6 cannot now be taken from the new 4, so again 1 is taken from the next higher digit giving 14. Now 14 − 6 is 8.

Step 4. The 1 is then taken from the next higher, changing 7 to 6 and finally 3 is taken from 6 giving 3.

The answer can be verified by adding the lower two numbers together. Thus 368 + 386 = 754.

TASK TWO

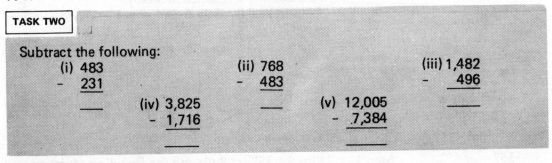

Subtract the following:

```
(i) 483        (ii) 768        (iii) 1,482
  - 231           - 483            -   496
    ___             ___                ___

(iv) 3,825        (v) 12,005
   - 1,716           - 7,384
     _____             ______
```

EXERCISE

Subtract the first quantity from the second:

(*a*) 135, 347
(*b*) 219, 478
(*c*) 1,687, 5,468
(*d*) 6,582, 8,140
(*e*) 747, 12,435
(*f*) 10,101, 110,000

Check your answers by addition.

MULTIPLICATION

When numbers are multiplied together the result can be obtained by adding a number to itself a specific number of times. For example, when 5 is multiplied by 3 the result may be obtained by saying 5 X 3 = 5 + 5 + 5 = 15. This method is not practical with large numbers. Suppose a business buys 2,500 articles each costing £15.75, finding the total cost would take a very long time if continous addition is employed.

The multiplication of the numbers 10 and under does not present a major problem. Difficulties occur when one or both of the numbers are greater than 10. These can however be overcome by treating each digit individually and then adding. Again the appropriate placing of digits is important. For example:

(*a*) Multiply 246 by 3

```
 246
 X 3
  18
 12
 6
 738
```

Step 1. 6 multiplied by 3 is 18. The 8 is placed directly below the 3, the 1 below the 4.

Step 2. 4 multiplied by 3 is 12. The 2 is placed below the 1 in 18, the 1 beside the 2 under the original 2.

Step 3. 2 multiplied by 3 is 6, and it is aligned under the 1, in 12.

Step 4. Add the results of the multiplication together.

Thus 246 X 3 = 738

This long approach is unnecessary, for addition can be completed mentally when multiplying by numbers less than 10.

(*b*) Multiply 246 by 3 once more:

```
 246
 X 3
 738
```

Step 1. 6 multiplied by 3 is 18. The 8 is placed under the 3 and the 1 retained mentally.

Step 2. 4 multiplied by 3 is 12. The 1 from Step 1 is added to the 12 giving 13. The 3 is placed under 4 beside the 8 and the 1 retained mentally.

Step 3. 2 multiplied by 3 is 6 and the 1 retained is added giving 7.

Thus 246 X 3 = 738

A combination of these two approaches may be adopted when multiplying by a number greater than 10.

(*c*) Multiply 357 by 48

```
   357
   X48
 2,856
 1,428
17,136
```

Step 1. Multiply 357 by 8 placing the first digit of the answer below the 8.

Step 2. Multiply 357 by 4, but since the 4 is in reality 40 the first digit of the answer is aligned under the 5.

Step 3. Add the results of the multiplications together.

Thus 357 X 48 = 17,136

(*d*) The same answer can be obtained by using the largest digit first.

357	Step 1.	Multiply 357 by 4, but since 4 is in reality 40 first place a zero at the right-hand end of the answer line below the 8 and align the first digit below the 4.
X48		
14,280		
2,856	Step 2.	Multiply 357 by 8 aligning the first digit of the answer below the 0.
17,136		
	Step 3.	Add each multiplication together.

Thus 357 X 48 = 17,136

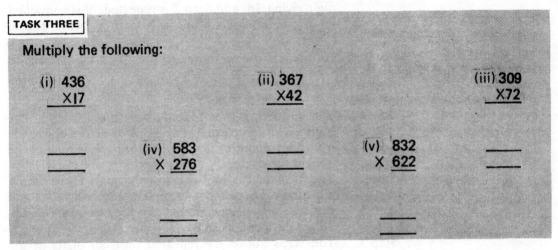

TASK THREE

Multiply the following:

(i) 436 X17

(ii) 367 X42

(iii) 309 X72

(iv) 583 X 276

(v) 832 X 622

EXERCISE

Multiply the following numbers together:

(*a*) 157 X 8
(*b*) 256 X 20
(*c*) 175 X 36
(*d*) 352 X 124
(*e*) 604 X 97
(*f*) 848 X 35
(*g*) 12,960 X 35
(*h*) 1,348 X 550
(*i*) 875 X 856
(*j*) 1,896 X 395

DIVISION

Just as multiplication in its simplest form is repeated addition, so division can be considered as repeated subtraction. Thus when 45 is divided by 9 the result will be the number of complete 9s that can be subtracted from 45.

i.e. 45 − 9 = 36 − 9 = 27 − 9 = 18 − 9 = 9 − 9 = 0

Therefore 45 divided by 9 is 5 since 9 can be subtracted from 45 on 5 occasions.

Again this approach is impractical where large numbers are involved but the same principle holds true. The number being divided, called the *dividend*, is reduced in size by subtraction until the dividing number has been removed as many times as possible. The result of removing this *divisor* is called the *quotient*. For example:

(*a*) For divisors less than 10:

Divide 576 by 9

```
9 | 576
     64
```

Step 1. Taking the largest digit 5 write down the number of times 9 is contained in it. If this digit is less than the divisor it is combined with the next digit.

Step 2. The number of times the divisor is contained in 57 is 6 since 9 X 6 = 54. This is written down below the 7.

Step 3. The excess of 3 (57 – 54) is combined with the next digit giving 36, and Step 2 is repeated. 9 is contained in 36, 4 times, and the 4 is written below the 6.

Thus 576 ÷ 9 = 64

(*b*) For divisors greater than 10 the steps are more detailed but the process is performed in the same manner.

Divide 3,419 by 13

```
     263
13 | 3419
     26
      81
      78
       39
       39
      nil
```

Step 1. The quotient is now placed above the dividend. The number of complete 13s in 34 (2) is placed above the 4. The product of 2 and 13 (26) is placed under the 34 and subtracted.

Step 2. The next digit is brought down giving 81 and Step 1 repeated. There are 6 complete 13s in 81 (78) and the result is placed above the digit brought down. 78 is subtracted from 81.

Step 3. The steps above are repeated until all digits in the dividend have been used.

Thus 3,419 ÷ 13 = 263

TASK FOUR

Complete the following:

(*a*) 4 | 936

(*b*) 5 | 8,525

(*c*) 29 | 41,586

(*d*) 145 | 37,410

EXERCISE

Answer the following:

(*a*) 2,954 ÷ 7
(*b*) 3,906 ÷ 9
(*c*) 532 ÷ 38
(*d*) 9,792 ÷ 64
(*e*) 4,610 ÷ 325
(*f*) 3,182 ÷ 86
(*g*) 25,288 ÷ 436
(*h*) 19,755 ÷ 11
(*i*) 41,888 ÷ 136
(*j*) 366,095 ÷ 365

CONCLUSION

Addition, subtraction, multiplication and division occur in many situations. The secret of accuracy lies in the way in which the information is arranged and by practice. An orderly layout gives the best results, even for the least experienced.

EXERCISE

(*a*) Complete the following sales table:

	August	*September*	*October*	*TOTAL*
Department A	3,346	3,679	3,248	(a)
Department B	4,327	4,378	5,021	(b)
Department C	7,733	7,745	7,465	(c)
	(d)	(e)	(f)	(g)

Note: (a) + (b) + (c) and (d) + (e) + (f) = (g)

(*b*) The number of articles completed by four employees in a radio components factory in one week is shown in the table below. Find the number produced by each employee for the week, the number produced each day and the total number produced in the week by the four employees.

Employee	*Number Completed*				
	Monday	*Tuesday*	*Wednesday*	*Thursday*	*Friday*
M. Able	42	38	46	34	36
N. Barker	39	50	50	43	47
O. Child	43	43	44	46	49
P. Dart	47	50	49	46	48

(*c*) The readings from the electricity and gas meters of a self-employed plumber are shown below. You are required to find his consumption of each per month.

Date	*Electricity*		*Gas*	
	Meter reading	*Units consumed*	*Meter reading*	*Units consumed*
June 1	6247		584460	
June 30	6397		585540	
July 31	6543		586380	
August 31	6801		587290	
September 30	6940		588300	
October 31	7025		589280	
November 30	7107		590530	
December 31	7325		593340	

(d) An electrical wholesaler buys 2,750 electronic calculators for £15 each. He sells them to a retailer for £23 each. His expenses amount to £2 for every calculator he sells to the retailer. Find:

(i) his total gross profit
(ii) his gross profit per calculator;
(iii) his total net profit;
(iv) his net profit per calculator.

SECTION III

STORING YOUR WORK

Throughout your course you will need to store the work you do outside this book so that it can be produced for assessment or checking at any time. You might well find this difficult if you are not properly organised. This first part of Section III is concerned with *one* method or system of storage which will assist you in keeping your work neat, orderly and accessible.

One of the most popular ways of keeping individual sheets of paper in order is to put them in a *ring binder* or *ring file*. These are convenient because they enable individual sheets to be removed from any section without disturbing the rest, and it is easy to add to any section or even continue a section in another file.

For your purposes, the first thing you must establish is how many different modules you will be studying during the course. This will indicate how many sections into which your file should be divided. You might feel it is desirable to have a separate file for the work of each module, but this is not absolutely necessary. It is relatively easy to expand your storage system as and when each file becomes full. Whole sections can be transferred to a new file, or one large section can be continued in a second file.

We will assume that you are going to start with one or two files. The first task is to split up the file into a number of sections. This is done by the use of *subject divider cards*. These are made to fit into the ring binder in the normal way, but they project beyond the sheets of paper, and are designed so that one part of each divider is visible at all times. It is on this visible part that you can indicate what is stored in that section.

The illustration on the facing page will give you some idea how these divider cards are designed, and how the section title can be recorded.

You will need one subject divider card for each module of work in your course of studies, and it might be useful to allow for one section in which you can keep special assignments. Once you have decided on the number of cards, and written in your section titles, put them into the file(s) and insert a suitable quantity of paper into each section to give you a good start. It is often necessary to use hole-strengtheners to prevent individual sheets of paper becoming damaged (the most commonly used size of file and paper is A4 (297mm × 210mm)).

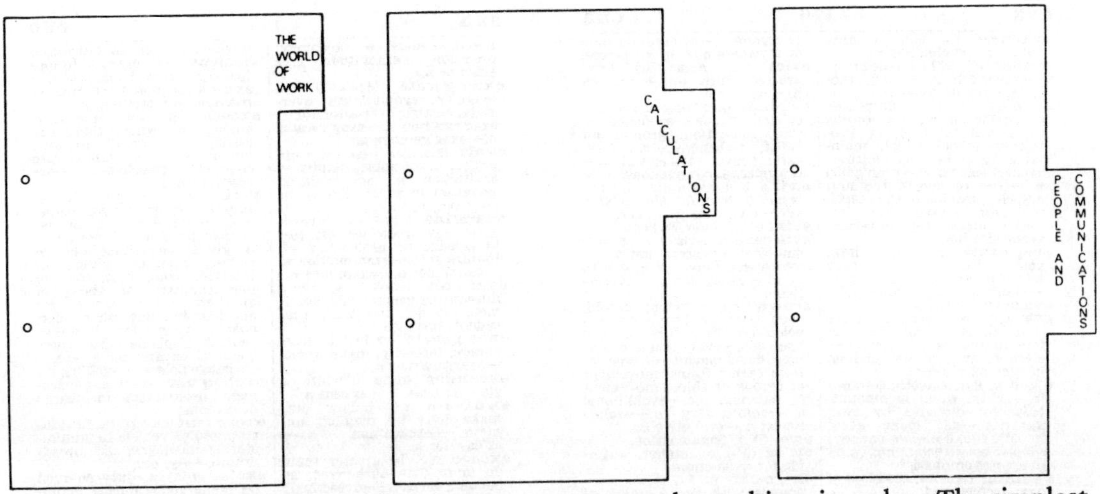

Within each section of the file it is also necessary to keep things in order. The simplest way of filing most information is in alphabetical order, but this is not suitable for your work. It is much easier for you to store things in *date order*. This means that as long as you put the date on every piece of work you do, it will be an extremely easy task to insert it in the correct place in the file because it will automatically follow on in sequence. You will then be able to retrieve the work from any part of your course easily, no matter when it was completed. If you make it a practice to put the date at the right-hand top corner of each piece of work, this will make it easier for you to find individual scripts at a later date.

This system will also enable your tutors to see how your work has developed and improved over a period of time. Remember that *all* work is important and should be kept in a suitable manner so that it can be easily checked at any time. It is quite possible that your tutor will feel that the orderliness, neatness and efficiency with which you store your course work is in itself a useful exercise for assessment purposes.

NOTE: Remember that the over-all contents of the file can be recorded on the outside cover, but this should be done in such a way that it can be altered if it is necessary to expand or re-arrange your storage system.

EXERCISE

After consultation with your tutor(s) arrange and label your own course file(s) in such a way that you will be able to insert, store and retrieve information quickly and efficiently.

DICTIONARIES AND WORDS

As you can see from the previous sections, a thorough understanding of any text depends upon your ability to put a particular meaning to words and phrases. If you find it difficult to understand any written passage, whether it is in a textbook or in a newspaper, you will need to use a dictionary quickly and accurately.

Most dictionaries rely on a system of abbreviations to give you information about a word. The extract from the *Collins Gem English Dictionary* on the following page looks almost as if it is written in code.

eva 176 **exa**

eval'uate *v.t.* find or state value of.—**evalua'tion** *n.*

evanesce' (-es') *v.i.* fade away.—**evanes'cent** *a.* fleeting, transient.—**evanes'cence** *n.*

evan'gel (-j-) *n.* gospel.—**evangel'ical** *a.* of, or according to, gospel teaching; of Protestant school which maintains salvation by faith.—**evangel'icalism** *n.*—**evan'gelist** *n.* writer of one of the four gospels; preacher of the gospel; revivalist.—**evan'gelise** *v.t.* preach gospel to; convert.—**evangelisa'tion** *n.*

evap'orate *v.i.* turn into, pass off in, vapour.—*v.t.* turn into vapour.—**evapora'tion** *n.*—**evap'orator** *n.*— **-ative** *a.*

eva'sion *see* EVADE.

eve (ēv) *n.* evening before (festival, etc.); time just before (event, etc.); evening.—**e'ven** *n.* evening.—**e'ven-song** *n.* evening prayer.

e'ven *a.* flat, smooth; uniform in quality, equal in amount, balanced; divisible by two; impartial.—*v.t.* make even; smooth; equalise.—*adv.* equally; simply; notwithstanding; (used to express emphasis).

e'vening (-vn-) *n.* the close of day; decline, end.

event' *n.* happening; notable occurrence; issue, result.—**event'ful** *a.* full of exciting events.—**event'ual** *a.* that will happen under certain conditions; resulting in the end; ultimate; final.—**event'ually** *adv.*—**eventual'ity** *n.* possible event.—**event'uate** *v.i.* turn out; happen; end.

ev'er *adv.* always; constantly; at any time.—**evermore'** *adv.*

ev'ery (-vri) *a.* each of all; all possible.—**ev'erybody** *n.*—**ev'eryday** *a.* usual, ordinary.—**ev'eryone** *n.*—**ev'erything** *n.*—**ev'erywhere** *adv.* in all places.

evict' *v.t.* expel by legal process, turn out.—**evic'tion** *n.*—**evic'tor** *n.*

ev'ident *a.* plain, obvious.—**ev'idently** *adv.*—**ev'idence** *n.* sign, indication; ground for belief, testimony.—*v.t.* indicate, prove.—**eviden'tial** *a.*—**in evidence,** conspicuous.

e'vil *a.* bad, harmful.—*n.* what is bad or harmful; sin.—**e'villy** *adv.*—**e'vil-doer** *n.* sinner.

evince' *v.t* show, indicate.

evis'cerate (-vis'er-) *v.t.* disembowel.—**eviscera'tion** *n.*

evoke' *v.t.* draw forth; call to mind.—**evoca'tion** *n.*—**evoc'ative** *a.*

evolve' *v.t.* develop; unfold, open out; produce.—*v.i.* develop, *esp.* by natural process; open out.—**evolu'tion** *n.* evolving; development of species from earlier forms; movement of troops or ships; movement in dancing, etc.—**evolu'tional** *a.*—**evolu'tionary** *a.*—**evolu'tionist** *n.*—**evol'utive** *a.*

ewe (ū) *n.* female sheep.

ew'er (ū'-) *n.* pitcher, water-jug for wash-stand.

ex-, e-, ef- *prefix,* forms compounds with the meaning of "out from," "from," "out of," "formerly" as in *exclaim evade, effuse, exodus.* Such words are not given here where the meaning may easily be inferred from the simple word.

exac'erbate (-as'-) *v.t.* aggravate, embitter, make worse.—**exacerba'tion** *n.*

exact' (egz-) *a.* precise, accurate, strictly correct.—*v.t.* demand, extort; insist upon; enforce.—**exact'ly** *adv.*—**exac'tion** *n.* act of exacting; that which is exacted, as excessive work, etc.; oppressive de-

māte, mēte, mīte, mōte, mūte, bōōt; bo͞on

exa 177 **exc**

mand.— **-ness** *n.* accuracy; precision.—**exact'itude** *n.*—**exact'or** *n.*

exag'gerate (egz-aj'-) *v.t.* magnify beyond truth, overstate; enlarge; over-estimate.—**exaggera'tion** *n.*—**exag'gerator** *n.*—**exag'gerative** *a.*

exalt' (egz-*awlt'*) *v.t.* raise up; praise; make noble, dignify.—**exalta'tion** *n.* an exalting; elevation in rank, dignity or position; rapture.

exam'ine (-gz-) *v.t.* investigate; ask questions of; test knowledge or proficiency of. inquire into.—**examina'tion** *n.*—**exam'iner** *n.*—**exam'inee** *n.*

exam'ple (-gz-â-) *n.* thing illustrating general rule; specimen; model; warning, precedent, instance.

exas'perate (-gz-) *v.t.* irritate, enrage; intensify, make worse.—**exaspera'tion** *n.*

excandes'cence *n.* white or glowing heat.— **-des'cent** *a.*

ex'cavate *v.t.* hollow out; make hole by digging; unearth.—**excava'tion** *n.*—**ex'cavator** *n.*

exceed' *v.t.* be greater than; do more than authorised; go beyond; surpass —**exceed'ingly** *adv.* very; greatly.

excel' *v.i.* be very good, preeminent.—*v.t.* surpass, be better than (*excelled'* (-seld') *p.t.* and *p.p.*—*excell'ing pres. p.*).—**ex'cellent** *a.* very good.—**ex'cellence** *n.*—**ex'cellency** *n.* title borne by viceroys, ambassadors.

except' *v.t.* leave or take out; exclude.—*v.i.* raise objection.—*prep.* not including; but.—*conj.* unless.—**except'ing** *prep.* not including.—**excep'tion** *n.* thing excepted, not included in a rule; objection.—**excep'tional** *a.*—**excep'tionally** *adv.*—**excep'tionable** *a.* open to objection.

excerpt' *v.t.* extract, quote (passage from book, etc.).—**ex'cerpt** *n.* a quoted or extracted passage.—**excerp'tion** *n.*

excess' *n.* an exceeding; amount by which thing exceeds; too great amount; intemperance or immoderate conduct.—**excess'ive** *a.*—**excess'ively** *adv.*

exchange' *v.t.* give (something) in return for something else; barter.—*v.i.* of officer, change posts with another.—*n.* giving one thing and receiving another; giving or receiving coin, bills, etc., of one country for those of another; thing given for another; building where merchants meet for business; central telephone office where connections are made, etc.—**exchange'able** *a.*— **-abil'ity** *n.*

excheq'uer (-kẹr) *n.* government department in charge of revenue.

excip'ient (ek-sip'-) *n.* food introduced as vehicle in administering medicine, as bread-crumb, jelly, etc.

excise' (-iz) *n.* duty charged on home goods during manufacture or before sale.—**excise'man** officer collecting and enforcing excise.—**exci'sable** *a.* liable to excise.

excise' *v.t.* cut out, cut away.—**exci'sion** (ek-sizh'-) *n.*

excite' *v.t.* rouse up, set in motion; stimulate, move to strong emotion; (electricity) magnetise poles of.—**exci'table** *a.*—**exci'tably** *adv.*—**excitabil'ity** *n.*—**excite'ment** *n.*—**excita'tion** *n.*—**exci'ting** *a.* rousing to action; thrilling.

exclaim' *v.i.* and *t.* cry out, interject.—**exclama'tion** *n.*—**exclam'atory** *a.*

thère, fâther, hẹr; *awl, oil, owl;* THine

TASK ONE

List nine abbreviations from this extract and say what you think they could mean. Use your own dictionary to help you because it will contain a section explaining what its own abbreviations mean.

Abbreviation	*Meaning*

If your dictionary has a method of showing how to *pronounce* words, find out exactly how this works. There should be an explanation in the front or at the back of the dictionary. You may find it useful to discuss this aspect of the work with your colleagues and with your lecturer.

When you are sure how your own dictionary works, refer back to the extract given earlier in this section. Study the words carefully and analyse the methods of explanation used in the extract. Say the words aloud so that the pronunciation is clear.

TASK TWO

The following passage has certain words missing. From the list below select those words which are most suitable, and write them in. Check the meanings carefully in your dictionary.

The term sole trader is frequently used when talking about sole proprietorship even though many __________ are engaged in professional or skilled __________ rather than in __________. Sole __________ may, of course, employ managers and others __________, but the full __________ for management policy, and the control over the business property, including the right to sell property or borrow on its __________, rest completely with one person – the owner or proprietor. Legally there can be no __________ between the owner's personal, private __________ and his business, although they are classed separately for __________ and __________ purposes. As a result, the __________ owner is fully responsible for all the __________ and debts of his business up to the extent of his personal property, including his __________ if he owns one.

distinction	taxation	sole	enterprises
services	security	owners	accountancy
employees	trade	house	liabilities
property	responsibility		

(T.A.C. Shafto, *Study Notes on Commerce*. McGraw-Hill)

You have now been involved in a basic process of communication – the written word. Communication means the process of conveying ideas and feelings, and involves the following.

The *communicator:* i.e. a person who is trying to convey some information to someone else;

The *message:* i.e. the actual information the communicator wishes to convey;

The *medium:* i.e. the method of conveying the information. This can be the written word, the spoken word, or simply a gesture;

The *receiver:* i.e. the person with whom the communicator wishes to make contact.

Our whole way of life is affected by our relationships with other people, and our ability to communicate with them. This communication can be *informal* as when we are dealing with people on a personal level, or *formal* as when we are conducting some kind of official business.

TASK THREE

Write in, and be prepared to explain your answers to the following questions.

(i) Do you think *gestures* are a formal or an informal means of communication? ____________________

(ii) Do you think *the spoken word* is a formal or an informal means of communication? ____________________

(iii) Do you think *the written word* is a formal or an informal means of communication? ____________________

(iv) In a sole-proprietorship do you think communications between the owner and his customers would be: *(a)* all informal? (YES/NO) *(b)* all formal? (YES/NO) *(c)* partly formal and partly informal? (YES/NO)

TASK FOUR

You are the proprietor of a small painting and decorating business. Describe a situation in which your communications with a customer could be classified under the following headings:

(i) written/formal; ____________________

(ii) spoken/formal; ____________________

(iii) written/informal; ____________________

(iv) spoken informal. ____________________

Much of the work in this book is concerned with the written word, but in any form of communication which involves words, the vocabulary you use has a direct effect on whether or not you are conveying your meaning efficiently. A dictionary is an essential aid to communication because there are many words which have more than one meaning. For example, some can be used in a business/commercial situation to mean one thing, and in a wider context to mean something completely different:

(*a*) The manager's secretary was *filing* the correspondence when she was called to the telephone.

(*b*) The engineering apprentice was *filing* the piece of steel to remove the rough edges.

EXERCISE

Write short sentences to show how the following words can be used in (*a*) the business/commercial sense, and (*b*) any other sense.

(a) staff;
(b) draft;
(c) reference;
(d) form;
(e) tax;
(f) report;
(g) address;
(h) union;
(i) capital;
(j) correspond;
(k) notice;
(l) frank;
(m) trade;
(n) punch;
(o) abstract.

The words in the next list can sometimes cause difficulty in pronunciation or meaning. Some of them are of foreign origin and have been adopted into our language to express particular ideas.

TASK FIVE

Find out how these words are pronounced, and give their meaning.

Debtor ______________________

Entrepreneur ______________________

Ancillary ______________________

Insolvent ______________________

Creditor ______________________

Oligopoly ______________________

Laissez-faire ______________________

Comptometer ______________________

Monopoly ______________________

Formalities ______________________

The previous tasks have helped you get used to the layout and structure of your dictionary, and you will have realised that such a text performs a number of functions or services for the user.

TASK SIX

Can you identify ten services that your dictionary provides? Give an example of each.

Service	*Example*
It gives the meaning(s) of words	Analogy – similarity in certain respects
__________	__________
__________	__________
__________	__________
__________	__________
__________	__________
__________	__________
__________	__________
__________	__________
__________	__________
__________	__________

In a former exercise you were dealing with words which have more than one meaning, and which can be used in a *specialist* way to convey a specific idea. The example used was *filing.* What were the two different meanings we gave to this word?

(*a*) ____________________

(*b*) ____________________

Most areas of work involve words which have specialist meanings. An awareness of these is essential to an understanding of the job.

TASK SEVEN

The following words are taken from the introductory section to the rules of number. Find them in your dictionary, and give the meaning as they are used in the context of this unit.

Word	Specialist Meaning
unit	__________
gross	__________
net	__________
overheads	__________
charges	__________

EXERCISE

(*a*) The following words are often confused in normal use because they *sound* the same. The correct term for this type of word is *homophone*. Write sentences for each of these words to show clearly that you understand their meanings and differences in meaning.

all ready	correspondence	practice
already	correspondents	practise
ascent	current	profit
assent	currant	prophet
buy	draft	sell
by	draught	cell
canvas	air	sum
canvass	heir	some
council	wholly	weather
counsel	holy	whether

(*b*) The passage below contains a number of words which are misused because they have/are homophones. Write a corrected version of the passage.

It became known that one of the directors didn't agree with the knew plans fore the factory, so a special bored meeting was called to consider his descent. His argument was that the scheme wood do nothing to rays the level of productivity, and would simply lead to a further waist of resources. The breeches of contract that would result from the delays caused by implementing the scheme indicated that it was wrong in principal.

You have seen from the use of your dictionary that words can often be used in different ways, and that different words can have different *functions* in a sentence. This is an important aspect of *grammar,* which can be defined as *the study of words in relation to one another in speech or writing.* It is not necessary to be too formal when considering aspects of grammar, but an understanding of how words work is essential if you are to communicate efficiently with other people. Each word in any sentence performs a particular "job", and the names which describe these "jobs" are classed under the general heading of the parts of speech.

THE PARTS OF SPEECH–NOUNS

Those which are used as *naming* words are called *nouns.* There are four types.

1. **Common nouns.** These give the names of objects and things as well as the general names used for persons. For example:

The *clerk* took the *file* into the manager's *office.*

EXERCISE

List ten common nouns which give the names of things you can see in your classroom.

2. **Proper nouns.** These are the names of particular places and persons. A proper noun should begin with a capital letter. For example:

Mr. Williams had to attend a sales conference in *Birmingham*.

EXERCISE

Give the names of five politicians, five cities and five European countries.

3. **Collective nouns.** The names of groups or collections of similar things or people with a similar interest come under this heading. For example:

The *committee* agreed that the *library* needed a further allocation of funds.

EXERCISE

(a) Give collective nouns for the following groups: people listening in a theatre; ships; islands; magistrates; bees.
(b) List ten more collective nouns, and explain what is being described.

4. **Abstract nouns.** These are often the most difficult to understand because they deal with ideas or qualities or states or actions. Only practice will enable you to identify them easily. Abstract nouns are sometimes described as those things (qualities, states, ideas or actions) which do not have a *physical presence*, i.e. we cannot touch, see or feel them. However, this description must be qualified by explaining that what we normally recognise is the *result* of one of these things. For example:

The woman showed great *fear* when she travelled by aeroplane for the first time.

In this sentence the abstract noun is *fear*. However, we cannot actually *see* fear. We can only see the *symptoms* or *results* of fear, e.g. face drained of colour, sweat, shaking limbs. It is only through the recognition of these symptoms that we identify the emotion being shown as *fear*.

The same situation applies to other abstract nouns – it is only because we can identify the symptoms or results of something that we are able to put a name to that particular quality, state, idea or action. For example:

The *bankruptcy* of the business was due to a combination of *inefficiency* and *incompetence*.

TASK EIGHT

Underline the abstract nouns in the following sentences.
(i) The accountant used his discretion when questioning his client.
(ii) The chief clerk showed great patience when he was disconnected because of the switchboard operator's incompetence.
(iii) Indifference is not a desirable quality of management.

EXERCISE

(*a*) Give abstract nouns corresponding to the following words: Industrial; agent; predict; prosperous; wise; mitigate; prepare; judge; dangerous; flexible.

(*b*) The words in italics in the following passage are all nouns. Say what kind of noun each is, and write a sentence of your own using the word correctly.

When two or more *people* join together to operate a business *enterprise* for the purpose of making a *profit,* they form a *partnership*. With this type of arrangement it is not necessary to have a formal or written *agreement*, although a partnership deed is desirable in order to avoid much *disagreement.* Partners are personally responsible for the debts of business, and must accept *responsibility* for the activities of fellow partners. Therefore one partner may suffer the consequences of another's *inefficiency*, *irresponsibility* or *dishonesty*.

THE PARTS OF SPEECH – VERBS

Every sentence is about somebody or something *doing* or *being* something, and the *verbs* are the words which express these actions. Verbs play a vital part in grammar, because the whole meaning and structure of a sentence depends upon them being used correctly, accurately, and in the right tense (e.g. past, present or future). Various aspects of verbs will be dealt with in future work, but for now you should make sure you can identify them and understand their function. For example:

When he *arrived* at the meeting he *discovered* that the other directors *were* already there.

The words which say that the persons being discussed *do* something or *are* something in the preceding sentence can be described thus:

arrived : past tense of the verb "to arrive"
discovered : past tense of the verb "to discover"
were : past tense of the verb "to be"

NOTE: The title of the verb is known as the *infinitive*, i.e. *to arrive; to discover; to be.*

The infinitive is often used in its standard form within a sentence, as can be seen in the following examples:

The clerk had *to go* into the next office *to answer* the telephone.

The insurance investigator hoped *to discover* the real cause of the fire.

After the accident the employee was asked *to write* a report of what had happened.

In order *to complete* the order we had *to transfer* stock from another branch.

TASK NINE

Complete the following tables which show the declension of two common verbs in the present and past tenses.

(i) To Be

present tense		past tense	
singular	*plural*	*singular*	*plural*
I *am*	we ______	I ______	we *were*
you ______	you ______	you *were*	you ______
he she ______ it	they *are*	he she ______ it	they ______

(ii) To Have

present tense		past tense	
singular	*plural*	*singular*	*plural*
I ______	we *have*	I ______	we ______
you *have*	you ______	you ______	you *had*
he she ______ it	they ______	he she *had* it	they ______

All verbs can be set out in this way. In the exercises which follow you will be working with some verbs which can cause confusion.

EXERCISE

(*a*) Set out the following verbs in tables which show their present and past tenses, as in the preceding task:

to write; to sell; to sing; to think; to drive.

(*b*) Identify the verbs in the following sentences, and write down the infinitive of each. Then find out what your dictionary says about each verb, making sure you know what any abbreviations mean. One verb is presented as an example at the end.

(i) Digits are symbols which represent numbers.
(ii) Numeration expresses numbers in words. (zero, one, two)
(iii) Notation gives numbers in figures or symbols. (0, 1, 2)
(iv) The result obtained when you add numbers is called the sum.
(v) When you subtract one number from another the result is called the difference.
(vi) The product is the name given to the result when you multiply one number by another.

(vii) Division consists of finding how many times one number is contained in another.
(viii) We refer to the number we want to divide as the dividend.
(ix) The number by which we divide the dividend is named the divisor.
(x) The quotient is the name we use for the result of the division.

Infinitive of verb		*Dictionary comment*
To represent	v.t.	call up by description or portrait; make out to be; act, play, symbolise; deputise; stand for.

THE PARTS OF SPEECH – PRONOUNS

These important words are inserted into sentences instead of nouns in order to avoid unnecessary and clumsy repetition. There are various types of pronouns, all of which are quite easily recognisable. You probably use them in written and spoken communication without even realising what they are. The following list gives many pronouns in everyday use.

I, me, mine, he, him, hers, ours, they,
them, theirs, you, yours, his, this, her,
she, yours, our, it, its, who, whom,
whose, which, that, we, us, my, their.

(*a*) *Personal* pronouns refer to people or things.
(*b*) *Possessive* pronouns show possession or "belonging".
(*c*) *Demonstrative* pronouns point out or indicate something or someone.
(*d*) *Relative* pronouns relate what you are going to say to a noun or pronoun you have already mentioned. For example:

(*a*) John said *he* couldn't find *it*. *(Personal pronouns)*
(*b*) He took *my* coat, and claimed it was *his*. *(Possessive pronouns)*
(*c*) *This* is your coat. *(Demonstrative pronoun)*
(*d*) That is the person *who* took my coat. *(Relative pronoun)*

TASK TEN

Put each of the pronouns listed earlier in this section under the appropriate heading. Consider each one carefully, and think how it is normally used.

Personal ____________________________________

____

Possessive __________________________________

____

Demonstrative _______________________________

____

Relative ____________________________________

____

NOTE: The words *this* and *that* are demonstrative pronouns only if they are used on their own *instead of* a noun. If they are used *in front of* a noun, they are *demonstrative adjectives.*

(*a*) *That* is what I am looking for. (Demonstrative pronoun)
(*b*) I have been looking for *that* book. (Demonstrative adjective)

EXERCISE

(*a*) Write a sentence using a personal pronoun.
(*b*) Write a sentence using a possessive pronoun.
(*c*) Write a sentence using a relative pronoun.
(*d*) Write a sentence which includes all four types of pronoun.

THE PARTS OF SPEECH – CONJUNCTIONS

Words which are used to link single words or groups of words together are called *conjunctions*. The most common ones are *and, but, because.* For example:

The chairman *and* the directors were present, *but* they had to wait for the secretary to arrive.

There will be exercises involving the use of conjunctions in Unit III when you are considering fluency and style. However, remember how a conjunction is used, i.e. as a *linking* word.

THE PARTS OF SPEECH – ADJECTIVES

When we want to describe something or someone, we often rely on adjectives. They can be said to limit or qualify the meaning or application of nouns or pronouns, i.e. they add to the meaning and make it more specific. For example:

A *public* company issues two types of shares – *ordinary* shares and *preference* shares.

TASK ELEVEN

Underline the adjectives in the following sentences, and use your dictionary to find their exact meaning.

(i) Co-operative societies originated as customer-owned, local, retail societies.
(ii) The retail societies established their own wholesale society to supply them.
(iii) One characteristic of local co-operative societies is the democratic nature of the management committees.
(iv) The original aim of this type of retail outlet was to provide a high standard of honest and reputable shopkeeping.
(v) In recent years the societies have faced increasing competition from efficient national, retail and supermarket groups.

THE PARTS OF SPEECH – ADVERBS

In the same way that adjectives add to the meaning of a noun, an *adverb* is used to modify or qualify or add to the meaning of verbs, adjectives or other adverbs. For example:

(*a*) The secretary typed *efficiently*. ("efficiently" tells us *how* she performed the action of the verb.)

(*b*) *Light* green paint was used to decorate our office. ("light" qualifies the adjective "green", and makes it clear what shade of green was used.)

(*c*) The new clerk worked *slowly, lazily almost,* until she realised how much work was accumulating. ("Slowly" is an adverb, and the following phrase brings an added dimension to our understanding of the situation.)

THE PARTS OF SPEECH – INTERJECTIONS

These words fall outside normal grammatical structure, and are usually "slipped in" to express feeling or emotion. For example:

"*Oh dear*, I've missed the bus and shall be late for work".

THE PARTS OF SPEECH – PREPOSITIONS

A preposition shows the relationship between one word and another, and often expresses *direction, position* or *cause*. For example:

(*a*) He took the letter *to* the post room. (Direction)
(*b*) The secretary put the client's file *on* the table. (Position)
(*c*) The managing director was angered *by* the board's decision. (Cause)

The list below gives you the most commonly used prepositions:

about, above, across, after, against, along, amid, amidst, among, amongst, around, at, before, behind, below, beneath, beside, between, beyond, by, down, during, except, for, from, in, into, near, of, off, on, over, round, since, through, to, towards, under, underneath, until, up, upon, with, within, without.

Points to bear in mind are as follows.

(*a*) It is often difficult to decide which preposition should be used in a particular context. There is no general rule – they must be remembered. For example, certain words *must* be used with a particular preposition: different *from,* not different *than*.

(*b*) Some words can be used with different prepositions to give a different meaning. For example:

I am *responsible for* checking the invoices.
The junior clerk was *responsible to* his supervisor.

(*c*) The style of your written work will suffer if you use prepositions unnecessarily. For example:

He started *(off on)* his inspection tour.
The representative met *(up with)* his client.

(*d*) Try to avoid ending a sentence with a preposition.

(*e*) If a preposition is used incorrectly, it can make nonsense of, or alter the meaning of a complete sentence. For example:

The manager's secretary sat *beside* him when taking dictation.
The manager's secretary sat *on* him when taking dictation.

In the following exercise a number of prepositions have been deliberately misused. Identify these, and rewrite the passage inserting the correct prepositions so that it can be clearly understood. All of them are obvious faults so as to help you recognise the use and misuse of these parts of speech.

EXERCISE

In Britain about two-thirds in the economy and about five-sixths up the commerce is conducted by private enterprise. The rest off the activities on the economy are conducted with State-controlled enterprises. Some, like the army, navy and air force, are clearly the sort of institutions that the State itself should control. Others are often performed between the State because they are non-profit making and are therefore unlikely to attract investment. Activities such as education, medical care and sanitation are operated as socially provided services without the benefit of all citizens. Upon the industrial and commercial fields certain goods and services are by their nature monopolies. Under these "natural" monopolies are gas, water supply and electricity. Such natural monopolies have come to be run in the U.K. by the State or amongst local authorities.

UNIT II

Achievement Checklist
When you have completed this unit, you should be able to:
- * Understand the differing roles and objectives or organisations;
- * Outline the features which typify the various kinds of organisations, and how they differ from one another;
- * Compare and contrast the main functions of the public and private sectors;
- * Perform the basic operations with fractions and decimals;
- * Perform basic operations using currency;
- * Recognise and write a simple, grammatically correct sentence;
- * Appreciate some of the advantages and disadvantages of using a diagram to present information;
- * Use appropriate vocabulary according to specialist or general requirements;
- * Explain relevant technical terms in non-technical language;
- * Understand the organisation of a library and use it effectively;
- * Use books efficiently.

SECTION I

THE MAIN FEATURES OF BUSINESS ORGANISATIONS

Unit I showed how economic activity in many countries is in the hands of a wide variety of business organisations. The illustration below gives an even more comprehensive list of the organisations involved although most of the "new" ones are similar to one or another of those already mentioned.

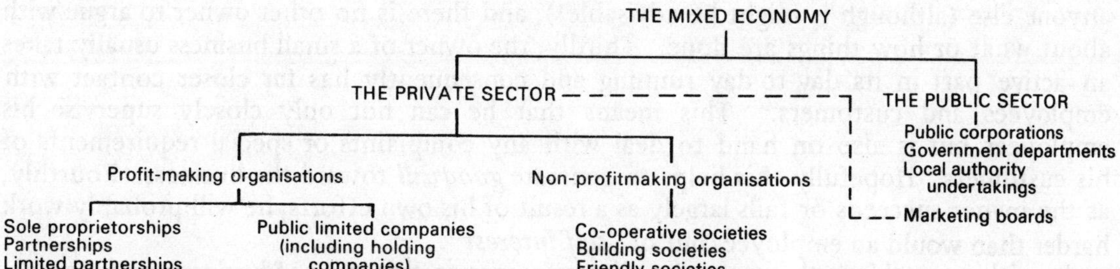

A. THE PRIVATE SECTOR – PROFIT-MAKING ORGANISATIONS

The Sole Proprietorship

This is the most numerous (although not necessarily the most important) type of organisation. The "sole proprietor" (or sole trader) is often thought of in terms of the local grocer or newsagent but a one-man business need not necessarily be that of a shopkeeper. There are very many small enterprises with a single proprieter in the professional fields of accountancy, law and estate agency, and there are also a large number of self-employed craftsmen such as painters, plumbers and electricians who tend to sell services rather than goods.

Whatever the nature of the business activity the proprietors will have to provide sufficient money to buy the essential things needed to enable the business to be started. For example, a butcher would need premises, shelving and counters, refrigerators and freezers, a cash till and perhaps a van besides his "tools of the trade" such as knives. The shopkeeper will also have to buy some stock so that he has something to offer potential customers when he opens the shop for business. The money provided by the owner is the (permanent) capital of the business but if he needs more money than he has personally available (either now or later) and providing he can show that his venture is likely to be successful, he may be able to negotiate a loan. Obviously if you borrow money you have to repay it at some time and the businessman is no exception. Such loan capital for the small firm can be obtained in the form of:

(*a*) personal loans from friends, relatives or business contacts;
(*b*) bank loans and/or overdrafts,
(*c*) trade credit (where goods and/or services are received immediately but payment is made at a later date – usually thirty days);
(*d*) hire purchase and leasing (particularly for vehicles and equipment);
(*e*) mortgages (on land and buildings);
(*f*) government agencies and departments (usually only in special cases).

As the use of funds from any of the above sources may be limited by conditions imposed by the lender, the proprietor may try to expand the permanent capital of the business by "ploughing back" part of his profits.

There are a number of advantages to setting-up in business as a sole proprietor. Firstly, they are easily established as there are few legal formalities, although planning permission for the premises may be needed from the local authority and an excise licence is required before tobacco or alcoholic products can be sold (it is also necessary to advise the Registrar of Business Names if a business is to be known by a name different to that of the owner). Secondly, decisions can be made very quickly. There is no need to consult anyone else (although it might be advisable!), and there is no other owner to argue with about what or how things are done. Thirdly, the owner of a small business usually takes an active part in its day-to-day running and consequently has far closer contact with employees and customers. This means that he can not only closely supervise his employees but is also on hand to deal with any complaints or special requirements of his customers. Hopefully this helps to generate *goodwill* toward the business. Fourthly, as the owner succeeds or fails largely as a result of his own efforts, he will probably work harder than would an employee, out of "*self interest*".

As with most things there are also disadvantages to this type of business organisation. The most important of these is that there is no legal distinction between the owner's "personal" and "business" property, and as a result if the business cannot pay its debts then the owner can be forced to meet them from his personal wealth – even if it means selling his home. This is usually referred to as *"unlimited liability"* and can cause the owner to be over-cautious, resulting in lost business opportunities. (It should be noted that the owner's "personal" and "business" affairs are kept separate for accounting and taxation purposes.) Another major disadvantage is that it is often difficult to obtain capital for expansion because of the limited size of the business. A small business does not usually make huge profits and, after providing for the owner's personal needs, there is not likely to be very much available for "ploughing back". If, on the other hand, the owner wishes to borrow money, then his limited means make it difficult for him to provide the prospective lender with collateral security (i.e. something the lender could sell to get his money back if the borrower defaulted). The small business could find it difficult to survive a trade or general economic recession as he will have little "fat" to live on. The owner may also be of limited ability and this may have an adverse effect on the business in such areas as the introduction of new ideas or coping with complicated legislation, because he has no-one immediately available to discuss his problems with. Sole proprietors often experience difficulties if they become ill or want to take a holiday. There may be no-one suitable (such as friends or relatives) that they can trust to run the business properly and employing "outsiders" can be a risky business because of the possibilities of theft, fraud or damage to customer relationships. Many of these difficulties can be overcome by spreading the ownership of the business amongst a larger number of people who, collectively, should be able to contribute larger amounts of capital than just one person. The simplest form for such an organisation to take is the partnership.

The Partnership

The obvious minimum for such an organisation is two partners but the maximum possible is twenty, although more are permitted in the case of accountants, solicitors and members of a stock exchange. It is also possible to have more than twenty members in special cases approved by the Department of Industry.

If a group of people decide to form a partnership then it follows that they will have discussed the aims and objectives of the business and agreed on the financial and administrative arrangements. Presumably all the partners are in agreement about the arrangements but it does not follow that this will always be so. People change their ideas and attitudes and at some time disagreements may need to be resolved. To avoid the worst effects of any such arguments and disagreements any partnership is well-advised to have a deed prepared and signed by all the partners to show that each of them agrees with its contents. The deed should specify the names of the partners (and of the firm, if different), their duties, and individual contributions of capital; the nature of the business the division of profits and losses and interest rates (if any) on capital, drawings or partners' loans to the firm. It should be stated if any of the partners is to receive a salary and any arrangements for drawing money out of the business. The deed should also include provisions for the calculation of a partner's share on death or retirement and the admission of new partners.
reference is made to the Partnership Act 1890 which lays down certain "rules" covering all the main points mentioned earlier.

The main disadvantage of the partnership is that the principals have unlimited liability, and in addition decision-making is a lengthier process than in the sole proprietorship because of the need for all the partners to be consulted. The death, bankruptcy or retirement of a partner may result in the firm having to close down because of the need to provide cash for that partner's "share". Furthermore, whilst in general more capital should be available than in a one-man business, it is still restricted to the amounts the partners can introduce themselves.

Two other points should be made about the constitution of a partnership. Firstly, there may be a sleeping (or dormant) partner with unlimited liability providing he takes no part in the management of the firm. Secondly, a limited partnership is one in which, as the name implies, partners can have limited liability provided they take no part in the running of the business and there is at least one partner with unlimited liability.

In general, there is considerable common ground between the sole proprietorship and the partnership, such as unlimited liability and the sources of loan capital. In both cases they are able to retain considerable privacy about their business affairs but they are increasingly under pressure to survive in this day and age. Principals often work longer hours for less money than if they worked for others; relatively small turnover restricts the opportunities for obtaining bulk discounts; difficulties are experienced in understanding and implementing complex legislation (e.g. VAT, Health and Safety at Work Act, etc.).

Nevertheless sole proprietorships and partnerships are particularly suitable kinds of business organisations for the small firm and enable those with limited resources to set up in business easily and cheaply.

The Limited Company

The restricted capital of small firms is (along with unlimited liability) a serious drawback for the ambitious entrepeneur and the need for more capital can provide the impetus for change. The formation of a limited company can help overcome these twin problems although it is quite a complicated matter as the procedure is governed quite strictly by the Company Acts of 1948, 1967 and 1976. The owners (or shareholders) acquire limited liability which means that they are not liable for the debts of the business beyond the amount they have invested in the firm. In addition more capital is usually available to these companies because they are able to extend ownership amongst larger numbers. Capital is invested in the company by individuals and institutions in return for a share of any profit made. The shareholder will, of course, also hope that the company will prosper and grow richer resulting in an increase in the value of his shares. The various advantages and disadvantages of limited companies are as follows.

Advantages

(*a*) They bring together those who wish to invest capital but who lack the knowledge to use it profitably and those who have the ability but perhaps not the capital.

(*b*) It makes it possible for small amounts of capital in the hands of many to be used to establish business organisations.

(*c*) As they tend to be large organisations they can achieve economies of scale and undertake projects which require large amounts of capital.

(*d*) As the company is a separate legal entity its "life" does not depend on particular individuals as a shareholder's death may result in a change only in the ownership of his shares – the company as such is unaffected.

(*e*) Shareholders have limited liability.

Disadvantages

(*a*) They may be affected by diseconomies of scale.

(*b*) They must comply with a considerable number of legal requirements, designed to protect shareholders and others with whom they do business, but which makes them expensive to establish.

(*c*) Shareholders owning small numbers of shares often lack the time and knowledge to take much interest in the company's affairs and therefore have little influence on the way in which it is run.

(*d*) In an increasingly complex world it is possible for the "specialists" managing the company to substitute their own priorities to the detriment of the owners.

(*e*) Companies operating in international markets may be adversely affected by events in other countries, e.g. wars, natural disasters.

The Formation of a Limited Company

This can be done by a special Act of Parliament but the overwhelming majority are formed by registration in accordance with the Company Acts. To effect registration the following documents must be lodged with the Registrar of Companies.

(*a*) The Memorandum of Association. This governs the relationship between the company and other firms or individuals. It must include:

(*i*) the name of the company including the word "limited";
(*ii*) the address of the registered office;
(*iii*) the objects of the company. These are the company's aims and objectives and if it acts outside these powers it is said to be *ultra vires*. An *ultra vires* contract is not enforceable;
(*iv*) a statement that the shareholders' liability is limited;
(*v*) the amount of capital the company wishes to be authorised to raise;
(*vi*) a statement signed by at least seven prospective members that they wish to be formed into a company;
(*vii*) the number of shares each of the above promoters have agreed to subscribe for.

(*b*) The Articles of Association. These are the internal rules of the company and state how the business is to be conducted. They include:

(*i*) the appointment and powers of directors;
(*ii*) the arrangements for shareholders' meetings;
(*iii*) the rights and responsibilities attached to different classes of shares;
(*iv*) the document must be signed by the same people that signed the Memorandum.

(*c*) A statement of the nominal capital (on which tax has to be paid).

(*d*) A list of directors and their written consents and promises to take up shares.

(*e*) A statutory declaration that the Company Acts have been complied with.

If all the above documents are in order the Registrar will issue a *Certificate of Incorporation* which gives the company its separate legal personality and it may enter into provisional contracts and, perhaps more importantly, raise capital. This is usually done by issuing a *Prospectus* which is an invitation to the public to subscribe for shares and is usually advertised in the "quality" press. The prospectus has to include all the information about the company which might be of interest to potential subscribers.

The next thing the company has to do is to obtain a *Certificate of Trading*, which the Registrar issues after it has been confirmed that the initial capital has been raised and that the directors have acted in accordance with their obligations. It only remains for the shareholders to have a statutory meeting within three months and the company is legally complete.

The Public Limited Company

This is the first of the two types of limited company – the second being the private limited company dealt with later. The main features of a public company are as follows.

(*a*) Capital is raised by selling shares directly to the public.

(*b*) There must be at least seven shareholders but no maximum is laid down.

(*c*) The shareholders liability for the debts of the business is limited to the amount they have paid for their shares (assuming they have been issued fully-paid).

(*d*) A company is a legal entity. This means that it can act as if it were a person and enter into contracts; as a result it can sue and be sued.

(*e*) The shareholders own the company and exercise control by electing a board of directors.

(*f*) Although the shareholders cannot withdraw their money from the company, they are free to sell their shares to anyone they wish.

(*g*) Companies are required, by law, to send the following documents to the Registrar of Companies every year:

(*i*) the annual accounts and balance sheet;
(*ii*) auditors' report (confirming the above are accurate);
(*iii*) directors' report.

NOTE: It appears that some companies do not comply with the strict requirements for these documents but that few are ever prosecuted as a result. It has been suggested that some recent company "crashes" could have been anticipated if such information had been available to the public as is intended.

The Private Limited Company

This type of company is very similar to the public limited company although it is usually smaller, particularly in terms of capital subscribed. This is largely due to the restrictions placed on membership by the Company Acts which specify a minimum of two and a maximum of fifty (not including past and present employees). In addition the company cannot offer shares to the public which restricts it to finding willing subscribers amongst relatives, friends and business contacts. Such companies are frequently formed to obtain more capital for small family firms and so that control is retained by the original owners the Articles of Association include provisions restricting the sale or transfer of shares. The Articles may state that the shares must first be offered to an existing shareholder or an even more restrictive requirement may be that any proposed change in ownership is subject to approval by the directors. As a private company may not offer its shares to the public it does not need to produce a prospectus nor is it possible to buy and sell the shares on a stock exchange. It is however permitted to start trading as soon as the Certificate of Incorporation has been received.

Holding Companies

If one company gains control of another by acquiring a majority of its shares, it is said to be a holding company. Usually the purpose of forming such a company is to build up a large-scale business and/or to make diversification easier. To achieve these aims the holding company is often involved in what is called *integration* which can be either *vertical* or *horizontal.* Vertical integration takes place when a company controls all stages of production and distribution of its output. For example, some oil companies control the entire process from the oil-fields to the petrol station, including all the intermediate stages such as refineries and road- and sea-tankers, etc. Horizontal integration occurs when firms engaged in the same stage of production are combined. This can take place at the manufacturing, wholesaling or retailing stage.

Holding companies that acquire controlling interest in a number of companies active in a wide range of industries are known as *conglomerates.* Those which have subsidiaries in a number of different countries are called *multinationals*. Some of the really big multinationals (e.g. the oil companies and the U.S.A. car companies) are bigger in most respects than some of the countries in which they operate, which gives them considerable influence in those countries' affairs.

Voluntary Co-operatives

For many years the pursuit of economies of scale has led to a general acceptance that "bigger is better" and many small businesses have found it increasingly difficult to survive in competition with the large organisations. This has been particularly evident in retailing where the growth of supermarket chains has led to many thousands of small grocers closing down. To increase competitiveness, and therefore the chances of survival, many small grocery retailers have joined wholesaler-inspired voluntary co-operatives (e.g. SPAR, Wavy Line, MACE, etc.). These organisations are similar to, but quite distinct from, the familiar "Co-op". Their aim is to provide the members with facilities for bulk-buying (both stock and fittings), group advertising and promotion whilst preserving the independence of the retailer to decide how his business is to be conducted on a day-to-day basis. Co-operatives have been formed on similar lines amongst farmers and the hardware, wallpaper and paint trades.

Trade Associations

These associations are not profit-making in themselves but they have been formed to promote the interests and welfare of their members who usually are. Independent firms, irrespective of size, active in a particular trade or industry often have similar difficulties and problems and have formed associations to protect their interests by such things as uniform prices (which may be considered to be "unfair" trading), standardisation of products and contract forms. The association may also act as the industry's spokesman in matters of public interest or in presenting information to government departments. Some are active in the promotion of education and training for their employees. Most associations are themselves members of a bigger association — the Confederation of British Industry (C.B.I.) which, in general, represents the views of its members and is often consulted by the government when formulating its policies. (The government will also consult with the Trades Union Congress (T.U.C.) which acts in a similar manner on behalf of its member trade unions.)

It should also be noted that some trade associations also act as employers' associations, in that they negotiate wage rates and conditions of service for employees in their particular industry. Usually the appropriate trade unions act for the employees.

B. THE PRIVATE SECTOR – NON-PROFIT-MAKING ORGANISATIONS

These organisations must of course make a profit (they must earn more than they spend), otherwise they would soon cease to exist, but they are organised and run for the benefit of members/customers, whereas those organisations classified as "profit making" are run for the benefit of the owners. Perhaps the best way of illustrating the difference is to compare the self-help nature of the former with the self-interest of the latter. This difference has been recognised by successive governments who have passed special Acts of Parliament (e.g. Building Societies Act) to govern their activities and by making them responsible to the Registrar of Friendly Societies rather than the Registrar of Companies.

Amongst the oldest and most important of these organisations that still subscribe to the original ideals that inspired their formation are the Co-operative Societies.

The Co-operative Societies

The success of the Rochdale Pioneers quickly led to retail co-operative societies being established in towns and villages all over the country. Each society was an independent unit and they were all organised on similar lines although slight variations in their rules did exist.

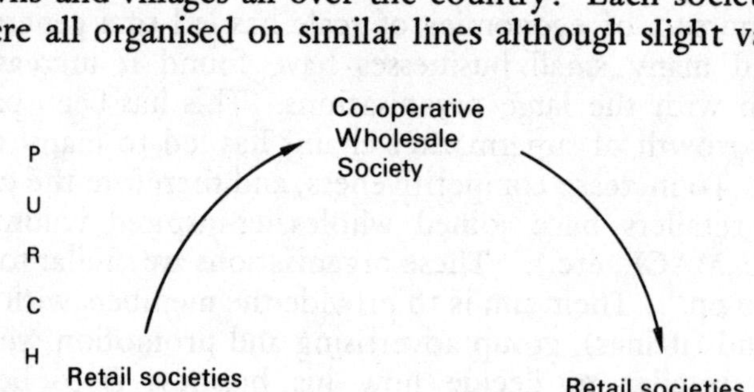

In recent years competition from larger public companies has led to the co-operatives improving what was a rather old-fashioned image by the adoption of modern marketing methods. Societies have also been encouraged to amalgamate to achieve economies of scale so that by 1976 there were some 220 retail societies (467 in 1968) with an annual turnover of about £2,500 million and nearly 11 million members.

The Co-operative Wholesale Society (C.W.S.) was formed in 1863 to meet the trading needs of the retail societies. The retail societies are members of the C.W.S. in much the same way that individual consumers are members of their retail societies and similarly the retail societies receive a share of C.W.S. profits in proportion to the value of their purchases.

As well as being the U.K.'s largest wholesaler, the C.W.S. is also manufacturer, farmer, overseas trader, banker, hotelier and travel agent. It owns or controls a number of subsidiary and associate companies with interests ranging from insurance to bacon production. The C.W.S. now controls over 120 factories, nearly 10,000 ha of farmland and employs nearly 30,000 people and with annual sales of £1,100 million it is one of the world's largest trading organisations.

Main Characteristics

(a) Each society is an independent self-governing body but the illustration below shows the interdependence the various branches of the movement and overall control of the consumer-members.

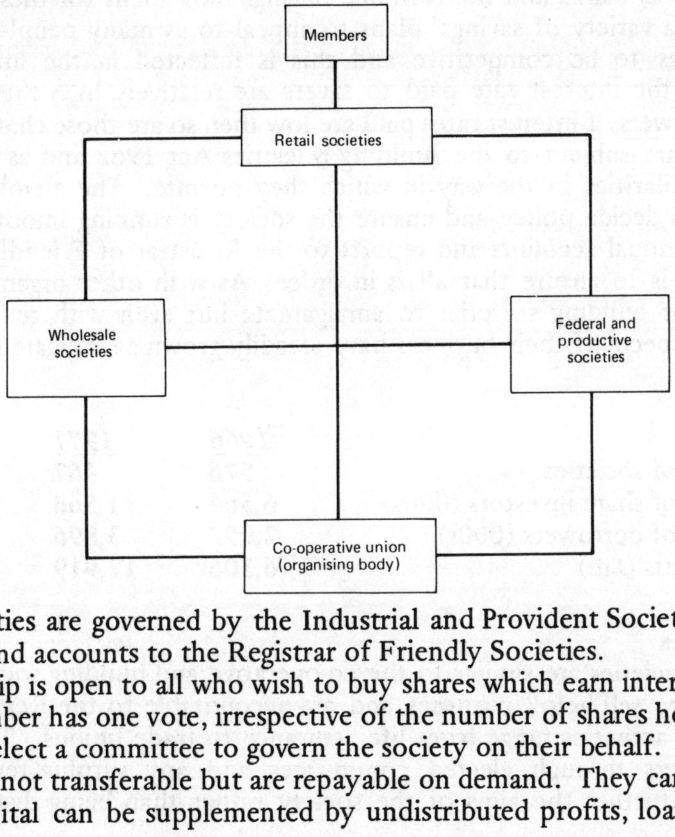

(b) The societies are governed by the Industrial and Provident Societies Acts and send annual returns and accounts to the Registrar of Friendly Societies.

(c) Membership is open to all who wish to buy shares which earn interest.

(d) Each member has one vote, irrespective of the number of shares held.

(e) Members elect a committee to govern the society on their behalf.

(f) Shares are not transferable but are repayable on demand. They cannot be sold.

(g) Share capital can be supplemented by undistributed profits, loans from members and the C.W.S.

(h) The traditional cash dividend paid in proportion to members' purchases has been replaced by the issue of trading stamps to all customers. This is cheaper and easier and stamps can be exchanged for cash or goods.

(i) The movement remains committed to the promotion of education and social welfare.

(j) The C.W.S. and the retail societies are actively promoting the amalgamation of retail societies through its offshoot, Co-operative Retail Services, which was originally established to develop trade in difficult areas. Now it comprises what were over 150 separate societies, has over 1,500,000 members and annual sales of £300 million.

The Building Societies

These societies were originally formed to help people buy their own homes and this is still their function today. Few people can afford to buy their houses outright and need to borrow in order to do so. Building societies lend money to house-buyers and the house itself acts as security for the loan. If the borrower defaults on his obligation then the society can sell the house to recover the money it is owed. Although that is their legal right, the societies are usually reluctant to take such a drastic step and will do all they can to help a borrower who finds himself in genuine financial difficulty. The finance for these loans is provided by the savings of many thousands of people who deposit funds with the societies in order to earn interest and perhaps obtain preferential treatment when they come to apply for a mortgage. The societies are in competition with other institutions such as banks and the National Savings movement for these funds and they, therefore, offer a variety of savings' plans to appeal to as many people as possible. The interest paid has to be competitive and this is reflected in the interest charged to borrowers. If the interest rate paid to savers are relatively high then so are the rates charged to borrowers; if interest rates paid are low then so are those charged.

The societes are subject to the Building Societies Act 1962 and as a result there are considerable similarities in the way in which they operate. The members elect a board of directors who decide policy and ensure the society is running smoothly. All societies have to render annual accounts and reports to the Registrar of Friendly Societies whose responsibility it is to ensure that all is in order. As with other organisations there has been a trend for building societies to amalgamate but even with reduced numbers of societies most aspects of their business have steadily grown as indicated by the following statistics:

	1966	1971	1976
Number of societies	576	467	364
Number of share investors (000s)	6,564	11,568	19,991
Number of borrowers (000s)	2,992	3,896	4,609
Total assets (£m)	6,306	12,919	18,202

Friendly Societies

Many of these societies are similar to the co-operative and building societies in that they were formed for "self-help" purposes and are accountable to the Registrar of Friendly Societies. Their activities range from life assurance to trade unions. They are governed by their members through elected committees and any surplus revenue is used to consolidate and further the aims of the society rather than being distributed to shareholders.

Sports and Social Clubs and Societies

There are numerous clubs and societies all over the country which have been formed by groups of people with a common interest in such diverse activities as gardening, model-making and a wide range of sports. The members formulate the rules and elect officers to organise and control activities and finance. The club relies on members' subscriptions for the bulk of its income although it is often supplemented by sales of refreshments and fund-raising events. Many clubs are affiliated to national federations which provide guidelines on how individual clubs should be organised and promote their welfare at a national level. The clubs have to be run in accordance with the laws of the land and, on election, the officers acquire a legal duty to ensure that this is done. If anything is amiss in the clubs' affairs then the officers are responsible.

C. THE PUBLIC SECTOR

In the U.K. the public sector of the economy is very important but the way in which central and local government activities are organised is not always very clear. Some activities are organised in such a way as to make it difficult to itemise specific characteristics whereas others are carried out by more easily identifiable organisations. The most important of these is the public corporation.

The Public Corporation

Most public corporations have been established by Act of Parliament to bring all or part of a specific industry under State control i.e. to nationalise. In most such cases the industry has a particular end product (National Coal Board, British Gas) or provides a commercial service (British Rail) that has been, or arguably could be provided by the private sector. However, for a variety of reasons (which will be discussed later) it has been considered necessary to bring these activities under direct government control.

Characteristics

(*a*) Established by an Act of Parliament which aims to meet the needs of the particular industry.

(*b*) Each organisation is expected to be economically viable "taking one year with another". In essence this means that it is acceptable to "average" profits and losses although short-term (and long-term!) losses have to be made good by the taxpayer through the Treasury.

(*c*) The appropriate minister responsible for each industry appoints a board to run the industry.

(*d*) The board is responsible for the day-to-day operation of the industry and the minister has no right to interfere but he does have considerable influence on matters of general policy.

(*e*) The board has to give a detailed annual report and financial statement to the minister who reports, in turn, to Parliament.

(*f*) Parliamentary control is exercised by:

(i) the Public Accounts Committe which examines the annual accounts;

(ii) the Select Committee for Nationalised Industries which keeps the various industries under review and has the right to investigate any matters which cause it concern. It has been argued that the Committee was a toothless watchdog but in 1978 the Chairman of the British Steel Corporation was *ordered* to appear before the Committee in connection with the publication of financial forecasts that were eventually found to be inadequate and misleading.

(iii) an annual debate in the House of Commons.

(*g*) Most industries have a consumers' council to represent the public's interests in matters of service, quality and price.

(*h*) The monopolistic nature of most corporations means that they can achieve economies of scale (but are also subject to diseconomies). It also makes it difficult to assess the industry's performance – making profits may simply mean that both costs and charges are too high.

Government Departments

Some State activities are controlled directly by the appropriate government department rather than by a public corporation. For example the Department of Health and Social Security organises the health and welfare services whilst the Ministry of Defence is responsible for the armed forces.

In some cases, such as education, control is effectively in the hands of the local authorities although there are large bodies of civil servants in Whitehall who control the purse-strings and co-ordinate implementation of government policy. Unlike the public corporations the minister responsible for a department is involved with day-to-day matters but is still ultimately responsible to Parliament. In recent years government departments have become increasingly important to the economy because of the enormous sums of money at their disposal (about £34,000 million in 1976/7). Even so government departments are not commercial organisations for their income is provided by taxation whilst they provide goods and services free (education, law enforcement, etc.) or at nominal cost (prescription charges).

Local Authority Undertakings

Local authorities act as agents in implementing government policies and directives at county and district levels, in such things as education and housing. In addition they also provide municipal services such as libraries and parks which are paid for out of the rates. Many authorities also provide commercially-run bus services, swimming-pools and restaurants which are usually expected to make an operating profit.

Finance for the authorities' activities may be obtained from:

(*a*) government grants and loans;
(*b*) rates (a local tax based on property);
(*c*) loans from the public;
(*d*) trading surpluses (deficits have to be subsidised from other sources).

Marketing Boards

Marketing boards were first introduced in this country in the 1930s when depressed economic conditions led to chaos in many primary markets. The aim of such boards is to provide a link between producers and users and to guarantee prices for both. They were formed mainly at the instigation of the government which retains some control over their activities although the boards are really producers' co-operatives.

This mixed parentage is reflected in the composition of the Milk Marketing Board which operates the Milk Marketing Scheme first established in 1933. Twelve board members are elected by milk producers on a regional basis, three special members are elected on a national basis by producers in England and Wales and the remaining three are appointed by the Minister of Agriculture. The board's policy decisions are put into effect by a management team consisting of a managing director and eight other directors.

As well as appointing board members, the government also controls the prices of liquid milk at every stage of production and as a result can exert considerable influence on the dairy industry, which is reinforced by the system whereby any surpluses on liquid milk trading have to be paid to the government which, in return, makes good any deficits.

TASK ONE

(i) What is meant by "ploughing back" profits? ______________________________

____

____

(ii) Explain what is meant by the term "trade credit". ______________________________

____

____

(iii) What is unlimited liability? ______________________________

____

____

(iv) State two disadvantages of the sole trader. ______________________________

____

____

(v) Why should a partnership deed be drawn up? ______________________________

____

(vi) State two likely sources of loan capital for the partnership. ______________________________

____

____

(vii) What is limited liability? ______________________________

____

____

(viii) Why should more capital be available to the limited company than to the sole trader or partnership? ______________________________

____

(ix) What is meant by the term "legal entity"? ______________________________

____

____

(x) Briefly explain the functions of the Memorandum and Articles of Association.

____

____

____

(xi) Define vertical and horizontal integration. ______________________

____

____

(xii) What is a conglomerate? ______________________________________

____

(xiii) Why do non-profit making organisations have to make a profit? ________

____

____

(xvi) How many members may there be in a limited company? ____________

____

(xiv) Why have some retailers formed voluntary co-operatives? ____________

____

____

(xvi) Distinguish between co-operative society and limited company shares.

____

____

(xvii) Why has there been a tendency for building societies to amalgamate? ________

____

(xviii) How does Parliament exercise control over the public corporations? ________

____

____

(xix) Who ultimately pays for any losses incurred by nationalised industries?

____

(xx) What sources of finance are available to a local authority? ____________

____

____

FUNCTIONS OF THE ECONOMY

The basic function of economic activity is to provide people with goods and services. In order to do this people in a community must be organised in such a way as to make the best use of their abilities. In primitive tribal societies, the fight for survival demands the full effort of every member of the community. Even so there is often only just enough food and other necessities to provide a meagre existence, and little or nothing is left over to trade with other tribes. Such self-sufficiency is known as *direct production* as everything depends directly on the skill and energy of the member of the community. Even in a primitive society, however, *specialisation* takes place with the strongest and fastest becoming the hunters whilst the weakest and slowest members of the group are responsible for the more menial domestic chores. Still others may be concerned with the production of crops.

Specialisation leads to surplus production – the hunter becomes increasingly skilled and catches more animals than he can eat but he spends so much time hunting that he cannot grow crops as well. The crop producer, however, has not the time to tend his crops *and* hunt. It is only a simple step for the hunter and farmer to exchange their surpluses to satisfy both their needs. This system of specialisation and exchange of "surplus" goods is known as *indirect production.* In a modern economy each of us specialises in a particular kind of work and the money earned is used to buy things we want but are unable to provide for ourselves. The increasing complexity of modern products and the introduction of mechanisation has led to increased specialisation and many workers, particularly in factories, only produce one small part of the finished item. Specialisation of this kind is often referred to as the *division of labour*. Nearly all modern societies depend on indirect production as a means of achieving the highest possible level of output and wealth. In general it leads to a higher average standard of living, although to some extent this will depend on the political and social structures of any particular society.

Historically, specialisation achieved its greatest advances with the coming of the Industrial Revolution from about 1750 onwards. The technological developments which took place in the following hundred years or so saw Britain change from an agricultural economy to an industrial one. The new mills and factories needed workers, and large numbers of people moved from rural areas to the towns and cities. They were attracted by the relatively high wages being paid and, as most were landless labourers, were trying to escape the grinding poverty and insecurity of everday life in the country. This migration, allied to a doubling of the population between 1801 and 1857 (10.5 and 20.8 million respectively), created overcrowding and conditions of appalling squalor and poverty in the towns. As a result, some people began to challenge the justice of a system which allowed many to suffer whilst a minority enjoyed great wealth and comfort. These ideas eventually took hold, and since then there has been gradual State intervention in our economic and social lives – improving working conditions by statutory means and slowly acquiring more and more direct responsibility for meeting social needs.

Such developments however have not been without their opponents, and until the Second World War (1939-45) economic activity was still left very much in the hands of private firms and individuals. It was believed that they would be motivated by the wish to make profits to put their capital into business ventures and, as a result, create employment and increase the wealth of the nation. Generally this was so, and the periodic economic depressions and the resulting hardship and deprivation were looked upon as unpleasant events which could not be avoided.

The Private Sector

Those in favour of private sector organisations argue that this is the best way to ensure that firms will use scarce resources in the most efficient manner possible, as to do so will result in the greatest possible profits. It is also said that the private firm is far more flexible and will enter or leave a market in response to a rise or fall in demand for any particular product, whereas a nationalised concern will lumber along regardless in the same old way. It is also suggested that the private organisation provides a means whereby the small savings of many can be channelled into productive organisations.

The idea that competition leads to maximum efficiency and that the less efficient firms will be forced to close down, may be partly true, although it ignores the possibilities that the increasing integration of firms into groups may help to camouflage the inefficient, whilst others may be prepared to continue in business at a lower level of profitability than the maximum possible. As a result of the increasing capital costs of new ventures it is doubtful if many firms have the capability of quickly switching from one product to another although they may be able to make minor adjustments to existing products without too much difficulty. If anything, the larger the organisation the more likely it is to have the capital and expertise to develop and market new products and ironically some of Britain's biggest firms are state-owned! Even so, it is often only the small firms that are prepared to take risks and provide goods and services which are of no interest to the large firm. Companies only acquire capital from the issue of shares at the time they are first made available to the public, and only then can any money be channelled into productive investment. In any subsequent sale of the same shares the company gains no benefit. Individuals try to save money in various ways much of the time, but a large part of this small-scale saving takes place through pension funds, trade unions and insurance companies, and most of their "investment" is in second-hand shares rather than new issues. These dealings constitute financial investment on a large scale, but as it is largely in the "second-hand" share market, it does not help one of our major recurring economic problems which is that not enough of the capital available for investment in manufacturing industry has been used because of its relatively high cost and manufacturers' reluctance to "gamble" on new projects.

Nevertheless, the first concern of the organisation in the private sector must be survival, and whilst in the short-term this may simply mean making a net profit each year, the firm must look ahead and try and plan for the future. If a business is to continue to be successful then it must be capable of anticipating and reacting to the changes that occur within its own industry and in the economy at large. It must be ready for changes in fashion, or increased competition from rivals. It must be able to absorb the impact of international events such as wars or national disasters in areas from which it obtains its supplies or where it sells its goods.

In general it is assumed that organisations in the private sector make as big a profit as possible but as mentioned in Unit I page 2 this may not always be so. However, the private firms' objectives may be fairly limited so far as the rest of the community is concerned and as a matter of self-interest the firm may try and circumvent policies or guidelines laid down by the government "in the national interest". An example of this might be the granting of wage increases outside the limits laid down, either openly or, more likely, in a way which is designed to disguise the true value of the increase. This may be done to retain a skilled and established workforce or to avoid industrial disputes and in some cases may occur with the connivance of the trade unions (who have little liking for wage controls).

The non-profit making part of the private sector consists of organisations which have some similarity to the profitmakers. The co-operatives and some friendly societies are in direct competition with these profit making organisations and provide goods and services in much the same way. The only difference is in the organisational structure. On the other hand trade associations are more concerned with promoting sectional interests no matter what form their member organisations take. However, one type of organisation within this group stands apart because its activities are both specialised and yet important to the economy as a whole.

The activities of the building societies have a direct bearing on very many people's lives. Borrowers are affected as the rate of interest they are charged on their mortgages determines what they can spend on other things. In addition, however, the societies exert a direct influence on the building and other industries as the more money they advance the bigger the demand for houses which, in turn, affects the demand for a variety of other things such as furniture, etc. Due to their origins the societies are very conscious of their social responsibilities and are still sensitive to the accusation that they encouraged the rapid rise in house prices that took place in the early 1970s. It is said that they granted loans too easily so that prospective purchasers were able to pay higher and higher prices for houses. For this and other reasons the government takes a close interest in mortgage interest rates, and whilst they can only influence the societies' decisions indirectly, the societies are aware that it would be relatively easy for any government to bring them under direct control. (Such knowledge also helps the government influence the activities of other industries such as banking.)

The Public Sector

State intervention in the economy really began with the Poor Laws of Elizabeth I, and thereafter an increasing variety of measures were introduced but they were largely designed to relieve the abuses of private enterprise rather than actively stimulate economic activity. However, the years following the First World War saw a world-wide depression which caused large-scale unemployment, hardship and suffering, and in 1936 Lord Keynes published a new economic theory which was to have far-reaching effects on the organisation of our economic lives. Keynes' view was that governments could directly influence the level of economic activity and consequently the level of unemployment. The acceptance of Keynes' views, the success of centralised planning during the Second World War and the election of a Labour Government in 1945 with a commitment to state intervention in the economy, all led to considerable nationalisation in the immediate post-war period.

In Britain the political persuasion of the government of the day is important in terms of the amount of state control of the economy. In general the political "left" is for government control, whilst the political "right" is against. However, both sides are in agreement about the major aims of government economic policy which are:

(*a*) full employment, *i.e.* in realistic terms for unemployment to be as low as possible;
(*b*) stable prices, *i.e.* no inflation;
(*c*) profitable export trade, *i.e.* we sell more abroad than we buy;
(*d*) economic growth, *i.e.* higher standards of living.

It is very difficult (if not impossible) to achieve all these aims simultaneously, particularly as other objectives have to be taken into account (such as defence and regional policies). However, it is more likely that the government will get nearer to its targets if it has a direct influence on how things are to be done, rather than leaving the economy to its own devices in the hope that all will be well. After all, it is this latter attitude which created so many problems in the past, and because of this, the *need* for government intervention in the economy does not seem to be a major cause of argument, although the extent and nature of that intervention certainly is. In some cases such as education, sanitation, defence and the maintenance of law and order there is little disagreement as they are socially necessary, but unprofitable, facilities which are unlikely to be provided by the private sector. Therefore any disagreements that do arise tend to be about the order of priorities. It is in the areas where the state has acquired control (through the public corporations) of industries that were previously in private hands that there is considerable controversy.

Why then have such industries been nationalised? There are a number of explanations.

(a) In a few cases the state was effectively ensuring their survival by the use of subsidies and grants before they were nationalised, *e.g.* coal and railways.

(b) Some industries are "natural monopolies" in that it would be wasteful to have more than one supplier, *e.g.* electricity, gas, railways.

(c) The capital requirements of some industries are so enormous that it is unlikely they could be obtained from private sources, particularly where it would be a long time before any profits might be made, *e.g.* railways, coal.

(d) Strategic industries may be in danger of collapse without government intervention, *e.g.* Rolls-Royce (1971) Ltd. – our only major aero-engine manufacturer and essential to defence plans.

(e) Services have to be provided to all members of the community although in some cases it is uneconomical to do so, *e.g.* electricity or telephones to remote farms.

(f) There are some cases where it could be dangerous to leave the industry in private hands, *e.g.* nuclear energy.

(g) There might be wholesale redundancy if the industry declined whilst in private hands. Nationalised industries can be directed to plan cut-backs so that the workforce declines at a slower rate - the private firm may have no such inclination.

(h) If the government's intervention is to be at all successful it needs agents to feel the economic pulse, *e.g.* Bank of England.

(i) A need for self-sufficiency in some very important resources in case of war, *e.g.* coal, transport.

A recent development in the extension of state influence has been the establishment of the National Enterprise Board. The aim is for the Board to act as a channel for government funds to selected parts of the private sector. The Board is required to develop the economy, promote efficiency and provide jobs whilst making an adequate return on capital employed. A recent example of the Board in action has been its rescue of British Leyland which is the only major British-owned car manufacturer and a large employer. If it were allowed to founder, not only would many thousands of jobs be lost but we would be completely reliant on foreign manufacturers (based here and overseas) for supplies – there would also be considerable "loss of face"; The company has received large sums of money and in exchange the Board has acquired shares in the company enabling it, and therefore the government, to influence the manner in which the company operates.

Opponents of nationalisation argue that it is inefficient because there is no profit motive and, in most cases, no competition either; that the industries are too big and suffer from too much bureaucracy and other diseconomies of scale. There is evidence to support these accusations but it must be borne in mind that the presence of the profit motive and competition does not automatically guarantee maximum efficiency – nor does their absence necessarily lead to total inefficiency. Furthermore it is often overlooked that the public corporations often suffer from government intervention in their investment and pricing policies, for reasons which have little to do with commercial viability. Investment in new plant may be deferred or cancelled if the government wishes to restrict public expenditure; prices may be pegged if it helps control inflation (and win votes!) even if it results in eventual losses, uneconomic plant and services may be kept open if a shut-down would result in increased unemployment or social hardships.

In conclusion, it is probably fair to say that the function of the public sector is to act in the national interest as interpreted by the government of the day.

TASK TWO

(i) Briefly explain the principal features of specialisation.

(ii) How does indirect production lead to a higher output than direct production?

(iii) State three arguments used in support of private enterprise.

(iv) State two reasons why firms may not aim for profit-maximisation.

(v) Give three examples of events that may have an adverse effect on the firm.

(vi) List as many products as possible for which demand might be affected by people buying new houses. ______

______

______

______

(vii) What are the four major aims of government economic policy? ______

______

______

(viii) Why are education and defence said to be unprofitable? ______

______

______

(ix) Explain the term "natural monopolies" in your own words. ______

______

______

(x) Why might it be dangerous to allow private firms to control the nuclear energy industry? ______

______

______

(xi) What are the aims of the National Enterprise Board? ______

______

______

(xii) How can political interference affect the profitability of nationalised industries? ______

______

______

______

(xiii) Why is it said that private sector firms make the best use of scarce resources?

______

______

______

(xiv) Explain in your own words the difference between "financial investment" and "productive investment". ____

____

____

(xv) Suggest two reasons why the private sector is more flexible than the public sector in meeting consumers' requirements. ____

____

____

SECTION II

FRACTIONAL FORMS

You are now aware of the nature of a partnership and it may be that the profit earned by a partnership is divided in the following manner: one partner receives one-half of the profits, the second partner receives one-quarter and the remaining one-quarter is to be kept in reserve. If the profits are considered to be 1 then the partners will receive ½ and ¼ respectively with ¼ going into reserve.

The Nature of Fractions
The division of the profits has been expressed in the form of each fraction being part of the whole profit. The fractions produced contain two elements; the number of parts the whole is divided into is called the *denominator* and the number of parts of the whole that we are considering is called the *numerator.*

$$\text{Thus} \quad \frac{\text{partners' share}}{\text{total profit}} = \text{fraction of the whole} = \frac{\text{numerator}}{\text{denominator}}$$

The fraction itself is called a *vulgar* or *proper fraction* and it may be recognised quite easily since the numerator is always smaller than the denominator.

Vulgar fractions are commonly used in everyday situations. We buy such things as ½ lb of butter, ½ kg of sugar, ¾ lb of cold meat.

TASK ONE

Give six examples of items purchased where the quantity is a vulgar fraction.

ANSWER (i) ____________ (ii) ____________ (iii) ____________

(iv) ____________ (v) ____________ (vi) ____________

But what quantities are we receiving? Suppose the profits from the partnership above amounts to £1,000 in a particular year, then we can find how much each receives and the sum kept in reserve.

The first partner receives ½ of £1,000 = £500
the second receives ¼ of £1,000 = £250
and the reserve sum is ¼ of £1,000 = £250

In order to find the sum received the whole profit is divided into the number of parts indicated by the denominator and then allocated as shown by the numerator. For example:

(a) Find ¾ of £240:

$$\frac{£240}{4} \times 3$$

Step 1: Divide the quantity by the denominator, giving £240 ÷ 4 = £60.

Step 2: The numerator 3 is now multiplied by the result of Step 1, giving £60 x 3 = £180.

Thus ¾ of £240 = £180

(b) Find $\frac{2}{7}$ of 1 week

$\frac{7}{7}$ days x 2

Step 1: Change the quantity to another form, giving 7 days.

Step 2: Divide the new quantity by the denominator, giving 7 ÷ 7 = 1.

Step 3: Multiply the result by the numerator, giving 1 x 2 = 2.

Thus $\frac{2}{7}$ of 1 week = 2 days

TASK TWO

Write down the values of

(i) $\frac{1}{5}$ of £1 = ____________

(ii) $\frac{3}{4}$ of £1 = ____________

(iii) $\frac{1}{3}$ of 1 hour = ____________

(iv) $\frac{5}{6}$ of 1 hour = ____________

(v) $\frac{7}{10}$ of 150 metres = ____________

(vi) $\frac{11}{20}$ of 1000 grams = ____________

(vii) $\frac{17}{50}$ of £250 = ____________

(viii) $\frac{7}{13}$ of £39 = ____________

(ix) $\frac{13}{15}$ of 540 litres = ____________

(x) $\frac{4}{9}$ of £750 = ____________

Simplifying Fractions

In the example concerning the partnership, one partner received £500 (½) of the profits, the other received £250 (¼) with £250 (¼) going into reserve. It is clear that the partner with the largest share receives the same as the other partner and the reserve combined.

£500 = £250 + £250

½ = ¼ + ¼

Therefore ½ is the same as $\frac{2}{4}$ and we can say that $\frac{2}{4}$ is ½ when reduced to its smallest terms. Similarly, $\frac{8}{12} = \frac{2}{3}$ when both the numerator and the denominator are divided by 4.

This reduction of a fraction to its smallest terms is called simplification and it may be necessary to reduce a fraction several times before it is in its simplest form. For example:

Simplify $\frac{126}{210}$

$\frac{126}{210} = \frac{63}{105}$ Step 1: Divide numerator and denominator by 2.

$\frac{63}{105} = \frac{21}{35}$ Step 2: Divide numerator and denominator by 3.

$\frac{21}{35} = \frac{3}{5}$ Step 3: Divide numerator and denominator by 7.

TASK THREE

Simplify the following fractions.

(i) $\frac{6}{8}$ = ____________

(ii) $\frac{25}{40}$ = ____________

(iii) $\frac{45}{65}$ = ____________

(iv) $\frac{68}{102}$ = ____________

(v) $\frac{275}{600}$ = ____________

(vi) $\frac{324}{486}$ = ____________

The simplification of a fraction does not alter its value; it only expresses that fraction in a more convenient form.

Thus $\frac{1}{2} = \frac{2}{4} = \frac{3}{6} = \frac{5}{10}$, etc.

TASK FOUR

Complete the following fractional forms.

(i) $\frac{1}{2} = \frac{\quad}{6} = \frac{\quad}{14} = \frac{9}{\quad} = \frac{15}{\quad}$

(ii) $\frac{1}{3} = \frac{\quad}{9} = \frac{6}{\quad} = \frac{\quad}{36} = \frac{16}{\quad}$

(iii) $\frac{2}{5} = \frac{\quad}{10} = \frac{20}{\quad} = \frac{\quad}{35} = \frac{16}{\quad}$

(iv) $\frac{3}{4} = \frac{\quad}{100} = \frac{\quad}{48} = \frac{21}{\quad} = \frac{\quad}{240}$

Improper Fractions and Mixed Numbers

You have seen that a proper fraction is one where the numerator is less than the denominator, but there are times when the fraction has, or requires the use of, a numerator that is greater than the denominator. These are called *improper fractions.* Thus $\frac{11}{3}$, $\frac{15}{4}$, $\frac{20}{5}$ are improper fractions and simplification of these creates *mixed numbers,* containing a whole number and proper fraction. For example:

Simplify $\frac{27}{4}$

Step 1: Divide the numerator by the denominator, to give the whole number. Hence $27 \div 4$ gives 6 remainder 3.

Step 2: The remainder is made the numerator in a proper fraction with the same denominator as the improper fraction, giving ¾.

Thus $\frac{27}{4} = 6\frac{3}{4}$

Where there is no remainder the result is a whole number only, thus $\frac{20}{5} = 4$.

TASK FIVE

Simplify the following improper fractions as mixed or whole numbers.

(i) $\frac{13}{6}$ ____________ (vi) $\frac{38}{8}$ ____________

(ii) $\frac{27}{8}$ ____________ (vii) $\frac{54}{18}$ ____________

(iii) $\frac{14}{7}$ ____________ (viii) $\frac{51}{9}$ ____________

(iv) $\frac{53}{11}$ ____________ (ix) $\frac{132}{11}$ ____________

(v) $\frac{18}{4}$ ____________ (x) $\frac{585}{55}$ ____________

It is often necessary to change a mixed number to an improper fraction. For example:

Change $6\frac{2}{3}$ to an improper fraction.

Step 1: Change the whole number to an improper fraction, using the denominator in the mixed number, by multiplication so that 6 becomes $\frac{18}{3}$

Step 2: Add the numerator of the original fraction. Hence $\frac{18}{3} + \frac{2}{3}$ becomes $\frac{20}{3}$

Thus $6\frac{2}{3} = \frac{20}{3}$

TASK SIX

Change the following to improper fractions.

(i) $2\frac{3}{4}$ ________ (v) $3\frac{7}{10}$ ________ (viii) $6\frac{5}{12}$ ________

(ii) $3\frac{5}{7}$ ________ (vi) $8\frac{1}{3}$ ________ (ix) $2\frac{11}{21}$ ________

(iii) $4\frac{5}{9}$ ________ (vii) $1\frac{8}{15}$ ________ (x) $5\frac{11}{16}$ ________

(iv) $9\frac{3}{5}$ ________

Addition of Fractions

The addition of fractions combines a number of techniques already used, with a number of supplementary operations. For example:

(*a*) simplify $\frac{1}{2} + \frac{1}{4} + \frac{1}{12}$

This can be achieved easily if the following is observed, i.e.

$\frac{1}{2} = \frac{6}{12}$ and $\frac{1}{4} = \frac{3}{12}$ Now $\frac{1}{2} + \frac{1}{4} + \frac{1}{12} = \frac{6}{12} + \frac{3}{12} + \frac{1}{12} = \frac{10}{12} = \frac{5}{6}$

This method hinges upon finding a denominator common to each fraction, in this case 12, which is called the *lowest common multiple* or LCM.

Applying this to a further example:

(*b*) Simplify $\frac{2}{3} + \frac{1}{8} + \frac{3}{4}$

Step 1: Find the LCM of 3, 8 and 4. This is 24.

$$\frac{(8) + (3) + (6)}{24}$$

Step 2: For each fraction find the number of times each denominator is contained in the LCM. Thus 3 is contained 8 times, 8, 3 times and 4, 6 times.

$$\frac{16 + 3 + 18}{24}$$

Step 3: Multiply each appropriate numerator by the values found in Step 2. So for $\frac{2}{3}$ 2 x 8 = 16; $\frac{1}{8}$ gives 1 x 3 and $\frac{3}{4}$ gives 3 x 6.

$$\frac{37}{24}$$

Step 4: Add the new numerators together (16 + 3 + 18).

$$1\frac{13}{24}$$

Step 5: Simplify the result.

(c) When whole numbers occur these are added first, then proceed as for example (b).

Simplify $2\frac{7}{10} + 1\frac{3}{4}$ — Step 1: Add the whole numbers (2 + 1 = 3).

$3 + \frac{14 + 15}{20}$ — Step 2: Find the LCM (20).

$3 + \frac{29}{20}$ — Step 3: Change $\frac{7}{10}$ and $\frac{3}{4}$ to the appropriate fraction of 20.

$3 + 1\frac{9}{20} = 4\frac{9}{20}$ — Step 4: Add the numerators, simplify and add to the whole number.

TASK SEVEN

Simplify the following.

(i) $\frac{1}{4} + \frac{3}{8} + \frac{1}{2} =$ ________________

(ii) $\frac{3}{5} + \frac{1}{10} + \frac{2}{15} =$ ________________

(iii) $\frac{4}{9} + \frac{7}{15} + \frac{3}{10} =$ ________________

(iv) $2\frac{2}{9} + 1\frac{7}{18} =$ ________________

(v) $\frac{5}{8} + 1\frac{1}{6} + \frac{11}{20} =$ ________________

(vi) $1\frac{5}{6} + 3\frac{5}{12} + 2\frac{4}{9} =$ ________________

(vii) $1\frac{15}{22} + 3\frac{1}{2} + 1\frac{3}{5} =$ ________________

(viii) $3\frac{4}{15} + 1\frac{3}{25} + 2\frac{11}{20} =$ ________________

Subtracting Fractions

The same steps are followed when fractions are subtracted. The whole numbers are dealt with first, the LCM is found and the numerators subtracted. For example:

(a) Subtract $2\frac{2}{3}$ from $5\frac{3}{4}$

$5\frac{3}{4} - 2\frac{2}{3}$ Step 1: Subtract the whole numbers.

$3 + \frac{9-8}{12}$ Step 2: Find the LCM and subtract.

$3\frac{1}{12}$ Step 3: Simplify, if required, and add to the whole number.

(b) When the proper fraction being subtracted is larger, the whole number is reduced by one, changed to a fraction and added to the smaller fraction.

Simplify $4\frac{1}{3} - 1\frac{3}{4}$ Step 1: Subtract whole numbers.

$3 + \frac{4-9}{12}$ Step 2: Find the LCM.

$2 + \frac{16-9}{12}$ Step 3: Since 9 cannot be taken from 4, one of the whole numbers is changed to $\frac{12}{12}$ and added to the smallest numerator.

$2\frac{7}{14}$ Step 4: Subtract and simplify.

TASK EIGHT

Simplify the following:

(i) $2\frac{4}{7} - \frac{5}{14} =$ ____________________

(ii) $6\frac{7}{10} - 2\frac{4}{15} =$ ____________________

(iii) $5\frac{3}{8} - 1\frac{7}{12} =$ ____________________

(iv) $2\frac{7}{30} - 1\frac{5}{6} =$ ____________________

(v) $8\frac{2}{3} - 5\frac{4}{5} =$ ____________________

(vi) $6\frac{3}{16} - 4\frac{7}{24} =$ ____________________

When addition and subtraction are combined the operations are no different, except that the fractions are arranged so that terms to be added and those to be subtracted are combined. (The subtracted terms always have the minus sign preceding them.)

For example:

Simplify $5\frac{3}{4} - \frac{1}{6} - 2\frac{3}{5} + \frac{7}{20}$

$3 + \frac{3}{4} + \frac{7}{20} - \frac{1}{6} - \frac{3}{5}$ Step 1: Rearrange the terms, and combine the whole numbers if necessary.

$3 + \frac{45 + 21 - 10 - 36}{60}$

$3 + \frac{66 - 46}{60}$ Step 2: Find the LCM and combine the terms.

$3\frac{20}{60} = 3\frac{1}{3}$ Step 3: Subtract and simplify.

EXERCISE

(a) Simplify

(i) $\frac{1}{3} - \frac{1}{6} + \frac{1}{2}$

(ii) $\frac{5}{6} - \frac{1}{3} - \frac{1}{2}$

(iii) $4\frac{1}{4} - 1\frac{2}{5} - \frac{9}{10}$

(iv) $4\frac{3}{8} - 1\frac{5}{16} - 2\frac{3}{4} + \frac{9}{48}$

(v) $8\frac{2}{3} - 4\frac{4}{9} - 2\frac{7}{15} + 2\frac{4}{5}$

(b) From a broadloom carpet 35 metres long, the following lengths are cut: 3¼ metres, 7¾ metres, 7½ metres and 6½ metres. How many metres have been sold? How many metres remain?

(c) Five men form a partnership be putting up the following sums of money: A – £5,000; B – £3,000; C – £2,000; D – £1,000; E – £1,000. They agree to share the profits in proportion to their investment. Find the fraction of total capital that each man invests. Find what each will receive when the profit in a particular year is £3,000.

Multiplying Fractions

This presents no problems when a logical approach is followed. This can be easily seen when a fraction is multiplied by a whole number. The number is considered to be an improper fraction with a denominator of 1. Thus 3 becomes $\frac{3}{1}$ 5 becomes $\frac{5}{1}$etc. When an "of" operation is required this indicates multiply. For example:

Find $\frac{3}{4}$ of 5

$\frac{3}{4} \times \frac{5}{1}$

Step 1: The whole number (5) becomes $\frac{5}{1}$ and the "of" becomes "x".

$\frac{15}{4} = 3\frac{3}{4}$

Step 2: Multiply the numerators together, then the denominators and simplify.

TASK NINE

Simplify

(i) $\frac{4}{5} \times 4 =$ __________ *(ii)* $\frac{3}{4} \times 12 =$ __________

(iii) $\frac{1}{6}$ of 8 = __________ *(iv)* $\frac{3}{8}$ of 24 = __________

(v) $\frac{5}{7} \times 3 =$ __________ *(vi)* $\frac{21}{73} \times 365 =$ __________

When multiplying fractions it is often easier to complete if simplification is carried out before any multiplication takes place. Again "of" operations are changed to multiply and any mixed numbers are changed to improper fractions. For example:

(a) Find $1\frac{1}{8}$ of $1\frac{1}{3}$

$\frac{9}{8} \times \frac{4}{3}$

Step 1: The mixed numbers are changed to improper fractions. Thus $1\frac{1}{8}$ becomes $\frac{9}{8}$ and $1\frac{1}{3}$ becomes $\frac{4}{3}$

Step 2: Common factors are simplified vertically or diagonally. Now 3 is common to denominator 3 and numerator 9, giving 1 and 3 after removal.

$\frac{\overset{3}{\cancel{9}}}{\underset{2}{\cancel{8}}} \times \frac{\overset{1}{\cancel{4}}}{\underset{1}{\cancel{3}}}$

Step 3: Common factor 4 is removed from denominator 8 and numerator 4 giving 2 and 1.

$\frac{3}{2} = 1\frac{1}{2}$

Step 4: With no further simplification, the numerators are multiplied together, then the denominators, and the results simplified if necessary.

(*b*) Simplify $4\frac{1}{5} \times 1\frac{2}{3} \times 1\frac{1}{4}$

$\frac{21}{5} \times \frac{5}{3} \times \frac{5}{4}$	Step 1:	Change the mixed numbers to improper fractions.
$\frac{{}^{7}\not{21}}{{}_{1}\not{5}} \times \frac{5}{\not{3}\,{}_{1}} \times \frac{\not{5}\,{}^{1}}{4}$	Step 2:	Simplify common factors. NOTE: A common factor can only be removed from two numbers. Thus denominator 5 is common with only *one* numerator 5.
$\frac{35}{4} = 8\frac{3}{4}$	Step 3:	Multiply and simplify.

TASK TEN

Simplify the following

(*i*) $\frac{4}{5} \times \frac{3}{8} \times \frac{5}{9} =$ ____________________

(*ii*) $4\frac{1}{2} \times \frac{2}{3} =$ ____________________

(*iii*) $2\frac{1}{3} \times \frac{8}{21} =$ ____________________

(*iv*) $2\frac{1}{4} \times 5\frac{1}{3} =$ ____________________

(*v*) $2\frac{4}{7}$ of $4\frac{2}{3} =$ ____________________

(*vi*) $1\frac{3}{5}$ of $6\frac{1}{4} =$ ____________________

(*vii*) $2\frac{1}{2} \times \frac{3}{10} \times \frac{3}{4} =$ ____________________

(*viii*) $5 \times 2\frac{1}{2} \times \frac{8}{75} =$ ____________________

(*ix*) $2\frac{2}{3} \times 2\frac{4}{7} \times 2\frac{1}{2} =$ ____________________

(*x*) $3\frac{1}{4} \times 8\frac{1}{3} \times 2\frac{4}{5} =$ ____________________

Dividing Fractions

When fractions are to be divided the first priority is to invert the divisor and then multiply. Thus, if dividing by $\frac{5}{6}$ it is necessary to multiply by $\frac{6}{5}$

This will apply if dividing by a whole number. For example:

Divide $\frac{4}{5}$ by 3	Step 1:	The 3 becomes $\frac{3}{1}$.
$\frac{4}{5} \times \frac{1}{3}$	Step 2:	The divisor is inverted and becomes a multiplier.
$\frac{4}{15}$	Step 3:	Multiply and simplify.

TASK ELEVEN

Simplify the following

(i) $\frac{1}{2} \div 5 =$ ____________ *(ii)* $\frac{4}{9} \div 16 =$ ____________

(iii) $\frac{11}{24} \div 22 =$ ____________ *(iv)* $\frac{9}{14} \div 36 =$ ____________

(v) $\frac{11}{12} \div 121 =$ ____________ *(vi)* $\frac{73}{80} \div 365 =$ ____________

As with multiplying fractions, it is often more satisfactory to simplify during the division operation if possible. Again the divisor is inverted and the fractions multiplied. For example:

(a) Divide $\frac{3}{8}$ by $\frac{4}{3}$

	Step 1:	Invert the divisors and multiply.
$\frac{3}{8} \times \frac{4}{3}$	Step 2:	Simplify common factors.
$\frac{\overset{1}{\cancel{3}}}{\underset{2}{\cancel{8}}} \times \frac{\overset{1}{\cancel{4}}}{\underset{1}{\cancel{3}}}$	Step 3:	Multiply and simplify.
$\frac{1}{2}$		

(b) When mixed numbers are dividing or being divided, they are first turned to improper fractions.

Divide $3\frac{3}{4}$ by $2\frac{1}{2}$	Step 1:	Turn the mixed numbers to improper fractions.
$\frac{15}{4} \times \frac{2}{5}$	Step 2:	Invert the divisor and multiply.
$\frac{\overset{3}{\cancel{15}}}{\underset{2}{\cancel{4}}} \times \frac{\overset{1}{\cancel{2}}}{\underset{1}{\cancel{5}}}$	Step 3:	Simplify common factors.

$\frac{3}{2} = 1\frac{1}{2}$ Step 4: Multiply and simplify.

TASK TWELVE

Simplify the following

(i) $\frac{5}{8} \div \frac{2}{3} =$ ____________

(ii) $\frac{2}{9} \div 1\frac{1}{3} =$ ____________

(iii) $2\frac{1}{3} \div 1\frac{3}{4} =$ ____________

(iv) $4\frac{1}{5} \div 3\frac{1}{2} =$ ____________

(v) $6\frac{3}{4} \div 7\frac{1}{5} =$ ____________

(vi) $7\frac{7}{10} \div 1\frac{5}{9} =$ ____________

(vii) $\frac{2}{3} \times \frac{3}{4} \div \frac{4}{15} =$ ____________

(viii) $3\frac{1}{2} \div 2\frac{4}{5} \times 2\frac{2}{3} =$ ____________

EXERCISE

(a) A tradesman sells a number of articles for a price $\frac{1}{3}$ greater than the price at which he bought them. If he sell the articles for £190, how much did they cost him? (Hint: he gets £$1\frac{1}{3}$ for every £1 of cost.)

(b) Tea is purchased in lots of 192 kilograms. During one week $\frac{3}{8}$ is sold on Monday, $\frac{1}{6}$ on Tuesday and on Wednesday $\frac{1}{8}$ of the remainder. How many kilograms are left?

(c) The cost of manufacturing a product is made up of three elements: the cost of raw materials, the cost of labour, and overheads. If raw materials cost £2,240, labour £3,500 and overheads £1,260, find what fraction of the total cost each represents.

(d) The manufacturing cost of the product in Question *(c)* is increased by 1. Find the new cost of manufacturing. The over-all increase is made up of a $\frac{3}{7}$ increase in the cost of materials, $\frac{1}{4}$ increase in the cost of labour, and the remainder increased overheads. Find the new cost of raw materials, labour and overheads.

(e) A stall holder sells 1 of his stock on Monday, 1 on Tuesday and 1 on Wednesday. The amount left is worth £65. What was the original value of the stock?

THE DECIMAL SYSTEM

The Nature of Decimals

The system of decimal numbers is an extension of the number system met in Unit 1 taking into account quantities which are less than one – another means of expressing quantities in fractional form. Just as the system of whole numbers is based upon one digit being ten times bigger than the preceding, so decimal fractions are based upon a relationship where each digit is one-tenth the size of the preceding digit.

The digits forming the decimal fraction are distinguished from the whole number by the use of the *decimal point.* Thus in the number 38.77 the digits 77 are the fractional part and the 7 farthest from the decimal point is ten times smaller than the 7 closest to the decimal point.

Viewed in another way a decimal fraction can be considered as a series of proper fractions whose denominators are 10 or a multiple of 10 (such as 100, 1,000, 10,000 etc). For example:

$$0.235 \text{ can be thought of as } \frac{2}{10} + \frac{3}{100} + \frac{5}{1000} = \frac{235}{1000}$$

The position of the decimal point is very important since the place value of digits is 10 times greater than a similar digit immediately to its right, and 10 times smaller than a similar digit to its left.

This factor enables the multiplication and division of numbers by 10 or a multiple of 10 to be completed with ease by moving the decimal point. When multiplying this means making the number larger by moving the decimal point to the right.

Thus:

3.823 x 10 = 38.23: move the decimal point 1 place right;
3.823 x 100 = 382.3: move the decimal point 2 places right;
3.823 x 1000 = 3823: move the decimal point 3 places right;
3.823 x 10000 = 38230: move the decimal point 4 places right;
adding a zero to complete the number of places.

With division the reverse is followed with the decimal point moving from right to left.

Thus:

56.93 ÷ 10 = 5.693: move the decimal point 1 place left;
56.93 ÷ 100 = 0.5693: move the decimal point 2 places left;
56.93 ÷ 1000 = 0.05693: move the decimal point 3 places left;
adding a zero(s) to complete the number of places;
56.93 ÷ 10000 = 0.005693: move the decimal point 4 places left.

A simple rule to remember for the number of places to move the decimal point is to count the number of zeros in the multiplying or dividing number and move the decimal point that number of times; to the right if multiplying and to the left if dividing.

TASK THIRTEEN

Insert the answers to the following.

(i) 3.63 x 100 =	________	*(ix)* 9.46 ÷ 100 =	________
(ii) 5.79 x 10 =	________	*(x)* 63.2 ÷ 1000 =	________
(iii) 135.6 x 1000 =	________	*(xi)* 3.41 x 20 (Mult by 2 then 10)	________
(iv) 28.056 x 100 =	________	*(xii)* 57.84 ÷ 300 (Div by 3 then 100)	________
(v) 80.08 x 1000 =	________	*(xiii)* 9.32 x 700 =	________
(vi) 43.6 ÷ 10 =	________	*(xiv)* 398.34 ÷ 900 =	________
(vii) 73.8 ÷ 100 =	________	*(xvi)* 110.121 ÷ 110 =	________
(viii) 52.13 ÷ 1000 =	________		

Addition and Subtraction of Decimals

The basic add and subtract operations with numbers containing decimals is little different from those using whole numbers. The essential rule of placing each digit in its appropriate place must again be followed and also the decimal points must be aligned with one another. For example:

(a) Add 357.91, 24.68, 100.02 and 12.34

357.91 24.68 100.02 12.34	Step 1: Align the numbers vertically, including the decimal points.
494.95	Step 2: Add in the normal way.

(b) Subtract 605.38 from 831.25

831.25 605.38	Step 1: Align the numbers.
225.87	Step 2: Subtract in the normal way.

TASK FOURTEEN

Add the following.

(i)	*(ii)*	*(iii)*
118.90	3.074	1018.92
782.65	32.901	591.02
317.18	90.77	911.66
______	______	______

Subtract the following.

(iv)	*(v)*	*(vi)*
4.063	1516.78	103.192
2.976	477.87	87.357
______	______	______

EXERCISE

Find the value of the following.

(a) 23.71 + 5.98 + 6.04 + 0.73
(b) 3.17 + 118.2 + 75.63 + 1.41
(c) 6.87 + 0.173 + 0.054 + 1.1205
(d) 11.8115 + 127.03 + 49.685 + 7.517
(e) 81.73 − 9.31
(f) 208.7 − 192.72
(g) 110.01 − 10.111
(h) 5.041 − 0.575
(i) 18.65 − 7.38 − 2.96
(j) 4.175 − 1.365 − 2.07

Multiplication of Decimals

The multiplication of numbers containing decimal fractions can be achieved if an additional step is included in the conventional multiplication of numbers. It is essential that the answer contains the same number of digits after the decimal point as there are in the numbers being multiplied together. For example:

(a) Multiply 2.83 by 14

```
  2.83
  x 14
  2830
  1132
  3962
```

Step 1: Ignoring the decimal point multiply 283 by 10 (2830).
Step 2: Multiply 283 by 4 (1132).
Step 3: Add the results of the multiplication (3962).
Step 4: Count up the number of digits after the decimal point in the numbers multiplied together. There are 2 (in 2.83).
Step 5: In the answer to Step 3 count 2 places from the right to the left and insert a decimal point.

Thus 2.83 x 14 = 39.62

(b) Multiply 8.17 by 5.7

```
  8.17
  x 5.7
 40850
  5719
 46569
```

Step 1: Ignoring the decimal point, multiply 817 by 50 (40850).
Step 2: Multiply 817 by 7 (5719).
Step 3: Add the results of the multiplication (46569).
Step 4: Count the decimal places. There are 3.
Step 5: Insert the decimal point 3 places from the right in the answer to Step 3.

Thus 8.17 x 5.7 = 46.569

TASK FIFTEEN

(i) 1.65 x 3 = ______ *(ii)* 3.15 x 7 = ______ *(iii)* 82.6 x 12 = ______

(iv) 5.76 x 16 = ______

(v) 13.3 x 24 = ______

(vi) 723 x 0.82 = ______

(vii) 74.9 x 5.28 = ______

(viii) 86.3 x 0.724 = ______

(ix) 0.0523 x 0.185 = ______

Division of Decimals

Like multiplication there is again little difference between dividing whole numbers and those containing decimal fractions. It is not possible to divide, initially, by a decimal fraction; it must be first changed to a whole number. Thus if dividing by 23.5 it is necessary to change the divisor to 235. This is easily done by multiplying the divisor by 10 which will move the decimal point to the extreme right of the number. However the divisor and the dividend are connected and any change in the size of the divisor must be matched by an equal change in the size of the dividend. For example:

(a) 11.68 ÷ 8

```
8 ) 11.68
     1.46
```

If the divisor is a whole number then division can proceed. The decimal point is inserted in the quotient, prior to division, adjacent to its position in the dividend.

(b) 2.94 + 1.4

```
        2.1
14 ) 29.4
     28
      14
      14
      ...
```

Step 1: Change the divisor to a whole number (1.4 x 10 = 14).

Step 2: Increase the dividend by the same amount (2.94 x 10 = 29.4).

Step 3: Divide 29.4 by 14 as if for whole numbers. Place the decimal point in the quotient above that in the dividend.

(c) 8.5995 + 0.273

```
        31.5
273 ) 8599.5
      819
       409
       273
       1365
       1365
```

Step 1: Make the divisor a whole number (0.273 x 1000 = 273).

Step 2: Increase the dividend by the same amount (8.5995 x 1000 = 8599.5).

Step 3: Divide 8599.5 by 273 as if for whole numbers. Insert the decimal point as appropriate.

TASK SIXTEEN

(i) 31) 47.12

(ii) 23) 214.36

(iii) 2.7) 65.07

(iv) 3.8) 8.084

(v) 1.35) 30.375

(vi) 13.55) 5.691

EXERCISE

Find the value of the following.

(a) 0.026 x 3.2
(b) 12.8 x 0.0004
(c) 0.4083 x 13.2 x 2.2
(d) 301.5 ÷ 40.2
(e) 874.5 ÷ 6.6
(f) 0.38078 ÷ 0.79
(g) 29.25 x 12.5 ÷ 3.65
(h) (0.026 x 3.2) ÷ (12.8 x 0.0004)
(i) (0.02 x 0.24) ÷ (4 x 0.006)
(j) (3.15 x 0.028) ÷ (0.36 x 4.9)

Decimal Places and Significant Figures

All the calculations up to this point have produced "real answers" but this is not always the case with decimal fractions. For example, if 9.61 is divided by 7, the result might appear as follows:

```
7 ) 9.6100000......
    1.3728571.......
```

with the division not reaching an end.

In order to deal with this impractical situation it is normal to halt the decimal fractions after a specified number of "decimal places", giving an answer *correct to . . . decimal places.*

If working to an answer correct to 2 decimal places then the answer to 9.61 divided by 7 would be 1.37. This is achieved by taking the answer to 3 decimal places, and if the third digit is 5 or more then the digit at 2 decimal places is increased by one; if not, the digit remains the same. Thus 9.61 ÷ 7 correct to 3 decimal places would be 1.373 since the 8 at 4 decimal places causes the 2 at 3 decimal places to be increased by 1. Any zeros occurring are treated in the same way as any other digit.

TASK SEVENTEEN

(i) Express the following numbers correct to
(a) the nearest whole number and
(b) correct to 1 place of decimals.

number	*whole number*	*1 decimal place*
4.809	________	________
7.057	________	________
2.116	________	________
3.989	________	________
19.602	________	________

(ii) Express the following numbers correct to
(a) 2 places of decimals and
(b) correct to 3 places of decimals.

number	*2 decimal places*	*3 decimal places*
8.51547	________	________
2.69971	________	________
3.09643	________	________
5.49803	________	________
4.90635	________	________

The accuracy of the answer can also be specified in terms of "significant figures". These are digits which are retained for any position of the decimal point and may apply equally well to whole numbers as well as those containing decimal fractions. For example: express correct to 3 significant figures:

(a) 2.0392 Each digit is significant, including the zero between 2 and 3. Thus 2.0392 correct to 3 significant figures is 2.04 (the 3 rounding up to 4).
(b) 0.0020392 The zeros before the 2 are *not* significant, but that between 2 and 3 is. Thus 0.0020392 correct to 3 significant figures is 0.00204 (the 3 rounding up to 4).
(c) 20392 The zero is again significant and is retained. Thus 20392 correct to 3 significant figures is 20400 (zeros are added until the decimal point is reached).

TASK EIGHTEEN

Express the following correct to
(i) 2 significant figures and
(ii) 3 significant figures.

number	*2 significant figures*	*3 significant figures*
2.7485		
4.8049		
0.05103		
305.008		
567.89		

Decimal Fractions and Common Fractions

The relationship between the two kinds of fractions is an important one and it is useful, in some calculations, to be able to change from one to the other. The relationship is perhaps obvious since both are a means of expressing the division of a whole into smaller quantities.

A decimal can be thought of as a fraction whose denominator is ten or a multiple of ten, the numerator consisting of the same digits as the decimal.

Thus $0.3 = \frac{3}{10}$, $0.53 = \frac{53}{100}$, $0.953 = \frac{753}{1000}$, etc.

It is a simple matter to change a decimal to a fraction. First make the digits in the decimal the numerator and for the denominator count 1 for the decimal point. For example:

(*a*) 0.6073 There are 4 digits after the decimal point. The denominator will be 10000 and the numerator 6073. Therefore $0.6073 = \frac{6073}{10000}$

(*b*) 0.091 There are 3 digits (the zero is significant) after the decimal point. The denominator will be 1000 and the numerator 91. Therefore $0.091 = \frac{91}{1000}$

TASK NINETEEN

Express the following decimals as fractions, and simplify where appropriate.

(i) 0.5 =	*(vi)* 0.375 =	*(xi)* 0.1428 =
(ii) 0.75 =	*(vii)* 0.0625 =	*(xii)* 0.74 =
(iii) 0.2 =	*(viii)* 0.005 =	*(xiii)* 0.315 =
(iv) 0.6 =	*(ix)* 0.15 =	*(xiv)* 7.875 =
(v) 0.125 =	*(x)* 0.66 =	*(xv)* 12.36 =

The reverse process, turning a fraction to a decimal, requires the division of the numerator of the fraction by the denominator. For example:

Express ¾ as a decimal

4) 3.00
0.75

Step 1: Insert a decimal point after the numerator and add as many zeros as required.
Step 2: Divide by the denominator.

TASK TWENTY

Express as decimals:

(i) $\frac{1}{2}$, 2) 1.0 *(ii)* $\frac{1}{4}$, *(iii)* $\frac{2}{5}$,

(iv) $\frac{7}{8}$, *(v)* $\frac{9}{50}$, 50) 9.00 *(vi)* $\frac{5}{16}$,

(vii) $\frac{23}{4}$, 4) 23.0 *(viii)* $\frac{21}{8}$,

Express as decimals, correct to 3 decimal places.

(i) $\frac{2}{3}$, *(ii)* $\frac{5}{6}$, *(iii)* $\frac{3}{7}$, *(iv)* $\frac{22}{7}$,

Decimal Notation and Currency

All the operations covered to this point will apply to any calculation involving currency. There is only one additional consideration necessary: the use of the halfpenny. The notation £5.86½ is confusing since it uses both a decimal and a proper fraction. This technique is, however, used widely in financial circles, not only nationally but also internationally.

With addition and subtraction the halfpenny is treated simply in terms of combining a number of halves or by the subtraction of a half from one or zero from a half.

TASK TWENTY-ONE

(i) Add horizontally to give the totals at *(i)*, *(ii)*, *(iii)* and *(iv)*, then add vertically to give the totals at *(v)*, *(vi)*, *(vii)* and *(viii)*.

£	£	£	£	
7.76½	27.81	98.72	______	*(i)*
10.16½	15.88½	91.21½	______	*(ii)*
6.49	39.57½	77.40½	______	*(iii)*
27.96½	16.48	69.59½	______	*(iv)*
______	______	______	______	
(v)	*(vi)*	*(vii)*	*(viii)*	

(ii) Subtract the following

(ix) £	*(x)* £	*(xi)* £
1963.41½	322.59	538.22½
− 875.36	− 209.65½	− 472.76½

The multiplication of values where the halfpenny appears may be treated in one of two ways. For example: £2.37½ x 12

(a) The pounds and whole pence are first multiplied, giving £28.44, and then the half is multiplied by 12 giving 6p. This is then added to the £28.44, giving £28.50.
(b) The alternative method involves turning the sum of money to a complete decimal, £2.37½ becoming £2.375, and then multiplying. Both methods are equally acceptable.

When dividing a sum containing a halfpenny, the sum should always be expressed as a full decimal. Thus £2.37½ ÷ 15 becomes £2.375 ÷ 15.

TASK TWENTY-TWO

Multiply the following:

(i)	*(ii)*	*(iii)*
£6.52	£15.75½	£2.82½
x 28	x 39	x 60

Divide the following:

(iv) £286 ÷ 52 *(v)* £70.40 ÷ 88 *(vi)* £18.37½ ÷ 21

= 52) 286

EXERCISE

(a) Find the total cost of the following articles purchased by a retailer from a wholesaler.
(i) 150 shirts at £3.75 each
(ii) 200 pairs of socks at 37½p each
(iii) 160 ties at £1.12½ each
(iv) 100 boxes handkerchiefs at £2.05 each

(b) A man earns £3,960 in a year. He does not pay tax on two-ninths of this income and he receives an additional tax-free allowance of £890. Tax is paid on the balance at an overall rate of 28½p for every £ earned. Calculate:
(i) the total tax paid;
(ii) his monthly income, to the nearest penny, after paying tax.

(c) A merchant mixes 35 kg of coffee costing £4.80 kg with another kind, 25 kg, costing £3.75 per kg. He sells the resulting blend at a total profit of £20. Find:
(i) the total cost of the blend;
(ii) the selling price per kg — answer to the nearest ½p.

SECTION III

SENTENCES

In the previous section on communication you saw that all words have a particular "job" to do. However, it is only when these words are combined in a *sentence* that they actually convey the full meaning to the reader or listener. For our purposes it is useful to define a sentence as *the clear expression of a single idea.* In any working situation it is vitally important that our ideas are expressed clearly and accurately so that there is no chance of them being misinterpreted. Many people think it is a sign of cleverness to write lengthy sentences - they hope to impress the reader with their command of the English language. Unfortunately, the result is often that their written work is jumbled and grammatically incorrect, thus creating the opposite impression, i.e. that they are careless, illogical and incompetent. This does not mean that long sentences do not have their place in written work, but it is essential for you to aim at accuracy and clarity *first*. Therefore your ability to construct a *basic sentence* which conveys a single idea or statement is the first thing to be developed. Once you understand the basic structure and have achieved grammatical accuracy at this stage, it is much easier to progress logically to more complex structures.

A simply structured sentence has two main sections — a *subject* and a *predicate.* The *subject* is the person or thing which *is* or *does* the action of the verb.
Therefore, to find the subject you must:
(a) identify the verb
(b) ask "who?" or "what?" of the verb.

e.g. The clerk fetched the files.
Stage *(a)* In this sentence the word of action, i.e. the verb, is *fetched.*
Stage *(b)* If you ask, "*Who* or *what* fetched . . . ?", the answer must be "*The clerk* fetched . . . ".

Therefore *the clerk* is the *subject* of the sentence.

In the next example you can see that such a sentence can convey a more complex idea. For example:
Department stores concentrate many "shops" in one establishment.
Stage *(a)* In this sentence the verb is *concentrate.*
Stage *(b)* Who or *what* concentrates?

Answer: *Department stores* concentrate . . . .

Therefore the subject of the sentence is *Department stores.*

The *predicate* of a sentence is what is said *about* the subject.

Given the same example, you will see that once you have established what the subject is, the predicate becomes obvious because you can easily identify *what is being said about the subject.*

e.g. Department stores (*subject*) Concentrate many "shops" in one establishment (*predicate*)

You will notice that *the predicate includes the verb.*

TASK ONE

In the following sentences, identify the verb by drawing a circle around it.; put brackets around the subject, and underline the complete predicate. Label each main part clearly, as in the example given.

e.g. (The Managing Director) (called) a meeting.

subject ***predicate***

(i) Department stores offer a wide range of commodities.

(ii) Departments are segregated within each store.

(iii) A "buyer" controls each selling department.

(iv) On larger items, credit facilities are offered.

(v) Large stores allow other firms to lease a portion of the floor space.

As you have seen, the fact that sentences are constructed simply and logically does not mean that they cannot convey important ideas. In fact this simplicity often makes the information have more impact, and therefore makes it more effective as a piece of communication. However, it can only be effective if the grammatical structure is correct. It is often (but not always!) easy to identify whether or not a sentence is correct by the sound of it.

EXERCISE

Read the following passage to yourself, and write out each complete sentence on a separate line. Make sure you begin each one with a capital letter, and finish it with a full stop. Although this basic punctuation will seem obvious to you, its importance must be emphasised. Many people have problems with communication because they become careless about the elementary rules of written English. You can see in this exercise how difficult a passage is to read and understand if these rules are not observed.

There are seven sentences here. Each one is grammatically correct and makes a clear, concise statement of fact.

A public corporation aims to operate " in the public interest" it is fully accountable to the public through Parliament the day-to-day management is in the hands of a board of directors some of these are part-time a Minister responsible to Parliament must approve all appointments accounts must be published capital can be acquired from accumulated profits, loans from the Government or direct borrowing from the public.

TASK TWO

Rewrite the following sentences in the space provided using the correct form of the verb indicated in brackets.

(i) There (*to be*) many methods of communication in business.

(ii) When we (*to write*) a message it should be clear and accurate.

(iii) Spoken communication is often (*to help*) by the use of gestures.

(iv) Diagrams and charts (*to present*) information visually.

You will have realised while you were completing the task above that one *particular* form of the verb is required in each sentence to make it correct. This is one of the most important discoveries you can make in written English – that the form of the verb is governed by the words to which it is related. The general rule that shows us how this relationship works is called the agreement of subject and verb.

The Agreement of Subject and Verb

In Unit II you spent some time setting verbs out in their various parts, and you will have seen that a verb can be used in its *singular* form or its *plural* form. The form you will require in any sentence will depend upon the subject.

If the *subject* is *singular*, the *verb* must be *singular*.

If the *subject* is *plural*, the *verb* must be *plural*.

For example: A large *variety* of socks *was* on sale.

In this sentence the important fact is not that there were socks on sale, but that there was a *variety* of socks. The phrase *a large variety* forms the *subject* of the sentence because the words "of socks" are put in only to show what type of merchandise is being discussed. In fact, these two words could be left out without altering the meaning of the main statement of fact in the sentence:

A large variety (of socks) *was on sale.*

In the original sentence, many of you will think that it would sound better to say "A large variety of socks *were* on sale". However, the word "variety" is singular the therefore the verb must also be singular, i.e. *was* (this is the singular form of the verb "to be" in the past tense).

The following example demonstrates the use of the same subject in its *plural* form, and the associated part of the verb "to be" changes accordingly.

Four *varieties* of butter *were* on sale.

The situation here is similar to the one before. The subject is "varieties", and as there are more than one being discussed, the subject must be *plural.* Therefore the plural form of the verb is required, i.e. *were.*

NOTE: The following words are *always singular* when they form part of the subject of a sentence: either, neither, every, kind, type, assortment.

For example: *Every* one of the letters *was* put through the franking machine.

So, there are some circumstances in which a sentence is made to *sound* clumsy, but *must* be constructed in this way to be correct.

The rule of agreement between subject and verb must be adhered to whenever you write a sentence.

EXERCISE

Decide which of the following sentences are wrong, and write out a corrected version.

(a) Local authorities has a definite effect on our daily living standards.

(b) They are responsible for maintaining national educational standards at a local level.

(c) Public health are an area in which local authorities must aim to maintain high standards.

(d) Clearly linked to the health services is the general social welfare services.

(e) All authorities provides police, fire and emergency services.

(f) Central government use the local authority as an agent for the repair and maintenance of roads.

(g) The upkeep and improvement of libraries come within the local authorities' responsibility.

(h) Outside London, the type of authority which wield most power is the "county" authority.

(i) There are six metropolitan counties and about thirty-nine counties in England.

(j) "District" authorities represents the second tier of the county structure.

EXERCISE

Identify 10 verbs in the following passage. For each verb you select, *write down the form of the verb used in the passage,* indicate its *subject, whether it is used in the singular or the plural, and show its infinitive.* For example:

Form used in passage	Subject	Singular/Plural	Infinitive
govern	regulations	plural	to govern

The Chairman of a meeting has a number of specific duties to perform. Some of these may be set out in the regulations which govern meetings, but many more are implicit in his appointment or arise out of common law.

Before a meeting commences he must satisfy himself that it has been called in the proper manner and that it is properly constituted. This means that his own appointment must be in order, and there must be a quorum During the meeting he must conduct the proceedings strictly in accordance with the rules, keep order and ensure that business is dealt with in the sequence set out in the agenda paper.

In dealing with sentences so far, you have seen how a single statement can be clearly expressed. However, there are times when you need to put in a little more information to support or expand the basic facts. This can easily be done by the addition of a clause or phrase to the main statement, There are many different types of clauses or phrases, but it is not really necessary for you to be able to analyse them in detail. The most important things for you to remember are that:

(*a*) the main statement in a sentence must be able to stand on its own as a complete sentence; and

(*b*) any additional information must conform to the established pattern of the sentence, i.e. it must *fit in with* and *be grammatically compatible with* the main statement.

For example:

The "district" authority, which is subordinate to the "county" authority, *is responsible for implementing national policy at a more local level.*

The main statement is in italics, and the additional information is put in between two commas at a suitable point in the sentence. If this additional clause is omitted, the rest of the sentence still makes complete sense. The additional information in this example is designed to indicate the relationship between the two types of authority without writing a separate sentence.

There are a number of standard methods of integrating and combining phrases, clauses and sentences, and these will be explained in detail in Unit III. For the moment, aim at simplicity of structure and include limited additional information in whatever way seems appropriate *only if absolutely necessary.*

EXERCISE

Read the following passage and complete the exercises given at the end.

THE STOCK EXCHANGE

Earlier in the unit it was stated that shareholders in public limited companies were not allowed to withdraw their capital from the company, but were able to sell their shares to others seeking to buy. The Stock Exchange provides the mechanism whereby the buyers and the sellers can be brought together. It is, in effect, a market place, and the prices of shares are determined by the laws of supply and demand. Briefly, this is rather similar to what happens with many agricultural products – if harvests are good more produce will be available than people really need; therefore the farmer will have to reduce the price to encourage people to buy more than they would normally. The reverse would happen if harvests were poor. There would be insufficient produce to meet people's needs, and they would tend to push the price up by bidding against each other for available supplies.

Members of the public are not allowed to go to the Stock Exchange themselves, but must arrange to buy or sell shares through a stockbroker. The broker is given the details of the shares to be bought or sold, and he contacts a stockjobber at the Stock Exchange to obtain details of the shares' current value.

Different classes of shares, e.g. banks; mines; industrials, are each dealt with by a small number of jobbers – experts in their chosen field – who are able to assess the value or price of a share according to the quantities being bought and sold. (The levels of supply and demand will themselves be decided not only by present levels of profitability of the issuing company, but also by other factors such as expected future performance.) The jobber quotes two prices to the broker before he knows if the broker wishes to buy or sell. The higher price is what the jobber is prepared to sell the shares for, and the lower price is what he is prepared to buy them for – the difference between the two is the jobber's "turn" or profit. The broker states his client's requirements and completes the deal on his behalf, charging a commission based on the total value of the transaction.

Many thousands of shares change hands in this way every day, but it is important to note that whilst ownership of the shares may change hands, and therefore ownership of at least part of the company, no part of the money changing hands is paid to the company. It is rather as if you were to sell a second-hand car – you would receive the money from the buyer, but you would not expect to have to pay any part of that money to the car's original manufacturer. He would have received his money when the car was first sold. In the case of company shares, the company receives the capital subscribed for the shares when they are first issued, and thereafter is only concerned with the change in ownership for the payment of dividends, etc.

The main advantage to the company in having a Stock Exchange quotation is that shareholders know that they can convert their shares back into cash at any time. This is a particularly important selling point for shares when they are first offered to the public.

Considerable importance is attached to Stock Exchange activity by the media, but it should be remembered that they are talking about what is primarily a "second-hand" market, and if share prices rise (or fall) it does not affect the amount of capital already carried by the company. However, it does reflect the level of confidence in the country's economic condition, and if share prices fall then lack of confidence may inhibit people's willingness to buy shares being offered for the first time.

Very little "new" capital (about 7½ per cent to 10 per cent) is raised by the direct sale of shares through the exchange, and this is usually done by means of a "rights issue", i.e. existing shareholders have the "right" to subscribe for new shares being issued by the company – usually at slightly preferential rates.

Earlier in this Section it was indicated that diagrams were a useful method of communication. The following diagram illustrates the mechanics of buying and selling shares.

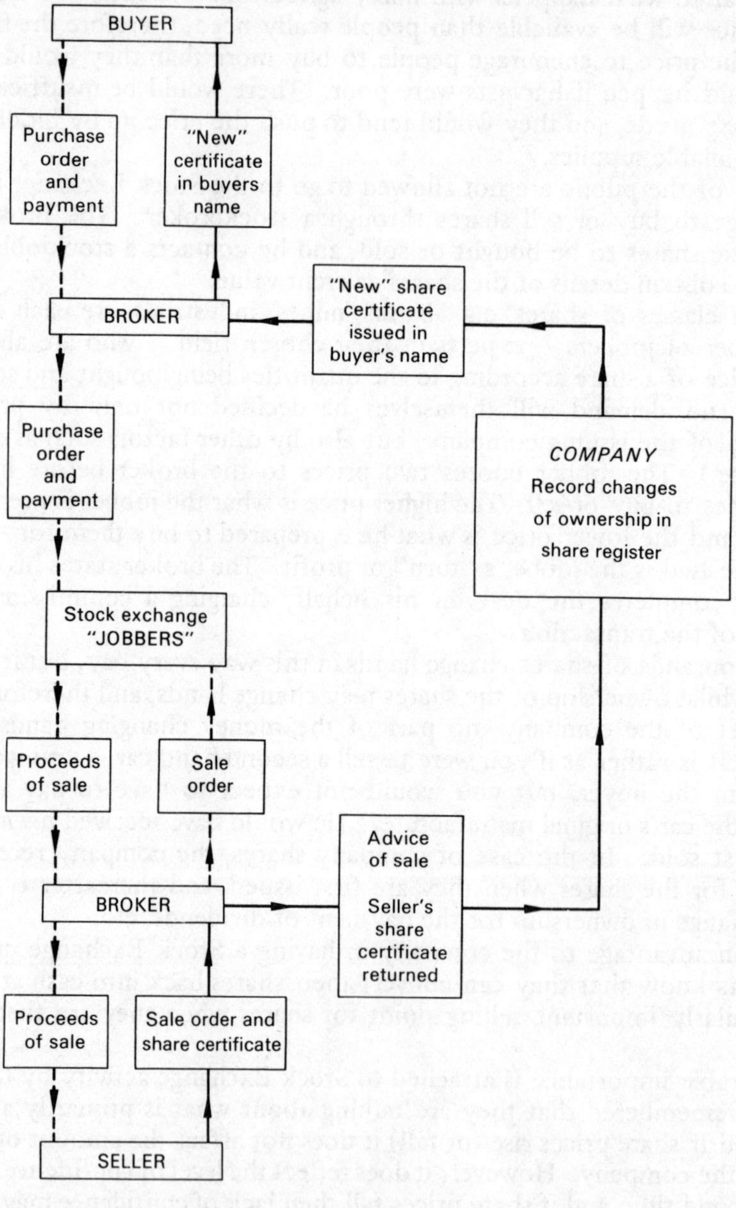

(*a*) Discuss whether or not the diagram presents the information more effectively than the written text, being prepared to explain the reasons for your point of view.

(*b*) Construct an alternative diagram to convey the same information as clearly and simply as possible.

TASK THREE

Complete the following sentences, basing your statements on the information given in the passage on the Stock Exchange.

(i) Shareholders in public limited companies cannot ______________________

____

(ii) Shareholders can dispose of shares by ______________________

____

(iii) The Stock Exchange is ______________________

____

(iv) The laws of supply and demand ______________________

____

(v) A stockbroker arranges ______________________

____

(vi) A stockjobber works ______________________

____

(vii) Stockjobbers specialise ______________________

____

(viii) Two prices are quoted ______________________

____

(ix) A broker charges commission ______________________

____

(x) When a company's shares change hands, the company ______________________

____

At this point it would be useful to recap on some of the points you considered in Unit I, in the section on using a dictionary. One of the important considerations when using words is whether or not they are given a specialist or technical meaning, or whether they are used in their general sense. The dictionary is an important aid to clarifying these meanings, as it is essential to avoid using a word in one sense when the other is intended. If you think a technical term will confuse your reader, you might find it easier to express yourself in general terms.

Consider the following sentences.

(a) A trader's capital is the excess of his assets over his liabilities.

(b) A trader ascertains his capital by deducting his liabilities from his assets.

(c) A trader is worth the amount by which what he owns exceeds his debts to others.

(d) By deducting what a trader owes from what he possesses we are able to ascertain his capital.

All of these sentences express the same idea, but the language is different. In the first two sentences, the technical or *specialist* language of the accountant is accurate and concise — as long as you understand the terms used. In the last two sentences, the same idea is expressed in terms which should be understood by *anybody* because they are *general* terms. Previously, you were asked to concentrate on the specialist meaning of particular words, but it is important that you should be aware of the need to express ideas in general terms in certain circumstances. Therefore the following tasks encourage you to consider *both* ways of expressing ideas while still aiming to keep the structure of your sentences as simple and concise as possible.

TASK FOUR

Using your dictionary to help you, write a short sentence to express the meaning of each of the following terms as used in the *business* sense. In the example, you are shown how such a sentence can be structured in different ways. This *variety* of sentence structure can make your written style more interesting, while retaining clarity and brevity. For example:

advance:

The word "advance" is often used in business to refer to a loan.

In business, it is common practice to refer to a loan as an "advance".

When used in the business sense, the word "advance" is used to mean a loan.

In your answers to the following questions you may use any suitable sentence structure as long as it is grammatically correct, accurate, and as brief as possible. If you have forgotten the desirable characteristics of basic sentences revise the earlier part of this section before you continue.

(i) assets: ______________________________

____

(ii) commission: ______________________________

____

(iii) interest: ______________________________

____

(iv) plant: ______________________________

____

(v) royalty: ______________________________

____

(vi) security: ______________________________

____

(vii) statement: ______________________________

____

(viii) stock: ______________________________

____

(ix) partnership: ______________________________

____

(x) depreciation: ______________________________

____

EXERCISE

Without repeating the definition of the words in the previous task, use each of them in an ordinary sentence to show that you clearly understand their *business* use. For example:

advance: The sole trader obtained an *advance* from his bank to expand his business.

EXERCISE

For each of the words above, write a sentence in which you show clearly the *general* meaning of the word. For example:

The development of electronics has led to a tremendous *advance* in communications.

TASK FIVE

This is a difficult task which will test your ability to express yourself clearly when you are unable to use specialist or technical terms. Explain in non-technical language, as if for a person who knows nothing at all about business, what is meant by each of the following sentences. Look back at the example on page 76 and be prepared to work out your answers "in rough" before you write them into this book. Use your dictionary to help you where necessary. The words in italics need special clarification.

(i) There is a *debit* balance of £50 on Mr Harding's account. ________________

____

____

(ii) The *gross* profit for the year was £7,200. ________________

____

____

(iii) Small payments are made from *petty cash*. ________________

____

____

(iv) I have an *overdraft* at the bank. ________________

____

____

(v) Cheques are not *legal tender*. ________________

____

____

LIBRARIES AND BOOKS

As well as being able to express youself clearly and accurately in writing, you will be required at many stages in your course to make use of a library for private study or research. The word *research* is often associated with people who are studying for a degree or who are involved in some other academic work. However, it also applies in a most practical sense to people in all walks of life who need to be able to use books, investigate problems and search for specific information. This is where libraries are invaluable, because they have far more resources at their disposal than any individual could ever hope to acquire.

If you are not used to libraries, you might feel a little uncomfortable at first because the atmosphere will almost certainly be quieter and more restrained than most other working situations. However, don't be over-awed by this seemingly restrictive situation – make the most of it. You have an ideal opportunity to work at your own pace, in your own way, and from you own chosen sources; you can explore any topic in depth, or quickly skim through a book to learn the major facts. Whatever approach you take, the library is one of your most important and useful sources of information.

There are many different types of library, but the ones you will have easiest access to are academic libraries, i.e. belonging to a college, school, etc., or public reference and lending libraries. These libraries contain much material of general interest such as encyclopaedias, newspapers and magazines, as well as many books and periodicals of

The storage of such quantities of material poses an enormous problem, and it is essential that a strict organisational system is adopted so that specific source material can easily be "tracked down". The easiest way to do this is to group publications together in different parts of the library according to type of publication and/or subject. The division by *subject* is usually used for books, and the library *classifies* each book before it is put into the library. The most commonly used system is a *decimal classification system* in which *subjects* are allocated a number between 1 and 1000. The main subject areas are as follows:

000 General Works	500 Pure Science
100 Philosophy	600 Technology
200 Religion	700 The Arts
300 Social Sciences	800 Literature
400 Language	900 History, Geography

There are obviously many divisions within these main subject areas, and these are catered for and numbered in a logical way, the aim being to allow for ten divisions within each main section. For example, Technology (600) is divided into General (600); Medicine (610); Engineering (620); Agriculture (630); Domestic Science (640); Office and Business Techniques (650); Chemical Technology (660); Manufacture (670); Specialised Trades (680); Building (690). Once this is done, the classification of more specific aspects of a subject follows a logical pattern. If you consider the Engineering division (620), this can be sub-divided to cater for the different branches of engineering technology, each one being numbered thus:

General Engineering	620	Railway/Highway	625
Mechanical	621	Hydraulic	626
Mining	622	Natural Waters	627
Military	623	Public Health	628
Civil	624	Transport	629

We now reach the stage where this system can be recognised as a *decimal* system, because a decimal point is introduced to allow for further specialisation, and figures can be added *after* the decimal point to cover even the smallest aspect of any subject.

TASK SIX

Go to your college library and find books which bear the following numbers. Give the name of the book, the author(s), and say which general section it is classified under. Complete as many as possible.

Number	*Title*	*Author(s)*	*General Section*
332.6			
791.45			
641.5			
621.3			
952.74			
111.13			
869.92			
248.84			
573.22			
485.1721			

Having completed Task Six you will have become accustomed to the general layout of your college library and will probably have noticed where magazines are displayed, where the newspapers are kept and where the reference section is situated. (The *reference section* contains books which are "for reference only", *i.e. they cannot be taken out of the library on loan.*) You should at some stage have noticed that there was a section which was made up of cabinets containing numerous small drawers. These are the library *catalogues.* The quickest way to find exactly where a particular source is located in a library is to make use of the catalogues and indexes.

Most libraries have an *author catalogue.* The index cards for this are arranged alphabetically according to the author's surname or the name of the organisation which issued the publication. This catalogue is particularly useful if you wish to discover how many books the library has by a particular writer, or if you want to find one or more publications by an individual author. The diagram at the top of page 81 shows an author catalogue index card.

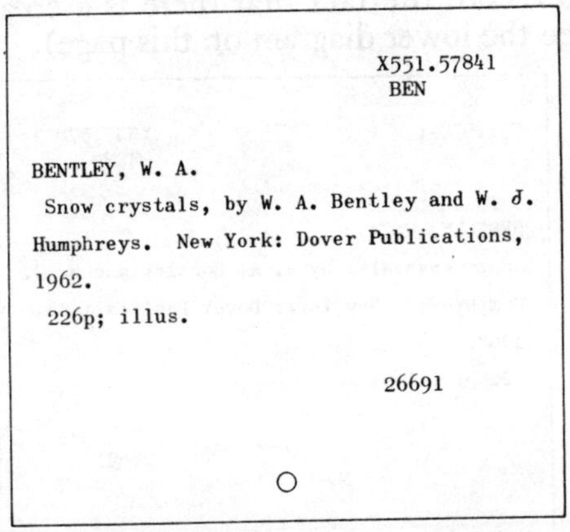

X551.57841
BEN

BENTLEY, W. A.
Snow crystals, by W. A. Bentley and W. J. Humphreys. New York: Dover Publications, 1962.
226p; illus.

26691

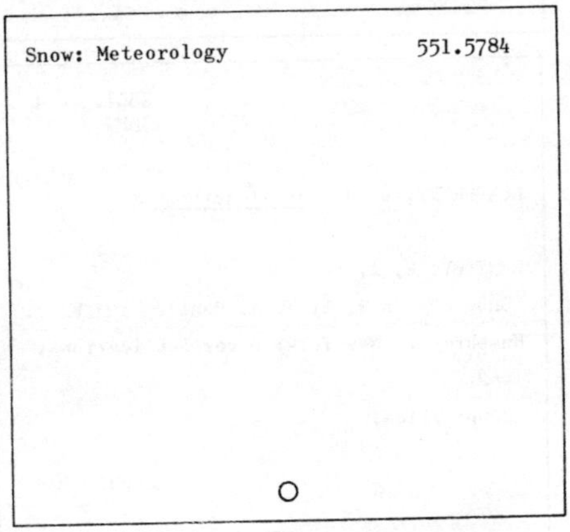

Snow: Meteorology 551.5784

The library will also have some form of *subject index*. If this is a card index, cards will be arranged to indicate subjects in alphabetical order and will give classification numbers for each subject so that you can discover exactly where to look for books dealing with any particular topic. The diagram immediately above shows a subject catalogue index card.

Once you have a classification number for a specific subject, you can find out what books are available on that subject by checking out the number in the *classified catalogue* which will have cards arranged in numerical order, i.e. in the same order as the books are arranged on the shelves. When you have found the relevant numerical section in the catalogue you will find a record of all the books – titles, authors and numbers – which deal with that subject area. You can then select the most suitable, and find it on the library shelves. A classified catalogue index card is shown at the top of page 82.

A thorough understanding of your library's catalogues and indexes is essential if you are to use this valuable facility to its best advantage. If you have difficulty finding or using the catalogues, the library staff will normally be extremely helpful in giving you guidance.

There is one type of entry in the catalogue which has not been mentioned yet, and that is an *added entry*. This is inserted into a catalogue if a book has more than one author.

It enables the librarian to record the fact that there is a co-author by entering the book under his name as well (see the lower diagram on this page).

```
551.57841                           X551.57841
                                       BEN

BENTLEY, W. A.
 Snow crystals, by W. A. Bentley and W. J.
Humphreys.  New York: Dover Publications,
1962.
 226p; illus.

                                    26691
```

```
                                    X551.57841
                                       BEN

HUMPHREYS, W. J.  joint author

BENTLEY, W. A.
 Snow crystals, by W. A. Bentley and W. J.
Humphreys.  New York: Dover Publications,
1962.
 226p; illus.

                                    26691
```

The exercises which follow are to help you get used to using your library effectively and with confidence.

EXERCISE

List the types of catalogues and indexes your library has, and give a brief indication of the information each gives.

EXERCISE

By using the relevant catalogue, answer the questions below.

(a) How many different authors called *Williams* have books in your library? Give the title and name the general subject area of one book for each of them.

(b) Find out how many books your library possesses written by each of these well-known authors: William Shakespeare; Oliver Goldsmith; John Steinbeck; George Orwell.

(c) Give the names of two books recorded under the following classification numbers: 133; 155.4; 215; 745.592; 643.3.

(d) Find out the classification numbers under which these subjects can be found: electricity; the manufacture of gas; office practice; building; transistors.

(e) By using the correct catalogue, find out whether your library has the following books in stock. Give the classified number and date of publication.

Book of Child Care	Hugh Jolly
The Child and the Family	Maria Montessori
Solar Energy for Man	Brian J. Brinkworth
World Resources and Energy	Michael Palmer
Tides	D. H. Macmillan

EXERCISE

(a) Name two weekly journals taken by your library.

(b) Are the following journals/periodicals taken by your library?

Design Engineering	*New Law Journal*
Mariner	*Visual Education*
Flora	*Housecraft*

(c) Give the names of all the newspapers your library takes.

(d) Are there any periodicals which appear to be specifically aimed at people interested in office work?

(e) Find out if your library takes specialist periodicals in any of the following fields. If so, give the name of one for each subject area.

Adult Education	Catering
Accountancy	Drama/The theatre
Law	Computers

The Use of Books

Once you have found a book which you think might contain some information you need, the problem is how to find that information quickly. If you approach a book in a logical manner you will save yourself time and effort. Obviously, you do not want to read right through the book, hoping to come across the required information. The following sequences of activities should help you find out whether or not the book contains what you want in as short a time as possible.

(a) Glance at the *title* page (this should indicate the general subject area).

(b) Read through the *table of contents*. This might be quite brief, but will sometimes contain a summary of the chapters themselves.

(c) If you are not successful so far, look at the *index* where, if you are lucky, the particular subject you are interested in will be listed. The index will normally be found at the back of the book, and subject areas are listed alphabetically with the relevant page numbers printed next to them.

(d) If the index is not very helpful, or the book has no index, the *preface* or *foreword* should outline what the author intended to cover in the book.

(e) Another section which many books have is that which contains an *appendix* or number of *appendixes*. These are designed to give you specialist or tabulated material to which brief reference is made in the text.

Remember a book is a "tool" which, if used effectively, can help you produce better work. However, bear in mind the following points which will help you decide whether or not the information you are collecting is useful to you.

(a) *When was the material written?* Some areas of study advance at such a rate that information can easily be out of date. Consider carefully whether the age of the material will affect its validity.

(b) *Has the book been revised recently?* You will find a publisher's note to this effect at the front of the book, near the title page. If a book has been revised recently it will mean that the necessary information has been updated.

(c) *Is the author a well-known person in his own particular field of study?* The "blurb" on the cover or flyleaf of a book will give you some idea of the author's background, qualifications and professional status. This is often a reasonable indication of his knowledge and ability.

(d) *Is the information in the book presented logically?* It is essential for a thorough understanding of any subject that it should be presented in a clear and orderly manner. If you are constantly puzzled by questions which do not appear to be answered in the text, or if there seem to be gaps in the development of ideas, it might be better to look for an alternative source.

EXERCISE

The following questions are based on the use of books, but will also require you to apply your knowledge of how the library works. If any of the books do not appear in your library, you should try to construct a similar question (and provide the answer) based on any suitable book which *is* on your library shelves. Therefore you will end up with the same number of questions and answers whether or not the particular book is available, and the exercise will have served its purpose of giving you useful practice in handling and using books correctly. You should copy out the question, and then give your answer as a complete, well constructed sentence, keeping it as simple in structure as possible. If there is more than one question in any section, write a *separate* and *complete sentence* in answer to each one. For example:

What is the title of chapter four in *A History of the English Language* by Albert C. Baugh?

Answer: The title of chapter four is "Foreign influences on Old English".

(a) On what page is the *Co-operative Union* mentioned in the book *Textbook of Commerce* by Hughes and Loveridge? Who are the publishers?

(b) Answer the following questions based on the *Foreword* to *World Energy Strategies* by Amory B. Lovin.

(i) What happened in autumn 1973?

(ii) What is the profession of the author of the book?

(iii) What are the two groups of problems that students of the energy problem should consider?

(iv) Who wrote the foreword, and from what country does he come?

(c) Find the book *Office Practice* by Swift and Stanwell, and answer the following questions. Say where in the book you find the information.

(i) What is the name of the currency used by each of the following countries:

Denmark; Switzerland; Yugoslavia; Austria; Poland?

(ii) What is the county town of Devonshire?

(iii) What is the county town of Gwent?

(iv) What is the county town of Caithness?

EXERCISE

Look for a book which gives information on the topics given below. You should aim to find one which presents the information in a manner you find reasonably easy to read, and which gives a fairly brief outline of each topic. There is no point in "ploughing" through an over-complicated textbook, when you require a broad understanding of the concepts only. Therefore bear in mind that the type of book you can successfully work from will be one aimed at CSE/"O" Level students, although the information *can* be found in books written for professional/"A" Level students.

You should find the information you want in a book dealing with commerce and/or economics. Glance through the preface to your chosen book to discover the *level* at which it is written.

Topic (a) Economies of scale (sometimes referred to as *the economies of large-scale production).*

Topic (b) Division of labour (also referred to as *specialisation).*

Your written work is to:

(a) List the *economies of scale,* and write a brief explanation of each.

(b) Describe what is meant by the *division of labour* in a few sentences, and list the advantages and disadvantages.

EXERCISE

Making use of the information you were given in Section I, and the book you were working with in the previous exercise, list as many public corporations as you can find. In this case you might be able to supplement your list by referring to other books of a similar type.

UNIT III

Achievement Checklist

When you have completed this unit, you should be able to:

*** Appreciate the activities of an organisation operating in the local and national sectors of the economy;**

*** Understand and use a variety of diagrammatic forms:**

(a) pictograms

(b) bar charts

(c) pie charts

*** Link ideas using a variety of devices;**

*** Achieve fluency and unity in longer sentences;**

*** Understand then put into practice the mechanics of note-making;**

*** Be aware and make use of standard words of reference.**

SECTION I

Introduction to Section I

As it is necessary for you to have an understanding of organisations operating in the local and national sectors of the economy, the unit contains a brief case study which covers both these requirements.

Much of the information has a regional bias, so we anticipate that your tutor will introduce supplementary material in order that you can relate your studies to your own area.

THE ELECTRICITY SUPPLY INDUSTRY – CASE STUDY

The industry, which is publicly owned, consists of the Electricity Council, the C.E.G.B., and twelve Area Electricity Boards in England and Wales (separate arrangements apply in Scotland and Northern Ireland).

The Electricity Council

The Electricity Council is the co-ordinating body for the electricity supply industry in England and Wales. Its main functions are to advise the Secretary of State for Energy, and to aid the Central Electricity Generating Board and the Area Boards in developing and maintaining an efficient, co-ordinated and economical system of electricity supply.

The Council also has certain specific functions, particularly in matters of finance, research and industrial relations.

THE CENTRAL ELECTRICITY GENERATING BOARD (C.E.G.B.)

The C.E.G.B. owns and operates the power stations and main transmission system, supplying electricity in bulk to direct consumers and the Area Boards, which distribute supplies to meet the needs of 49 million people. The C.E.G.B.'s assets are valued at over £3,850 million, and its interconnected "grid" power system is among the largest in the world.

The C.E.G.B. has over 60,000 employees, most of whom are located in the five regions which are responsible for the power stations and transmission system in their areas. The overall structure of the organisation is shown in the diagram below.

Coal is the C.E.G.B.'s principal fuel for electricity generation and over half the coal produced in Britain is consumed in C.E.G.B. power stations. Oil and gas provide about one-quarter of electricity supplies and hydro-electricity less than one-thousandth with nuclear fuel providing the remaining one-eighth. This proportion will increase as the nuclear power stations being built are completed.

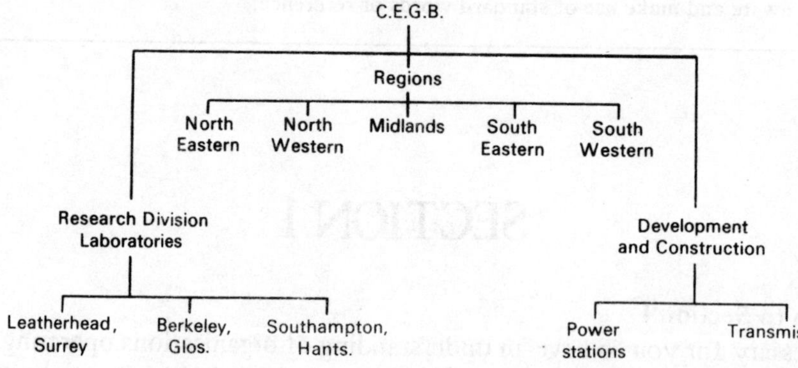

The power stations and the bulk supply points from which Area Boards and direct consumers take their supplies are linked by the "grid" transmission system. It comprises transformers, substations and a network of overhead lines and underground cables which is controlled from the National Control Centre in London.

As one of the largest electricity undertakings in the world, the C.E.G.B. has much to offer in terms of skill and experience and consequently has close relations with many inter-governmental bodies; it participates in the work of international conferences and collaborates with numerous overseas utilities. These activities are co-ordinated through the overseas relations service of the Secretary and Solicitors' Department at Headquarters.

Since 1976 assistance and advice to overseas countries has been co-ordinated through British Electricity International Limited (B.E.I.), a wholly-owned subsidiary company of the Electricity Council which represents the overseas consultancy work of the U.K. electricity supply industry as a whole.

The South Western Region of the C.E.G.B.
This region, which includes South Wales, has twenty-one power stations generating electricity from different forms of energy as follows:

Oil	8
Coal	6
Nuclear	4
Hydro	3
	21

The four nuclear power stations in the region are all located along the Severn Estuary, at Berkeley, Oldbury and two at Hinkley Point (A and B). This area is ideal for power generation by nuclear means since geological conditions are suitable for the very heavy structures which are needed for all large modern power stations and the land is of little agricultural value. In addition the Severn provides the large quantities of cooling water which these stations need, and the slight rise in temperature which results is soon lost when the water is returned to the estuary.

A further advantage of siting nuclear stations in the Severn area is that if coal-fired stations were built there all the fuel would have to be brought in from coalfields in the Midlands and the North, as all the available South Wales coal suitable for the purpose is already being used. This would obviously be expensive and also introduce environmental problems through the handling of very large quantities of coal in an area where this has not been common practice. The Severn Estuary sites are also relatively remote from large centres of population and in the early days of nuclear power this was felt to be an advantage in the unlikely event of an accidental release of radioactivity. However, a lack of such accidents and improved safety measures has led to this restriction on siting being less strictly applied. Nevertheless the stations do produce highly radioactive nuclear waste that has to be handled with great care.

Oil is no longer as economic as it was, following the four-fold increase in price that has taken place over the last few years. However, the advent of North Sea oil means that the stations will be able to use our own supplies which are not only less likely to be interrupted but will also mean major savings on our overseas spending. Even so North Sea (and other) oil supplies will not last for ever and we shall then have to look to alternative sources of energy to use.

The small hydro-electric scheme harnesses the energy of the River Tavy on Dartmoor.

THE "GRID"

The grid is part of a system which transports electricity from the power stations to the areas where people want to use it.

Any transport system, for example roads, needs routes of different sizes for handling different volumes of traffic. It needs motorways, trunk roads, minor roads, lanes and streets. It also needs a system of traffic control. The grid provides the "main roads" along which electricity is moved, subsequently being fed (via substations) into the local lower voltage networks, the "minor roads" of the elctricity distribution system. As well as transporting electricity to wherever it is needed the grid brings further benefits.

(a) It makes electricity supply more reliable by providing an interlocking network of power lines over the whole country so that if one power station or line breaks down, power can be drawn from other power stations along alternative routes.

(b) It cuts out unproductive capital development by reducing the amount of reserve plant needed to cover breakdown and maintenance.

(c) It reduces the cost of electricity because at night and over weekends, when power demands are lower, high-cost stations can be shut down and production concentrated at the lowest-cost stations with efficient modern plant and low fuel costs.

In short the grid is enormously important in helping to provide a reliable and efficient supply of power to the public, and the operational flexibility it provides is invaluable because, unlike other products, electricity cannot be stored. Most manufacturers can stock goods to even out the fluctuation of demand, but electricity must be made as it is used, and must have an instant transport system capable of giving immediate delivery.

AREA ELECTRICITY BOARDS

The twelve Area Boards in England and Wales are responsible for the distribution networks and for the retail sale of electricity to customers. In addition they undertake contracting work and the sale of electrical appliances.

The territory served by the Area Boards covers 151,000 square kilometres with a population of 49 million, and with a wide variation in topography and population density. Rural areas represent as much as seventeen-twentieths of the total area of the country, but account for only about one-fifth of the total population. One of the Boards – dealing with the South West – is now considered in more detail.

THE SOUTH WESTERN ELECTRICITY BOARD

Organisation

The South Western Electricity Board was set up in 1948, along with eleven other Area Boards in England and Wales, when the Electricity Supply Industry was transferred to public ownership. Its main function is to purchase electricity in bulk from the C.E.G.B. and to distribute it to about 1 million consumers throughout the South West.

The members of the Board determine overall policy aided by four chief Officers (the Chief Engineer, the Commercial Manager, the Chief Accountant and the Secretary and Solicitor) who are also reponsible for policy implementation. Specialist services are provided through the Personnel Manager, the Management Services and Development Officer and the Purchasing and Stores Controller.

The Area is divided into thirteen Districts (*see facing page*), each controlled by a manager who also contributes to Board policy and who is responsible for applying it at local level. He is also responsible for good consumer and staff relations in the District. Each manager has senior officers responsible for the engineering, commercial and secretarial accountancy functions respectively. To assist with the co-ordination and implementation of engineering and commercial policy, the Districts are sub-divided into four Groups. Each Group has a comparatively small number of out-posted Head Office staff, some of whom control the electricity distribution system. The chart on the facing page summarises the general organisation of the Area,

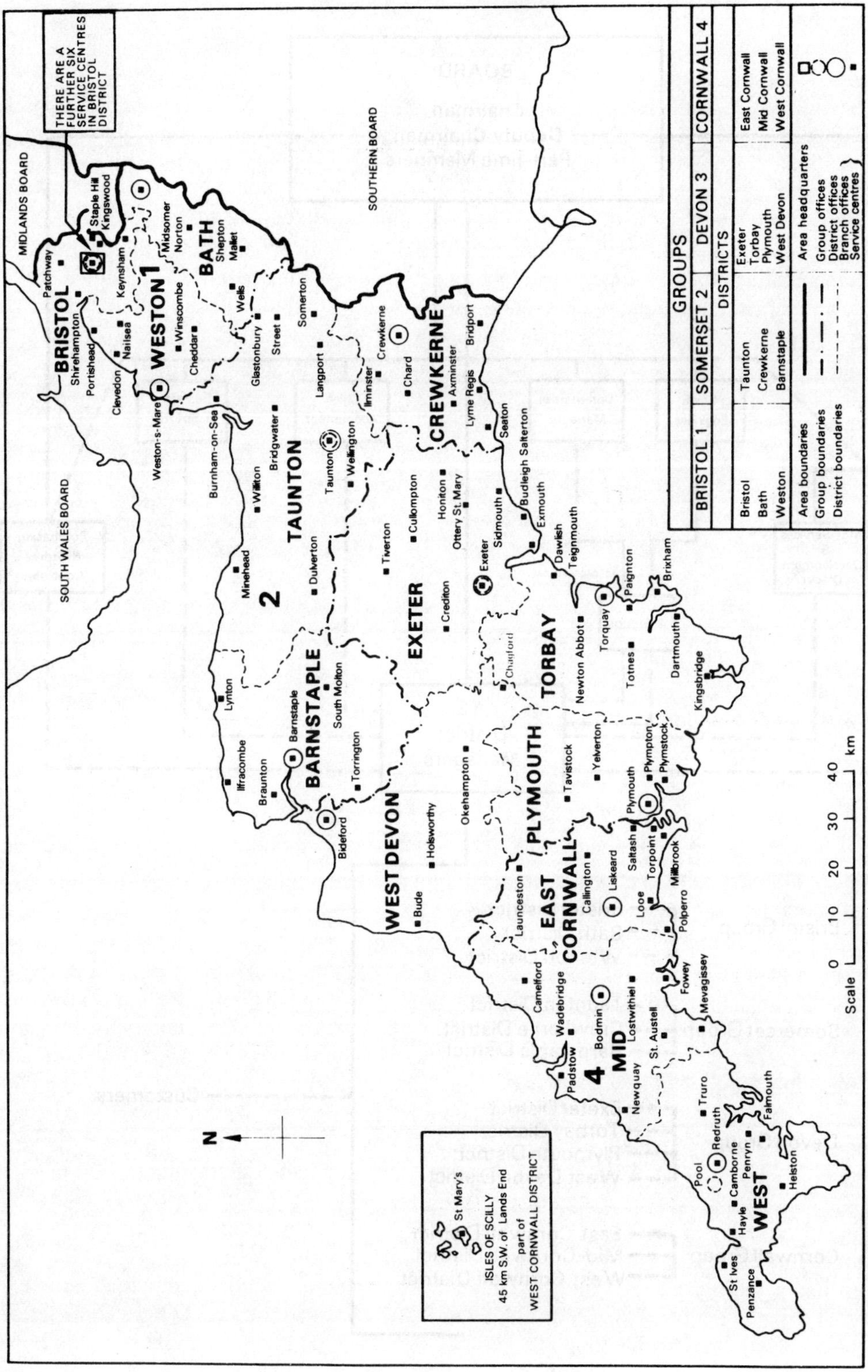
MIDLANDS BOARD
SOUTH WALES BOARD
SOUTHERN BOARD
THERE ARE A FURTHER SIX SERVICE CENTRES IN BRISTOL DISTRICT
BRISTOL
WESTON
BATH
1
TAUNTON
2
CREWKERNE
EXETER
BARNSTAPLE
TORBAY
WEST DEVON
PLYMOUTH
EAST CORNWALL
MID
4
WEST
Patchway
Staple Hill
Kingswood
Shirehampton
Portishead
Clevedon
Nailsea
Keynsham
Midsomer Norton
Shepton Mallet
Winscombe
Cheddar
Wells
Glastonbury
Street
Somerton
Weston-s-Mare
Burnham-on-Sea
Bridgwater
Williton
Minehead
Langport
Ilminster
Crewkerne
Chard
Axminster
Bridport
Lyme Regis
Seaton
Taunton
Wellington
Dulverton
Tiverton
Cullompton
Honiton
Ottery St. Mary
Sidmouth
Budleigh Salterton
Exmouth
Dawlish
Teignmouth
Exeter
Crediton
Chagford
Newton Abbot
Torquay
Paignton
Brixham
Totnes
Dartmouth
Kingsbridge
Lynton
Ilfracombe
Braunton
Barnstaple
South Molton
Torrington
Bideford
Holsworthy
Okehampton
Bude
Tavistock
Yelverton
Plympton
Plymstock
Plymouth
Saltash
Torpoint
Millbrook
Launceston
Callington
Liskeard
Looe
Polperro
Camelford
Wadebridge
Bodmin
Lostwithiel
Fowey
Mevagissey
St. Austell
Padstow
Newquay
Truro
Falmouth
Redruth
Pool
Camborne
Penryn
Helston
Hayle
St Ives
Penzance
ISLES OF SCILLY 45 km S.W. of Lands End part of WEST CORNWALL DISTRICT
St Mary's
N
Scale
0 10 20 30 40 km
GROUPS
BRISTOL 1
SOMERSET 2
DEVON 3
CORNWALL 4
DISTRICTS
Bristol
Bath
Weston
Taunton
Crewkerne
Barnstaple
Exeter
Torbay
Plymouth
West Devon
East Cornwall
Mid Cornwall
West Cornwall
Area boundaries
Group boundaries
District boundaries
Area headquarters
Group offices
District offices
Branch offices
Service centres

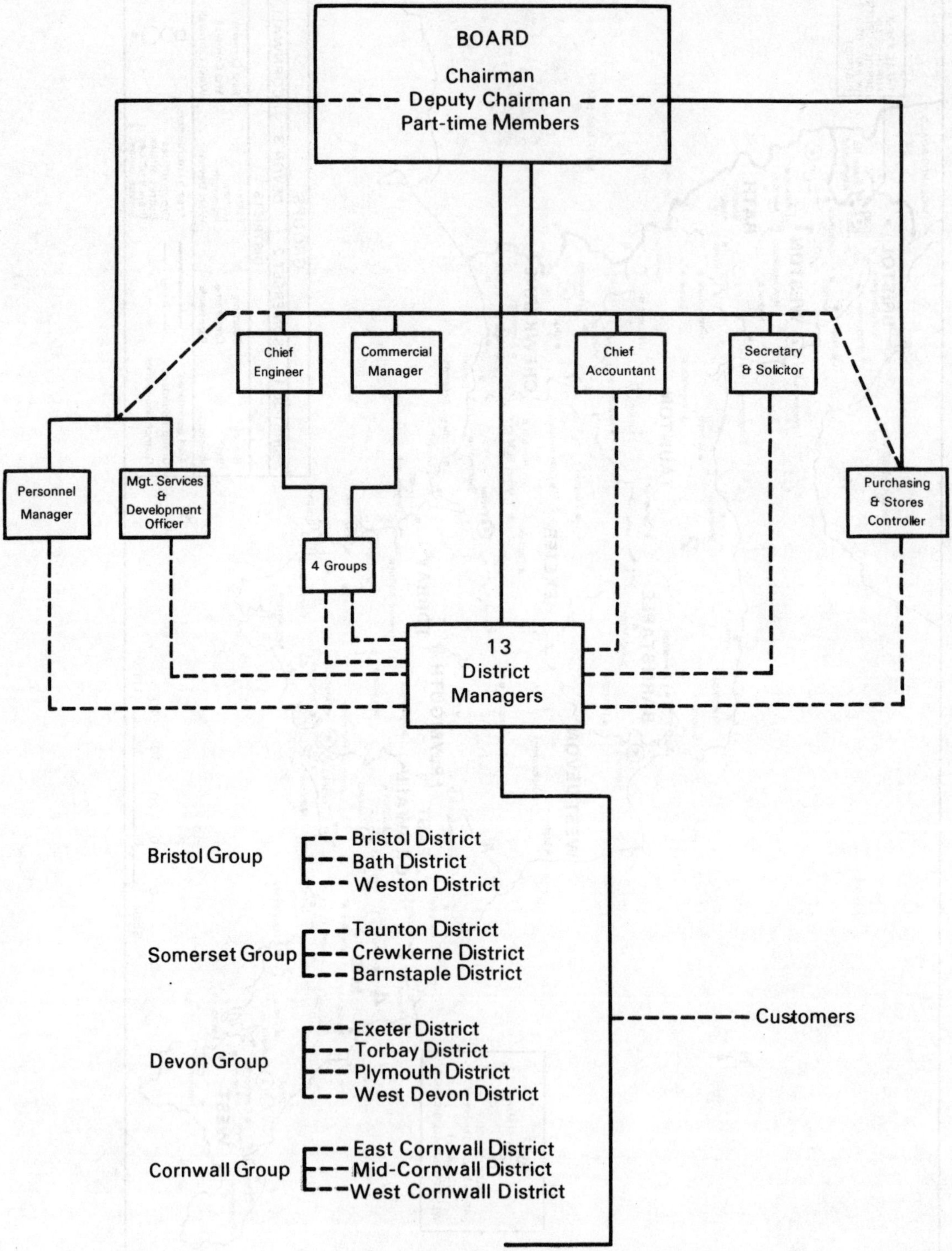
BOARD
Chairman
Deputy Chairman
Part-time Members
Chief Engineer
Commercial Manager
Chief Accountant
Secretary & Solicitor
Personnel Manager
Mgt. Services & Development Officer
Purchasing & Stores Controller
4 Groups
13 District Managers
Bristol Group
Bristol District
Bath District
Weston District
Somerset Group
Taunton District
Crewkerne District
Barnstaple District
Devon Group
Exeter District
Torbay District
Plymouth District
West Devon District
Cornwall Group
East Cornwall District
Mid-Cornwall District
West Cornwall District
Customers

Activities

Electrical Supply to Consumers	*Electricity sold (millions of units)*	*Total Customers at 31/3/77*
Domestic	4,610.4	918,107
Farm	353.9	32,068
Commercial	1,667.3	84,365
Combined domestic and commercial	134.1	11,278
Industrial	2,592.8	8,722
Public lighting	79.8	391
Sales to other Boards	0.1	–
	9,438.4	1,954,931

NOTES:

(*a*) Total revenue from sales of electricity for 1976/77 amounted to £199,171,000.

(*b*) Average cost of units purchased from C.E.G.B. = 1.498p. Average revenue per unit sold = 2.110p.

Extracts from the Chairman's Annual Report 1976/77

The Board welcome the continued improvement in their finances and the return to a profit of £3.5 million after several years of losses.

It is also significant that, after a period of decline, sales of electricity to industrial customers have increased during the year. This improvement on previous trends has resulted in total sales only marginally different from 1975/76, despite a substantial fall in domestic sector sales at the beginning of the year.

Industrial and commercial advisory services of the Board have, throughout the year, been available for advice to customers in the effective use of electricity and this service is regarded as particularly significant in current circumstances when industry and commerce may now be seeking to achieve expansion of their activities with the maximum efficiency in the use of energy.

Under the slogan of "The Way Ahead", staff, Trade Unions and management have participated in joint discussions aimed at improvements in organisation, working methods and technical practices. The programme of studies based on this participative approach is still in its infancy but early results are encouraging.

In the Board's marketing and contracting activities speed and flexibility of response to the customer remain paramount. Strenuous efforts to reduce overhead expenses are continuing to be made in an effort to keep prices and repair charges as low as possible.

For a number of years now, the Board have publicly emphasised their recognition of the difficulties some customers face in paying electricity bills that have become larger as tariffs have increased. Those with genuine problems have been encouraged to make an early approach to the Board for help in solving them. The Board's Budget and Flexible Payment Plan methods and the increasing availability of easy payment stamps have been actively promoted during the year and there are now nearly 27,000 customers participating in the Flexible Payment Plan. Sales of easy payment stamps, which are now available through over 400 retail outlets and 100 Board shops, increased by 24 per cent and amounted to over £3½ million.

Commercial

(*a*) Contracting and sales of appliances activities during the year were affected by reduced consumer expenditure due to the general economic situation. Total turnover for the year was £20.6 million made up of £12.7 million for appliance sales and £7.9 million for contracting resulting in a loss of £212,000 (£510,000 in 1975/76).

(*b*) The SWEBWarm Insulation Service is available to consumers. This service aims to improve the thermal insulation of houses (particularly those built pre-1974) to reduce heat loss – and therefore save energy – which is estimated to be in the following proportions:

walls	$\frac{7}{20}$	roof	$\frac{1}{4}$
ground	$\frac{3}{20}$	windows	$\frac{1}{10}$
draughts (doors and windows)			$\frac{3}{20}$

The remedies recommended are:

walls – foam-filling outside-wall cavities.
roofspace – laying insulation between the joists.
draughts – weather-stripping doors and windows.

In addition:

hot water tank to be properly lagged.

(*c*) Other energy conservation steps taken include resetting time-switches to reduce electricity used; checking and adjustment of heating control system; improvement of lighting installations and general advisory services to customers.

(*d*) The Board operates maintenance and service schemes whereby domestic appliances are regularly checked and serviced for a fixed quarterly sum.

(*e*) Other activities include the design of an all-electric bakery, catering shows and competitions and barn hay-drying systems.

(*f*) The Board offers a wide range of domestic electrical appliances for sale, both "own brand" and others, at its various branches.

Research and Development

(*a*) Progress continues on the introduction of network management by computer.

(*b*) More than 10,000 meters taking 50p coins have been issued and over 27,000 meters taking 10p coins have been fitted with coin boxes holding up to £70.

(*c*) An engineering exhibition "EE76" was held at Taunton. It featured mechanical aids to construction work, technical aids to fault location and maintenance and the network management system.

(*d*) The Board have purchased an instrument for measuring very accurately the temperature of equipment at a distance – even from the Board's helicopter.

Staff

SWEB staff 1976/77

	Reductions	Number at 31st March 1977	Number at 31st March 1976
Managerial and Higher Executive	(+)3	51	48
Technical	36	717	753
Executive, Clerical, Accountancy, Sales, etc.	90	2505	2595
Industrial	213	3654	3867
Technical Staff Trainees	9	13	22
Apprentices	32	147	179
TOTAL	377	7087	7464

NOTES:

(*a*) The total salaries bill (excluding related expenses) for the year amounted to £24.4 million compared with £22.7 million in 1975/76;

(*b*) The staff reduction of 377 was the result of non-replacement following natural wastage coupled with early retirement and selective severance arrangements.

(*c*) Both staff and management have spent considerable time in joint discussions from which ideas for developing the organisation and procedures of the Board are beginning to emerge. It is hoped that the discussions will help to further already close working relationships.

(*d*) In view of the reduced number of trainees appointed in recent years, more emphasis has been given to using training resources for the further development of existing staff.

(*e*) The Board has also been able to provide training on a fee-paying basis to UK companies and overseas organisations. Thirty overseas trainees commenced training during the year.

The South Western Electricity Consultative Council (SWECC)

This is a statutory body established to look after and protect the interests of existing or prospective electricity users in the South West. The members, who serve voluntarily, are appointed by a Government Minister from a broad cross-section of the community including local councillors and representatives of domestic, agricultural, commercial and industrial consumers, trade unions, women's organisations and so on. The Council is entirely independent SWEB and has its own staff and offices in Exeter.

The Council must be consulted by SWEB on any proposed changes in tariffs and on other major matters of policy affecting consumers before decisions are reached. As a result SWEB informs the Council of its general plans and proposals for the future so that the consumer's viewpoint can be obtained and allowed for. In addition SWECC looks into individual complaints from consumers who are not satisfied with the outcome of their earlier complaint direct to SWEB.

There are four local committees consisting partly of Council members appointed by the Minister and partly of other people appointed by the Council on a similar basis from a wide range of local interests. The committees are:

Bristol and District Local Committee	–	covering Bristol and environs.
Cornwall Local Committee	–	covering Cornwall.
Devon Local Committee	–	covering Devon.
Somerset Local Committee	–	covering Somerset, most of Avon and part of south-west Dorset.

SECTION II

NOTE: For successful completion of this section, you will require a ruler, pair of compasses and a protractor.

DIAGRAMMATIC PRESENTATION

It is possible, at any time, to draw up a statement showing the financial state of any business, no matter how large or how small it might be. This statement is known as a *balance sheet* and is little more than a list of *assets* (the things the business *owns*) and *liabilities* (the things the business *owes*).

R. U. BUSY
BALANCE SHEET
(as at 31.12.19——)

Capital (at 1.1.19——)	£10,000		*Fixed Assets*		
Add net profit	600		Buildings	£5,100	
			Machinery	1,900	
	10,600		Vehicles	1,800	£8,800
Less Drawings	1,000				
		£9,600			
Long-term Liabilities			*Current Assets*		
Bank loan		900	Stock-in-trade	1,400	
			Trade debtors	570	
Current Liabilities			Cash-in-hand	330	2,300
Creditors for stock		600			
		£11,100			£11,100

You will notice the orderly arrangement in columns and the itemised totals, so that the financial position can be easily seen.

TASK ONE

You are required to complete the following balance sheet by inserting the missing values (marked by an asterisk).

I. M. SOLVENT
BALANCE SHEET
(as at 31.12.19––)

Capital (as at 1.1.19––)	£48,200		*Fixed Assets*		
Add Net profit	7,300		Land and buildings	28,000	
	*		Fixtures and fittings	8,000	
			Vehicles	*	£48,000
Less Drawings	4,600	£ *			
Long-term Liabilities			*Current Assets*		
Bank loan		8,300	Stock-in-trade	7,000	
			Trade debtors	4,500	
Current Liabilites			Cash in bank	2,000	
Trade creditors		2,800	Cash in hand	5,000	£ *
		£ *			£ *

For people familiar with book-keeping or accounting, the balance sheet provides an immediate picture of the state of the business. For those without any experience the balance sheet is simply a mass of words and figures. The same can be said of any information relating to aspects of business or commerce that is numerical in nature. However if this numerical information is presented in a different form it can be much easier to understand.

The world we live in is essentially a visual world with pictures and diagrams in many instances conveying more to a person than the written word.

PICTOGRAMS

Diagrams appropriate for use with business information are based upon a small number of very simple types which can be added to in order to show more detail.

This can be illustrated using the balance sheet for R. U. Busy:

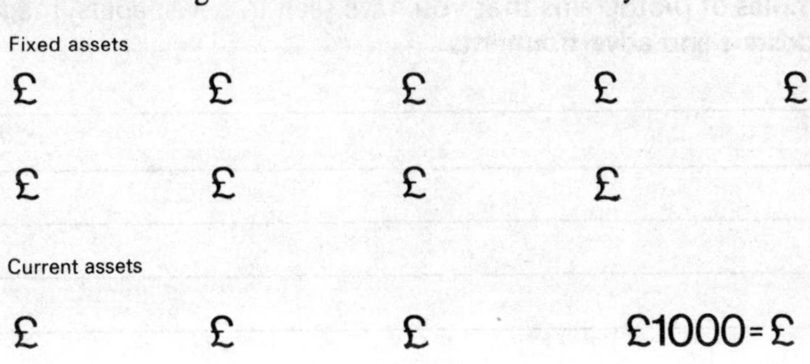

Fixed assets

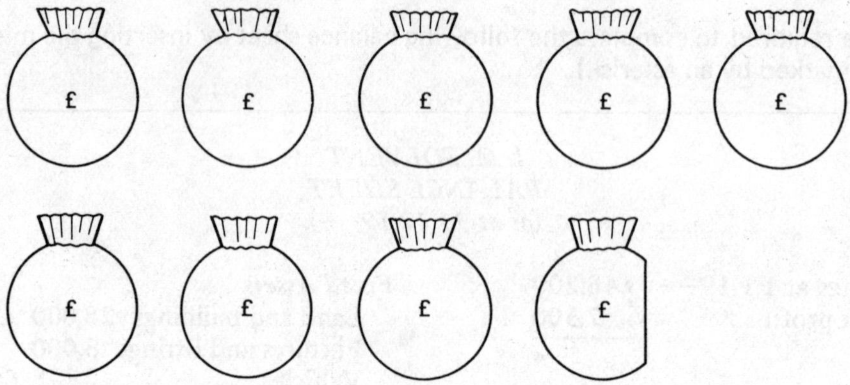

Current assets

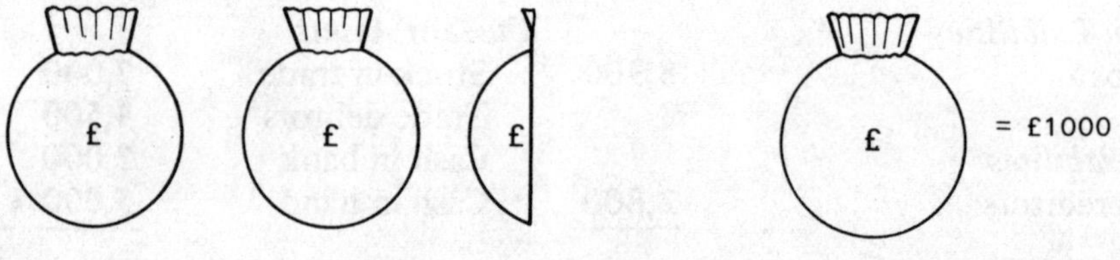

The information is shown here as two examples of a *pictogram* and involves the use of pictures to represent numerical data. There are several different ways in which information can be shown pictorially. These illustrations are the easiest to understand; the same picture being repeated an appropriate number of times, with part of a picture representing fractional amounts. Thus a complete "£"sign or money bag represents £1,000 and £800 is represented by $\frac{8}{10}$of a "£" sign or money bag and £300 is represented by $\frac{3}{10}$of a "£" sign or money bag.

In order to convey its full meaning each pictogram must, besides being as simple and clean as possible, have a title and an indication of the quantity each picture represents.

A more complicated way of producing a pictogram is to use pictures of changing size; the value is indicated by the size of picture shown. The construction of such pictograms is not recommended, since for example a doubling of the figure being represented involves increasing the area of the picture four times, and lies outside the scope of this book.

TASK TWO

List five examples of pictograms that you have seen in newspapers, magazines and books or on posters and advertisements.

(i) ______________________________

(ii) ______________________________

(iii) ______________________________

(iv) ______________________________

(v) ______________________________

EXERCISE

Illustrate the information below in the form of pictograms.

(a) The cars produced by a company in each of three years was as follows:
Year 1 – 120,000 Year 2 – 145,000 Year 3 – 180,000

(b) The number of passengers carried by four different coach companies in a particular week was:

Easirider & Sons	3,250
C. & S. Traction Company	2,500
Tinajen Omnibus Company	2,000
Travellers Coaches	1,800

BAR CHARTS

The pictogram is designed so that the numerical information can be seen and appreciated at a glance. This may also be achieved by the use of *bar charts*. In this diagrammatic form the information is represented by rectangles. The appearance of the rectangles varies according to the complexity of the information that is being shown.

The essential property of the bar chart is that the height (or length) of the rectangle represents the *size* of the information being illustrated.

Simple Bar Charts

Using R. U. Busy's balance sheet the total fixed and total current assets may be illustrated as follows:

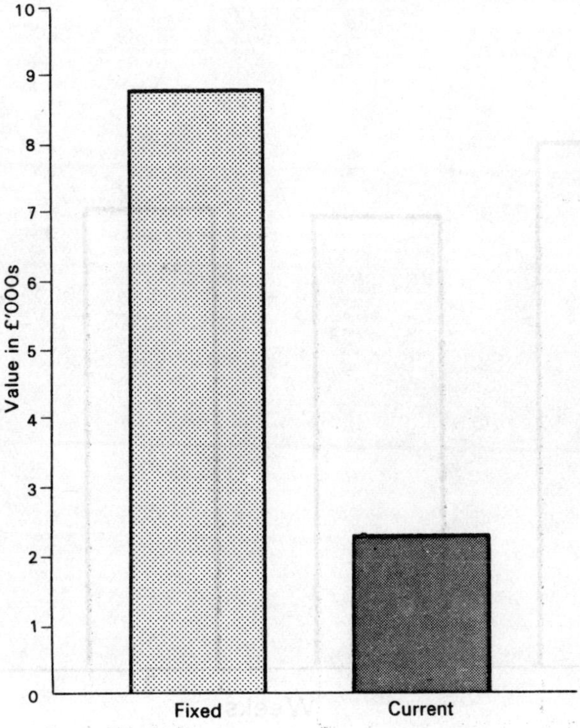

The bar chart is produced in order that it may be easily and quickly understood. To achieve this it is presented in as clear and bold a manner as possible. This means that the heights (or lengths) of the rectangles must be capable of rapid assessment by referring to a line drawn to the same scale. In the example above 1 unit of height represents £1,000 and fractions of 1 unit represent sums less than £1,000.

The scales used will always depend upon the space available for the illustration.

Again for clarity each rectangle is drawn with the same width and labelled. This prevents any possible confusion about what is being presented. Finally the bar chart is *always* given a title so that the person looking at it will immediately know what the bar chart is about. For example:

The commission, to the nearest £, earned by a sales man during one month is given below:

Week	1	2	3	4
Commission (£)	52	45	46	61

Step 1: Draw two straight lines (axes) perpendicular to each other near the bottom and left-hand side of the space being used.
Step 2. Scale the vertical line (axis). 1 unit height equal to £10.
Step 3: Prepare widths for the four rectangles representing the four weeks.
Step 4: Draw the rectangles to the appropriate heights – Week 1 = £52 = 5.2 units of height.
Step 5: Label the axes and give a title.

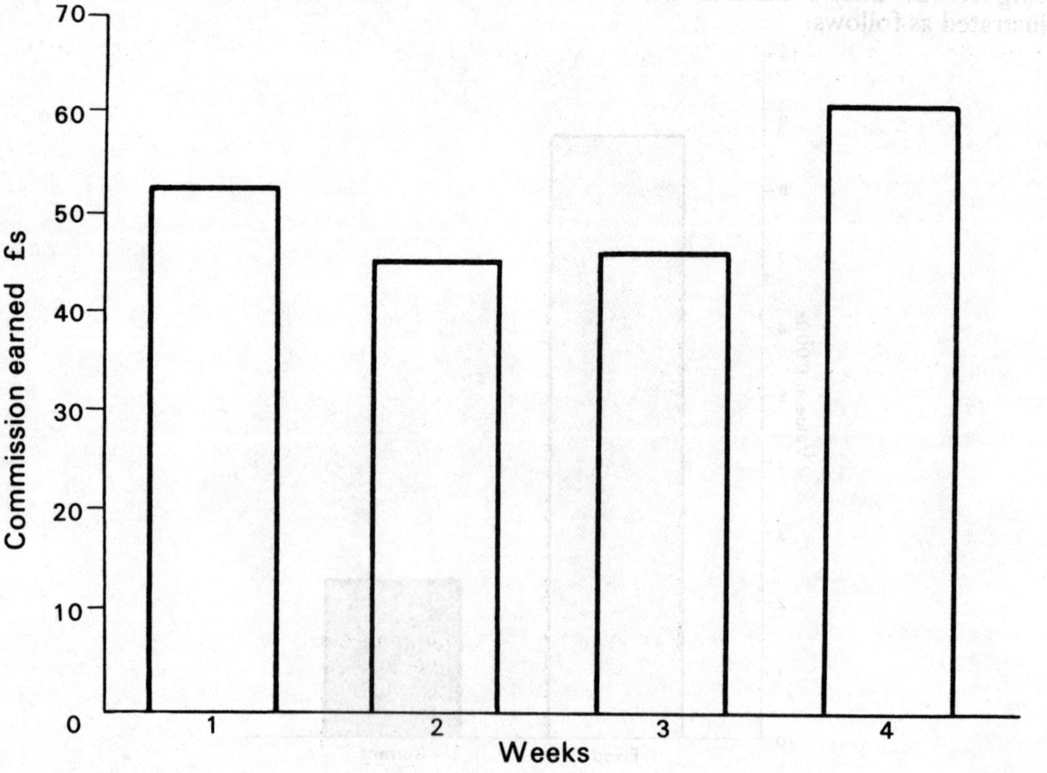

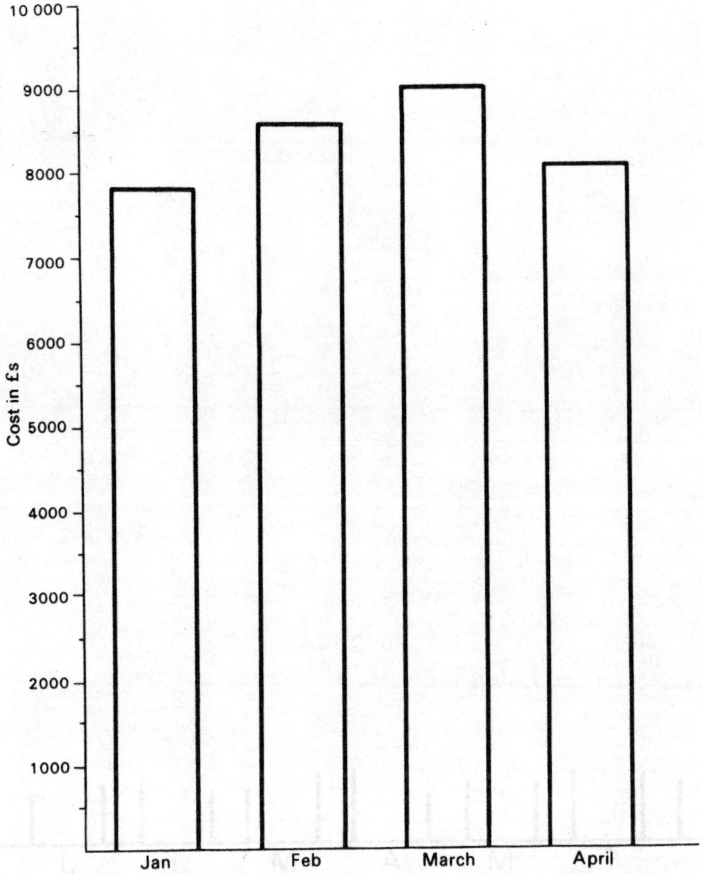

TASK THREE

For the bar chart above write, within each rectangle, the value of manufacturing costs represented by each rectangle.

EXERCISE

Illustrate using bar charts.

(a) Total sales of "Blue Jeans" by Vie & Co. were as follows:

Monday	£68	Tuesday	£78	Wednesday	£30
Thursday	£72	Friday	£96	Saturday	£121

(b) The number of guests staying at an hotel during each month of a year, was:

January	52	February	40	March	59	April	60
May	104	June	149	July	157	August	180
September	166	October	85	November	0	December	78

(c) The assets of I. M. Solvent at the beginning of this Section on page 95.

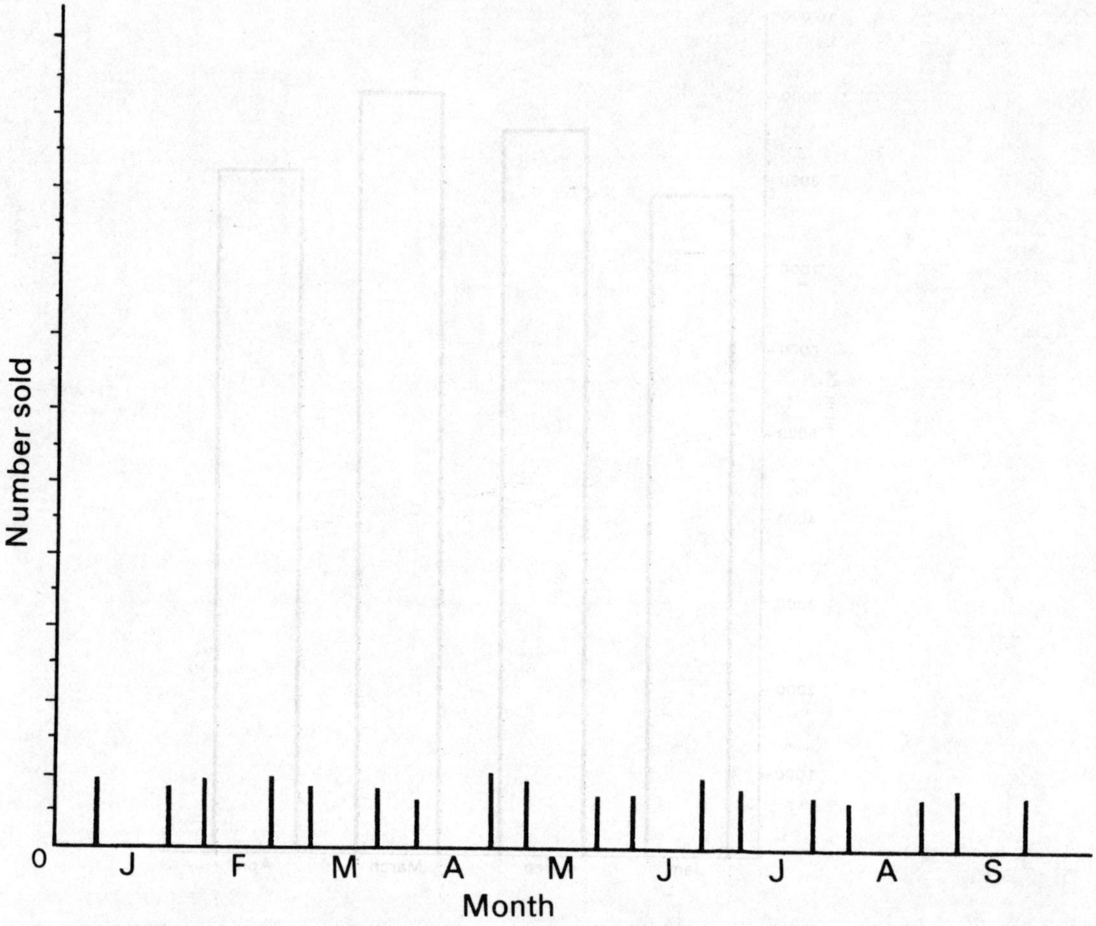

TASK FOUR

Using the framework above, illustrate the data below as a simple bar chart. The number of electronic calculators sold by a retailer during the first nine months of a year were as follows:

January	80	April	45	July	80
February	70	May	60	August	95
March	60	June	65	September	65

Component Bar Charts

The simple bar chart is intended to convey quickly the totals being represented. The totals, however, may contain a number of items which may also require illustration. The *components* form the total and therefore the overall height of the rectangle. This is sub-divided in order to show the components.

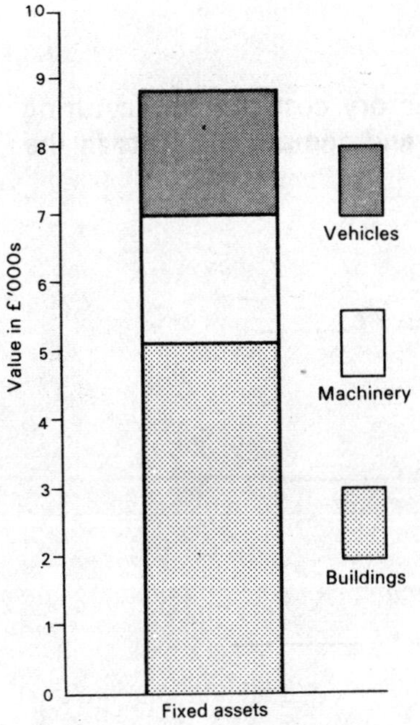

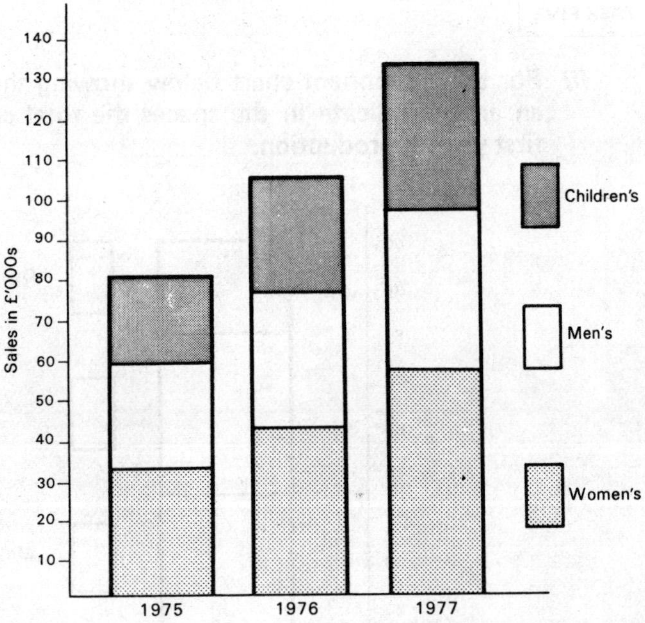

For example the fixed assets for R. U. Busy, totalling £8,800, are made up of buildings – £51,000, machinery – £1,900, and vehicles – £1,800. The *component bar chart* for the fixed assets will appear in the form shown above (left). This type of bar chart is used to illustrate totals and in particular changes in total. They are also intended to give an indication of the size of each component part. For example:

The sales recorded in the three departments of a shop selling shoes are shown in the table:

	Sales in £'000s		
Year	*Women's*	*Men's*	*Children's*
1975	32	26	21
1976	41	34	29
1977	55	40	36

As a component bar chart this information relating to the value of sales would appear in the form shown in the right-hand illustration above.

Step 1: The total sales for each year are represented first by drawing rectangles of an appropriate height, as for a simple bar chart.

Step 2: Each rectangle is sub-divided to illustrate each component. The division is determined by the size of each component. Thus for 1975 the rectangle is divided at 3.2 units of height (women's) and then 5.8 (women's and men's combined) The remainder of the rectangle represents children's. It is usual to put the largest component at the bottom of the rectangle to give an impression of "steadiness".

Step 3: The axes are labelled, a title given and a key to the components is completed.

TASK FIVE

(i) For the component chart below showing the factory cost of manufacturing an article indicate in the spaces the total cost and component costs in the first year of production.

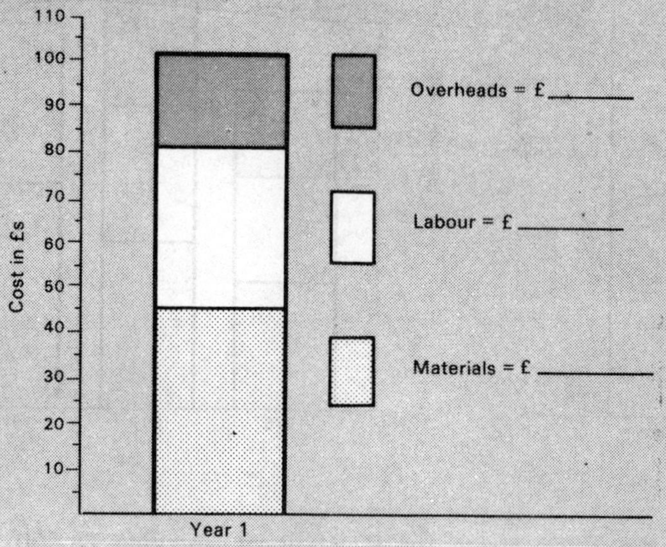

(ii) Using the outline below, draw a component bar chart to illustrate the number of typewriters repaired each week during one month by three men.

	Week 1	*Week 2*	*Week 3*	*Week 4*
R. Smith	31	27	29	32
S. Jones	32	32	35	36
C. Brown	36	38	37	37

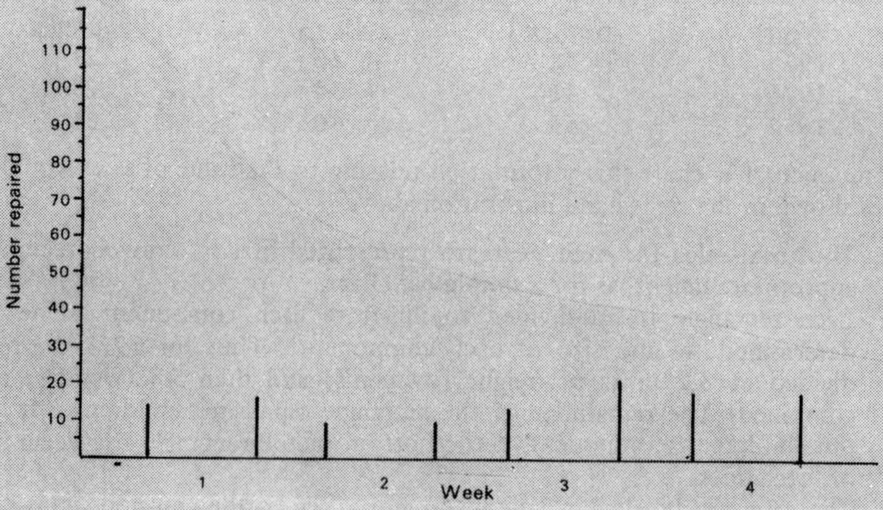

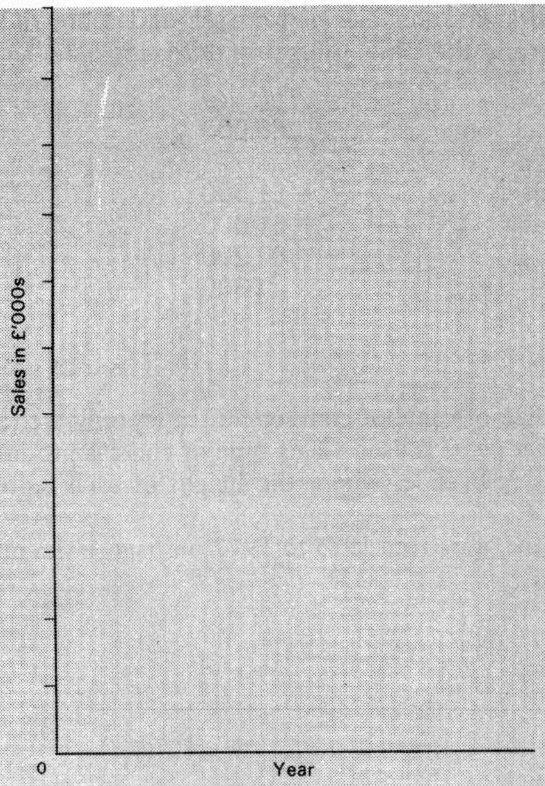

(iii) Illustrate, using the component bar chart above, the sales over four years by the four shops in a small retail group (sales in £000s).

	Year 1	*Year 2*	*Year 3*	*Year 4*
Shop A	300	400	550	690
Shop B	240	320	380	400
Shop C	200	220	280	360
Shop D	180	200	250	280

EXERCISE

(a) Illustrate the fixed and current assets of I. M. Solvent as component bar charts. (Use the balance sheet on page 97.)

(b) Show as component bar charts the changes between two months in total output and indicate changes in the factory outputs in a group of companies producing electrical components.

	September	*October*
Company A	15	18
Company B	25	30
Company C	19	24
Company D	22	27

(c) The costs of producing and revenue from selling 1 tonne of steel this year and last year is shown in the table. Illustrate this using bar charts.

	This year	*Last year*
Revenue per tonne	£5,000	£5,200
Costs:		
Materials	£1,500	£1,200
Overheads	£1,000	£1,100
Labour	£2,200	£2,800
Profit	£300	£100

Multiple Bar Charts

Where changes in the size or value of component values only are required, not the overall total, then a *multiple bar chart* is used. This type of chart is produced by drawing a series of simple bar charts, side-by-side, where the height of each represents the value of the component.

Using the data for shoe sales from 1975 to 1977 on page 103 a multiple bar chart would appear as follows:

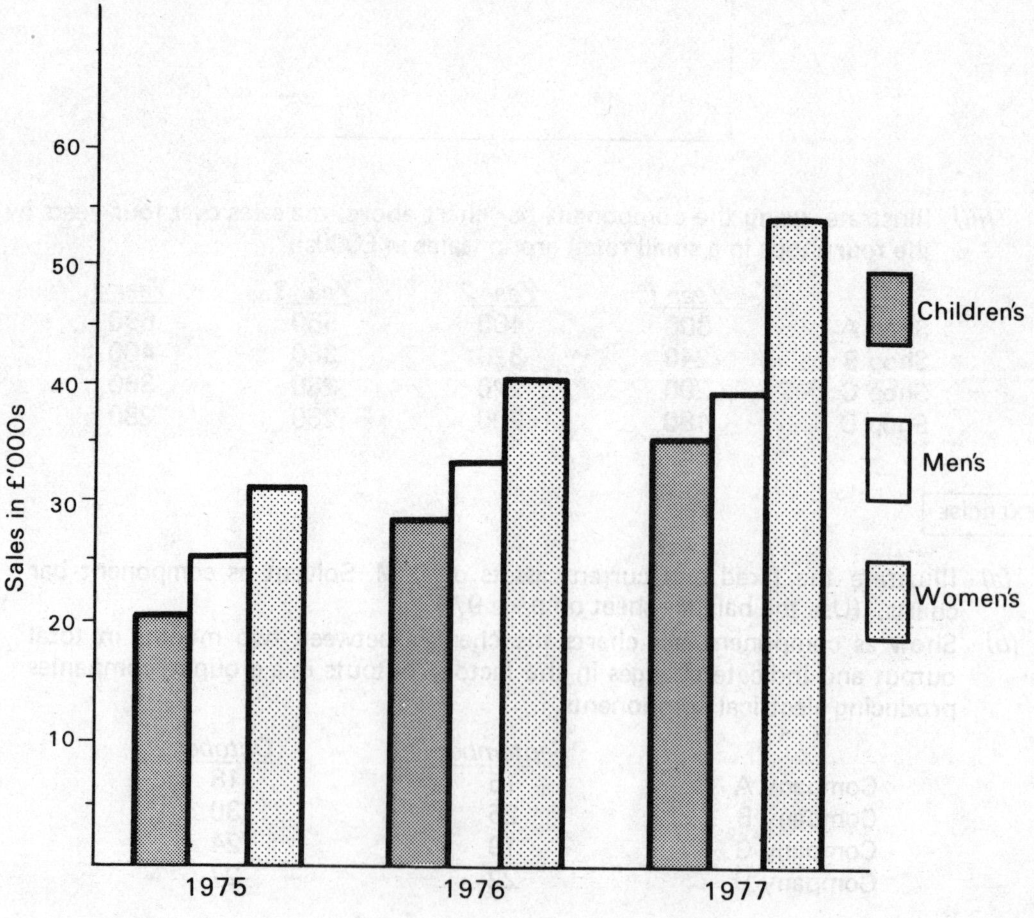

TASK SIX

(i) Using the axes in the illustration below complete the multiple bar chart showing the value of sales of computer equipment in three major sales areas during one year.

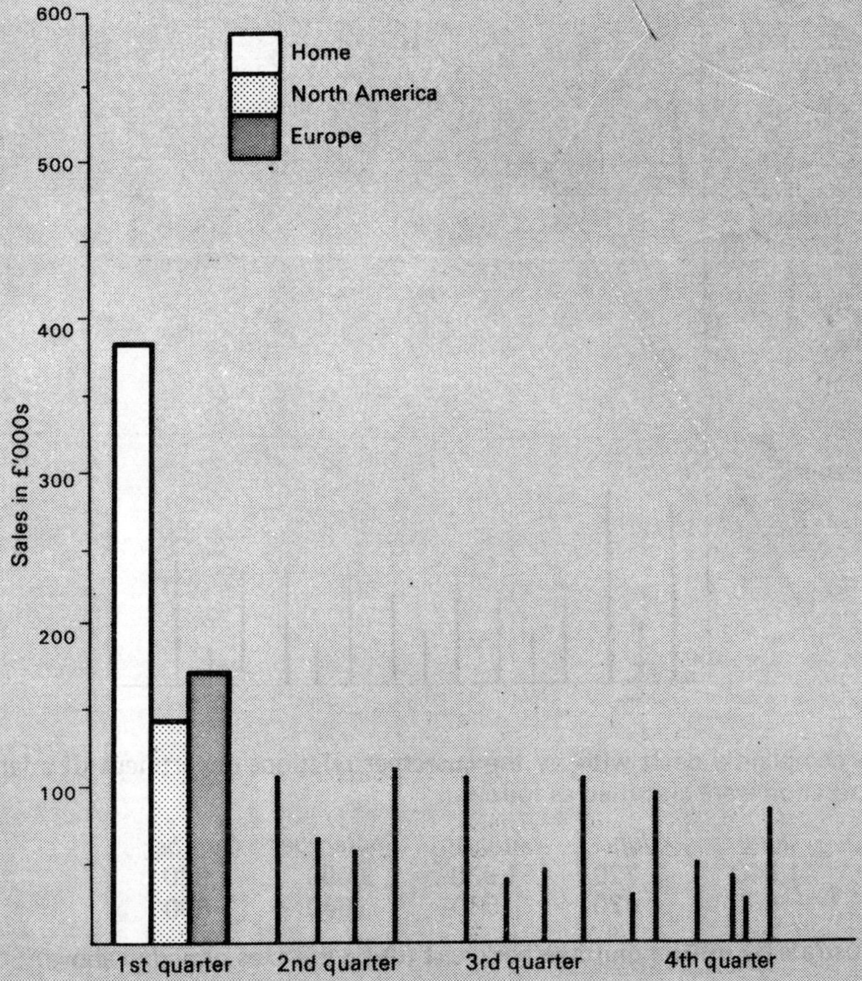

	Sales in £'000s			
	1st Quarter	2nd Quarter	3rd Quarter	4th Quarter
Home sales	390	300	575	405
North American sales	145	135	160	150
European sales	175	160	190	175

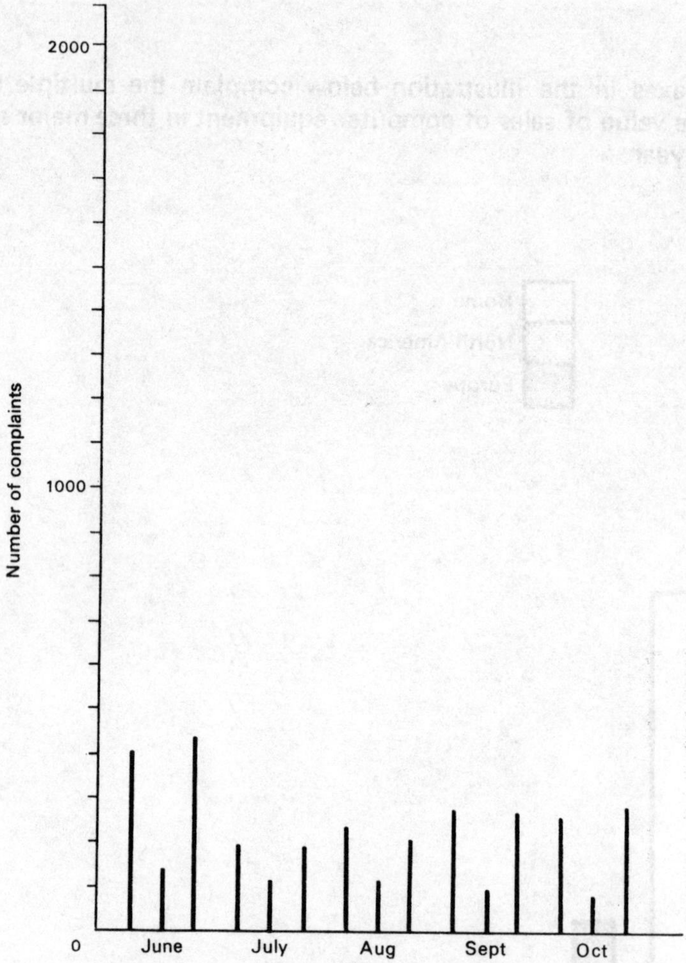

(iii) The complaints dealt with by the customer relations department of a large corporation were classified as follows:

	June	*July*	*August*	*September*	*October*
Postal	1,840	1,720	1,930	2,090	1,920
Personal	680	420	530	640	600

Illustrate by using a multiple bar chart (using the axes provided above).

PIE CHARTS

The component bar chart and multiple bar chart are useful ways of showing information in a diagrammatic form, the component bar chart showing how totals change with an indication of the size of each component making up the total, the multiple bar chart showing changes in the actual values of each component without being concerned with the overall total.

These two charts can only be used when there are not more than three or four components; if more are shown then the chart becomes too complex and the impact of the chart is lost. When a large number of components have to be shown a *pie chart* is more suitable.

A *pie chart is a divided circle,* each component being contained between two radii of the circle. The area of the circle represents the overall total and the area of each section is proportional to the size of the component being represented.

Using the balance sheet of R. U. Busy, his total assets of £11,100 can be shown as a pie chart. The £11,100 will be represented by the total area of the circle and each individual asset by a portion of the area.

The portion of area represented by each asset can be easily found by expressing each asset as a fraction of the total assets and multiplying the fraction by 360° (there are 360° contained within a circle). This will give the appropriate portion of the circle being used as an angle contained between the two radii at the centre of the circle.

Thus Buildings $= \frac{5100}{11100} \times 360^{\circ} = 165^{\circ}$

Machinery $= \frac{1900}{11100} \times 360^{\circ} = 62^{\circ}$

Vehicles $= \frac{1800}{11100} \times 360^{\circ} = 58^{\circ}$

Stock-in-trade $= \frac{1400}{11100} \times 360^{\circ} = 45^{\circ}$

Trade debtors $= \frac{570}{11100} \times 360^{\circ} = 19^{\circ}$

Cash-in-hand $= \frac{330}{11100} \times 360^{\circ} = 11^{\circ}$

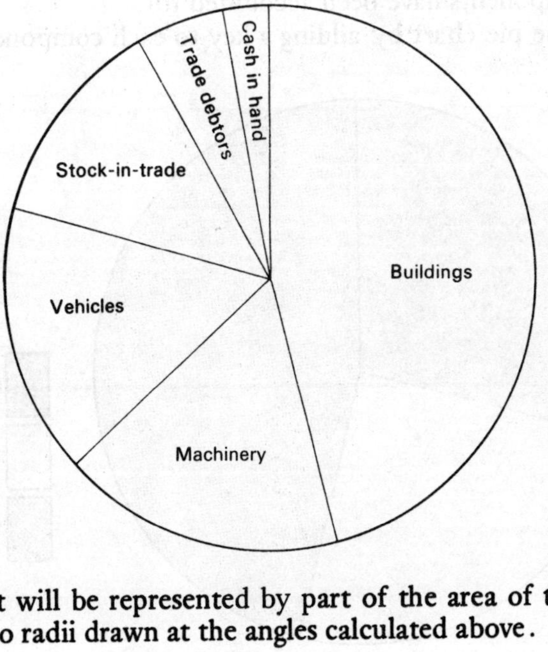

Now each component will be represented by part of the area of the circle. The area is contained between two radii drawn at the angles calculated above.

Commence by drawing a radius at 12 o'clock, followed by a second radius at the angle calculated which will have the proportion of area represented by buildings (165°) and repeat for each component. For example:

The sales of clothing in a large retail store in one month were as follows: women's £55,000, men's £30,000 and children's £35,000. Represent this on a pie chart.

Step 1: For each component express its value as a fraction of total sales.

Thus Women = $\frac{55,000}{120,000}$, Men = $\frac{30,000}{120,000}$ and Children = $\frac{35,000}{120,000}$

Step 2: Multiply each fraction by 360° to find the angle between each pair of radii.

Women $\frac{55,000}{120,000} \times 360^{o} = 165^{o}$

Men $\frac{30,000}{120,000} \times 360^{o} = 90^{o}$

Children $\frac{35,000}{120,000} \times 360^{o} = 105^{o}$

(Simplify the fractions as follows before multiplying, $\frac{55,0\not{0}\not{0}}{12\not{0},\not{0}\not{0}\not{0}} \times \overset{3}{\not{3}\not{6}\not{0}^{o}} = 165^{o}$)

Step 3: Draw a circle and commencing at 12 o'clock draw a radius. Measure the angle for women (165°) using a protractor and draw a second radius. This portion of the circle now represents the sales of women's clothing.

Step 4: From this radius measure the next angle, men 90°, draw another radius. Repeat until all components have been accounted for.

Step 5: Complete the pie chart by adding a key to each component and inserting a title.

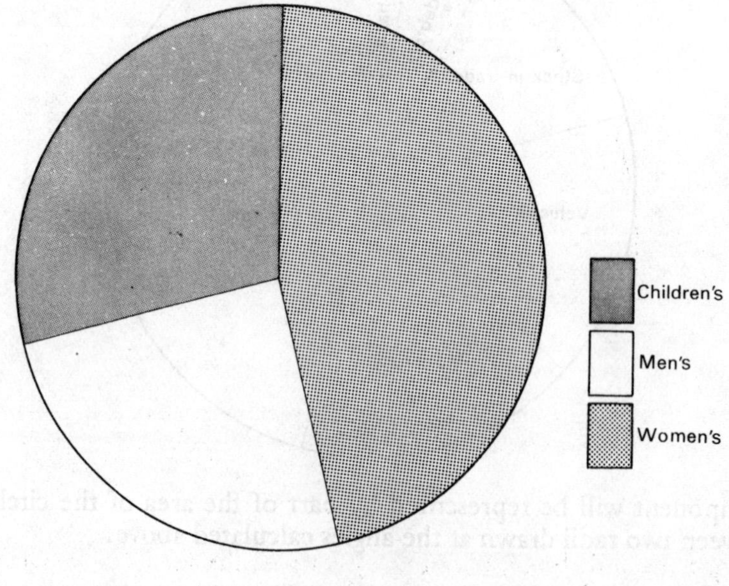

TASK SEVEN

(i) The employees of a small business travel to work by bus, car, on foot or by train. The proportion of each, if the total number of employees is represented by the area of a circle, is as follows: bus 160°, car 90°, foot 60°, train 50°. Represent this as a pie chart using the circle below.

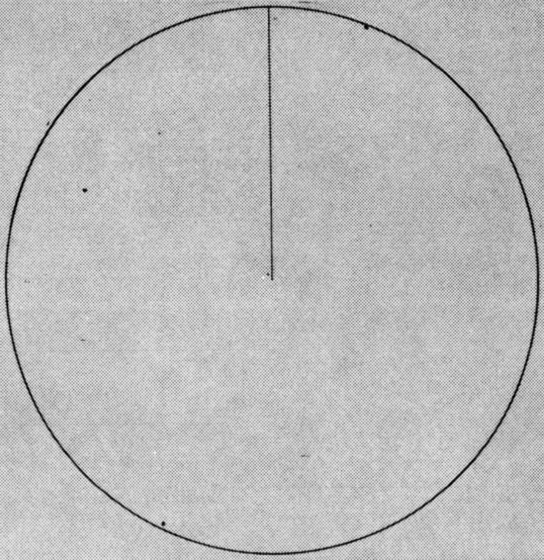

(ii) A survey of absence in a company during one week gave the following information.

No. of days absent	1	2	3	4	5
No. of employees absent	17	25	15	10	5

Represent this information below after finding the angles for each component.

Days absent	*Angle of circle*
1	$\frac{17}{72} \times 360^{\circ} = 85^{\circ}$
2	$\frac{25}{72} \times 360^{\circ} =$ __________
3	$\frac{15}{72} \times 360^{\circ} =$ __________
4	$\frac{10}{72} \times 360^{\circ} =$ __________
5	$\frac{5}{72} \times 360^{\circ} =$ __________

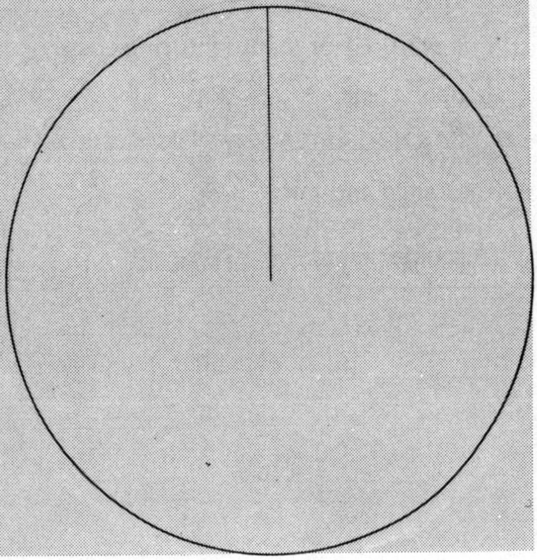

(iii) Represent the last year's trading analysis of the Rochub Fishing Tackle Company on the pie chart below.

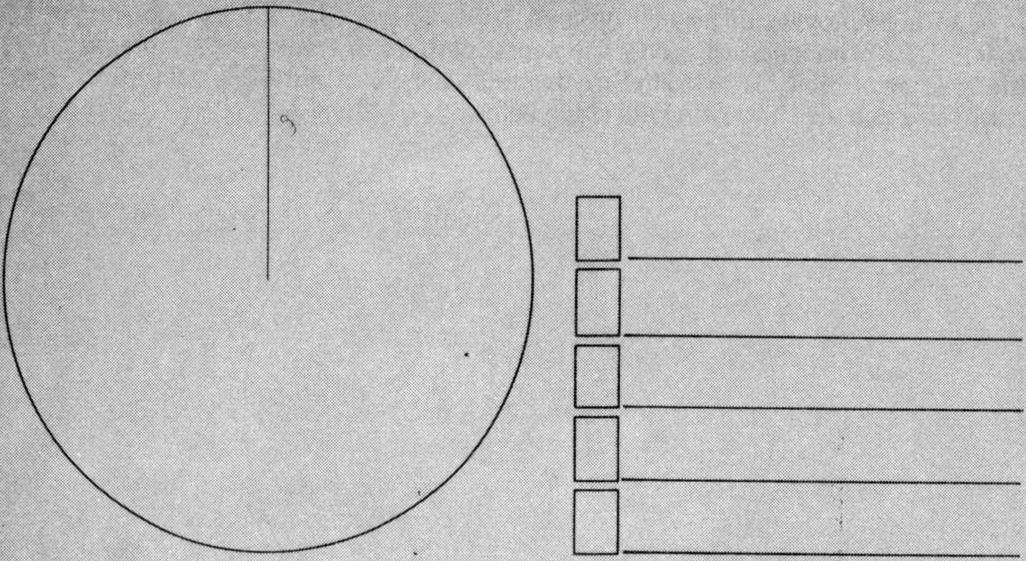

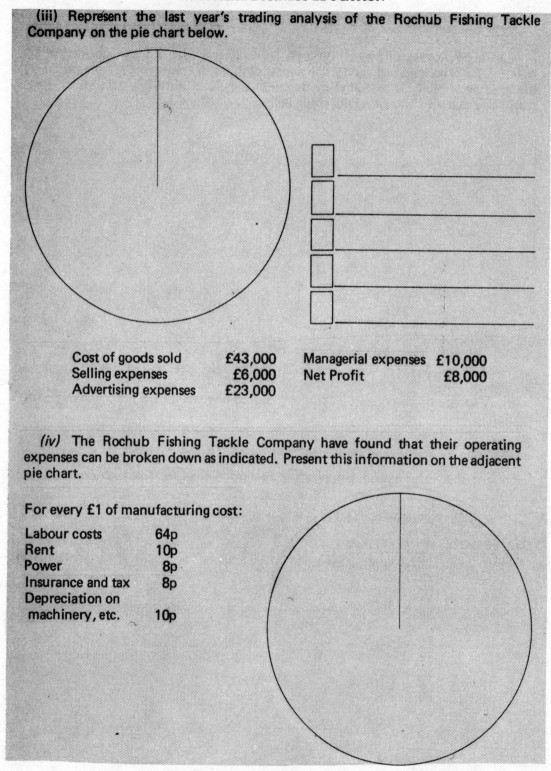

Cost of goods sold	£43,000	Managerial expenses	£10,000
Selling expenses	£6,000	Net Profit	£8,000
Advertising expenses	£23,000		

(iv) The Rochub Fishing Tackle Company have found that their operating expenses can be broken down as indicated. Present this information on the adjacent pie chart.

For every £1 of manufacturing cost:

Labour costs	64p
Rent	10p
Power	8p
Insurance and tax	8p
Depreciation on machinery, etc.	10p

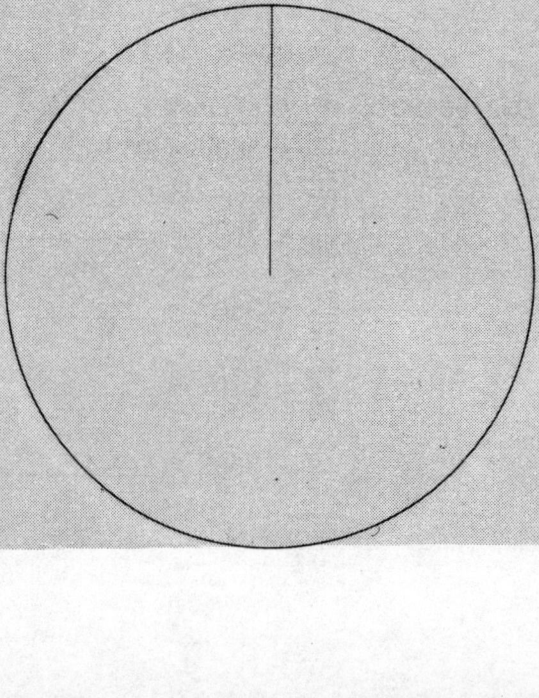

EXERCISE

(a) A manufacturer employs the following personnel: 180 unskilled employees, 120 craftsmen, 80 clerical workers and 20 sales representatives. Construct a pie chart for this information.

(b) Compare the costs of production and revenue of 1 tonne of steel this year with the costs of production and revenue last year using pie charts.

	This year	*Last year*
Revenue per tonne	£5,000	£5,200
Costs: Materials	£15,000	£1,200
Overheads	£1,000	£1,100
Labour	£2,200	£2,800
Profit	£300	£100

SUPPLEMENTARY WORK

This section commenced with the financial statement of a sole proprietor – a balance sheet. These statements are also produced for partnerships and companies; they differ only in the quantity and complexity of the information presented. The same principles of an orderly arrangement in columns and rows and itemised sub-totals and totals apply. Below is an example of the balance sheet for a partnership. It differs from that of the sole proprietor only in that the capital is itemised according to each partner's investment, share of the profit and drawings.

TASK EIGHT

(i) Complete the balance sheet below by inserting the missing values marked by an asterisk.

SLOW AND EASY BALANCE SHEET (as at 31.12.19—)

Capital (at 1.1.19—)			*Fixed Assets*		
Slow	£25,000		Land and buildings	£30,000	
Add ½ share of profit	3,640		Plant and machinery	10,700	
	*		Fixtures and fittings	3,850	
Less Drawings	3,500	£ *	Vehicles	*	£50,460
Easy	25,000		*Current Assets*		
Add ½ share of profit	3,640		Stock-in-trade	*	
	*		Trade debtors	3,990	
Less Drawings	3,500	£ *	Cash in bank	2,840	
		£ *	Cash in hand	110	£11,540
Long-term Liabilities					
Bank loan	£2,900				
H.P. loan	3,850	£ *			
Current Liabilities					
Trade creditors		4970			
		£ *			£ *

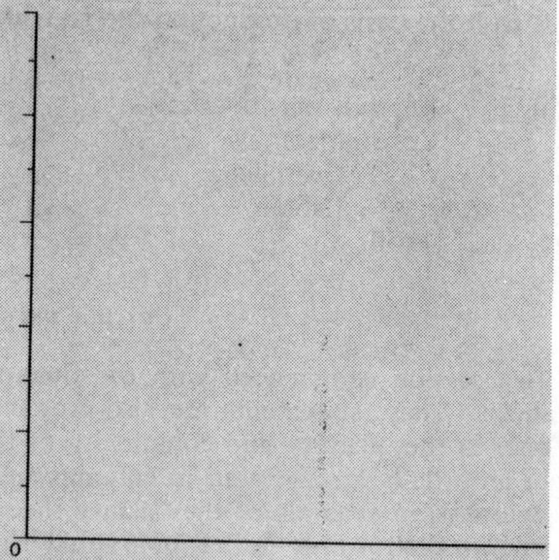

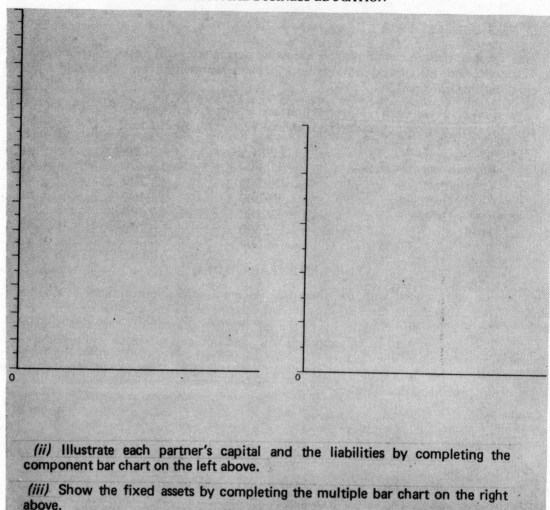

(ii) Illustrate each partner's capital and the liabilities by completing the component bar chart on the left above.

(iii) Show the fixed assets by completing the multiple bar chart on the right above.

The balance sheet of a company is more complex than the sole trader or partnership balance sheet because the Company Acts contain quite detailed instructions on what information must be included. These disclosures are intended to protect existing and prospective shareholders. (The example given would not meet the requirements of the Acts.)

The following exercises are to be carried out using the balance sheet for the Chalk and Talk Company, shown at the top of the facing page.

(a) (i) Draw simple bar charts to show the authorised share capital for Chalk and Talk.

(ii) Using these bar charts show on each the proportion of the issued share capital.

(b) Draw component bar charts to illustrate the original cost, depreciation and net value of the fixed assets.

(c) Illustrate the current liabilities by means of a circular diagram.

THE CHALK AND TALK CO. LTD. BALANCE SHEET

(as at 31.12.19––)

Share Capital		
Authorised		
80,000 Ordinary Shares of £1 each		80,000.00
20,000 8% Preference Shares of £1 each		20,000.00
		100,000.00
Issued		
65,000 Ordinary Shares of £1 each		65,000.00
15,000 8% Preference Shares of £1 each		15,000.00
		80,000.00
General reserve		5,000.00
Ten per cent loan stock		15,000.00
Current Liabilities		
Creditors	12,000.00	
Loan interests (10%)	1,500.00	
Preference dividend (8%)	1,200.00	
Proposed ordinary dividend (20%)	13,000.00	27,700.00
		£127,700.00

Fixed Assets	*Cost*	*Depreciation to date*	*Net*
Premises	48,000.00	–	48,000.00
Plant and machinery	17,600.00	5,800.00	11,800.00
Fixtures and fittings	9,800.00	3,400.00	6,400.00
Motor vehicles	22,700.00	7,600.00	14,700.00
	97,700.00	16,800.00	80,900.00
Current Assets			
Stock		13,700.00	
Debtors		16,300.00	
Bank		16,600.00	
Cash		200.00	46,800.00
			£127,000.00

NOTES
(*a*) "Authorised capital" is the *total* amount the company is *allowed* to raise by the Memorandum of Authorisation.
(*b*) "Issued capital" is the amount the company has actually raised from the public by the issue of shares.
(*c*) "Unissued Capital" is the difference between 1 and 2 above *and can be* issued if the company wishes to raise more capital
(*d*) "Depreciation to date"is the estimated loss in value of the assets through "fair wear and tear" from the time they were bought to the date the balance was prepared.

SECTION III

FLUENCY AND STYLE

So far in this book, most of the written communication work has asked you to concentrate on keeping your sentences and statements as simple and as concise as possible. In some of the exercises and tasks, however, you might have found it rather restricting to write in such a way because you felt there was more information needed than could be "squeezed" into a simple sentence. The passage which follows is an exaggerated example of how simple statements can sometimes make the style of any written work very difficult to read. Each of the simple sentences is grammatically correct.

> The retail trader is a link. The retail trader is a link in the chain of distribution. The retail trader is the final stage in the progress of an article from manufacturer to consumer. The retail trader is important to the consumer. He provides the consumer with conveniently situated shops. The consumer is offered a variety of goods.

The problem with writing in this style is that you are likely to *repeat* yourself unnecessarily; also, the fact that the reader has to keep stopping wherever you have put a full stop is likely to *interrupt his train of thought* if it happens too frequently. It would improve the style of the passage, and make it easier for the reader to follow if it was written like this.

The retail trader is the final link in the chain of distribution between the manufacturer and the consumer. The retailer is important to the consumer because he provides a conveniently situated shop which contains a variety of goods.

TASK ONE

(i) How many sentences are there in the second version of the passage on the retail trader? ______________________

(ii) Apart from the fact that the reader doesn't have to keep stopping, can you suggest any other reason why this passage can be understood more easily and more quickly than the original?

____

____

(iii) Refer back to the sections of Unit I which give you an explanation of *conjunctions* and *relative pronouns* (see p. 23 and p. 24). Then find two conjunctions and one relative pronoun in the second version of the passage.

(a)______________ (b)______________ (c)______________

If you look carefully at the functions of these two parts of speech, as given in Unit I, you will see that they are actually fulfilling these functions in the passage.

TASK TWO

For each of the words you have selected in (iii) above, explain what function each is fulfilling in its sentence.

(i) ____

____

(ii) ____

____

(iii) ____

____

You will now have realised that a sentence can often be *improved* by expanding it beyond a simple statement, and including some useful and relevant *additional* information. In the passage you have been studying, many of the simple statements were *combined* in order to link together ideas which were then easier to understand because they are related to each other. This *linking* of ideas is designed to increase the *fluency* of written material.

You will now have realised that a sentence can often be *improved* by expanding it beyond a simple statement, and including some useful and relevant *additional* information. In the passage you have been studying, many of the simple statements were *combined* in order to link together ideas which were then easier to understand because they are related to each other. This *linking* of ideas is designed to increase the *fluency* of written material.

TASK THREE

Look up the word *fluency* in your dictionary. It will probably appear as part of the section on *fluent.*

What part of speech is "fluency"? ______________________

Give a definition of "fluent". ______________________

____

Explain in your own words what you think "fluency" is when it is used to refer to written English ______________________

____

____

In order to help you make your written work more fluent, it would now be useful to consider a number of different methods or devices, which can help you *link ideas together.* You have already looked briefly at conjunctions in Unit I, so let us deal with them first of all.

Conjunctions

Examples of these are *and, but, because.* These "linking" words are easy to use because they are simply inserted between ideas in order to bring them together. For example:

(a) The chairman stood up. He addressed the meeting. He could not be heard at the back of the room.

(b) The chairman stood up *and* addressed the meeting, *but* he could not be heard at the back of the room.

NOTE: *It is often necessary to leave out words to avoid repetition when you combine sentences* (e.g. "he" in the second sentence).

In the example above, the full stops and the capital letters are replaced, where necessary, by the appropriate conjunction. Many words can be used as conjunctions but the following list gives you a few of the more common ones which should be easily recognisable. You will notice that the column on the right indicates conjunctions which are used *in pairs.* If you want to use this type of structure, remember that these *correlative conjunctions* can be paired only with their opposite numbers as shown:

or	both ... and
although	either ... or
while	neither ... nor
if	if ... then
unless	not only ... but also
whereas	whether ... or

Examples of the use of Correlative Conjunctions

(a) The junior clerk was reprimanded *not only* because he was unpunctual, *but also* because he was insolent.

(*b*) The Board discussed that the company should seek more capital *either* by offering a new issue of ordinary shares *or* by issuing a loan stock.

NOTE: In order to avoid grammatical problems, you should aim to use each half of a pair of correlative conjunctions in front of a part of speech similar to the other half, as in the examples above.

TASK FOUR

In each of the following sections you will see more than one simple sentence. By using *conjunctions*, join these sentences together so that they form a single, fluent sentence. Underline the conjunction you use, and try to use a different one in each sentence.

NOTE: Although you can leave out indivdual words, *all the main ideas must appear in your answer*.

(i) Building societies were established to satisfy a social need. They developed as local societies. ______________________________

____

____

(ii) Many building societies are now national organisations. They have become very large, powerful financial institutions.______________________________

____

____

(iii) Building societies have encouraged the rapid growth of home ownership. They are prepared to lend more money to many prospective buyers.______________________________

____

____

As you saw in Task One, the relative pronoun is another part of speech which can be usefully employed as a device for linking ideas.

Relative Pronouns

In Unit I we said that these parts of speech relate what you are going to say to a noun or pronoun you have already mentioned. The following example will once more demonstrate how they are used: For example:

(*a*) Mrs Weston is the accounts clerk. She is responsible for balancing the statements.
(*b*) Mrs Weston is the accounts clerk *who* is responsible for balancing the statements.

NOTE: The relative pronoun "who" has been placed in the most obvious position in order to link these sentences. The sentences could be combined in different ways, as you are shown in the following examples, but this involves *rearrangement* of the information which can lead to a slight change in emphasis or meaning. This is explained more fully in the sub-section on rearranging and omitting words (*see* p. 122). For example:

(*a*) Mrs Weston, *who* is the accounts clerk, is responsible for balancing the statements.
(*b*) Mrs Weston, *who* is responsible for balancing the statements, is the accounts clerk.

As well as considering the use of the relative pronoun in these sentences, you have an opportunity to appreciate the specialised use of words we discussed in Unit I, i.e. "balancing" and "statements".

TASK FIVE

(i) What do these terms mean when used in the business sense?

balancing: ______________________________

____

statements: ______________________________

____

(ii) Use the two words from *(i)* in sentences which show their general meaning. Try to construct sentences which are fairly long, and involve the use of at least one relative pronoun and one conjunction.

balancing: ______________________________

____

____

statements: ______________________________

____

____

TASK SIX

Use relative pronouns to combine the following sentences. Underline the linking word you use.

(i) The Post Office is an important organisation. It came under public control in 1968. ______________________________

____

____

(ii) Like other forms of business organisation, public corporations need employees. These are not classed as civil servants.

____

____

____

____

The Participle of a Verb

This method of joining ideas is more sophisticated than the previous two, and requires a little more skill. There are two forms of participle which we need to consider, *the present participle* and *the past participle.*

(a) *The present participle* can be formed by adding the letters *ing to* the basic form of the verb, e.g. if the infinitive of the verb is "to walk", the present participle is formed by taking the word *walk* and adding *ing*, i.e. *walking.* Remember that some verbs might need to change slightly in order to make the spelling correct. For example.

To run: run + ing = runing. This is wrong. Therefore an extra n must be inserted to make it correct, i.e. running.

(b) *The past participle* is rather more awkward, because there is no rule that can be applied in order to help you form it. The past participle of any verb *must be learnt.* The following examples should help you to recognise the type of word you are looking for:

to speak	: spoken	to run	: run
to walk	: walked	to climb	: climbed
to ride	: ridden	to write	: written

There is one test you can use as a guide when thinking about a past participle: you should be able to use the word *having* in front of it.

NOTE: The past participle can also be used with other parts of the verb "to have" such as "has" and "had". For example:

Having spoken to the customer, the salesman fetched the manager.
The clerk was exhausted after he *had walked* to the bank to pay in the cash.

Now you have seen examples of these two types of participle, you can probably identify how they are used as a linking device in order to improve fluency. The following sentences demonstrate this. In the first instance you are given two short sentences. These are linked by the use of the present and then the past participle.

He returned to his office. He made a telephone call.
Returning to his office, he made a telephone call. *(present participle)*
Having returned to his office, he made a telephone call. *(past participle)*

TASK SEVEN

The following sentences would be improved in style if they were combined. Attempt this, using either the present participle or the past participle of the verb. Be careful which you choose because you must aim to keep exactly the same meaning as the original statements.

(i) I have dealt with the firm for many years. I have no hesitation in recommending them.

____

____

(ii) The wallpaper is liable to discoloration. It is unsatisfactory.

____

(iii) The cargo ship left Hamburg. It followed a course for Southampton.

____

____

(iv) The clerk labelled the parcels. He then took them to the post-room.

____

____

One problem which often arises with the past participle of a verb is that it is confused with the simple *past tense.* The past participles of most verbs can be identified quite easily, as we saw earlier, by putting such words as "have", "had" or "having" in front of them. The difficulties are that:

(a) in some verbs the past tense is spelt the same as the past participle;
(b) in others it is confusingly similar, but differs by the changing of one letter;
(c) in still others, it is completely different.

Three examples you were given earlier are set out below to demonstrate this.

	Infinitive of verb	*Past tense*	*Past participle*
(a)	to walk	walked	walked
(b)	to run	ran	run
(c)	to write	wrote	written

The important thing to bear in mind is that each is a completely different part of the verb, and they are *not interchangeable.* Don't fall into the trap of using the past tense, when you actually want to use the past participle. It is easy to make this mistake sometimes, particularly when you are talking to someone rather than writing something down. Remember, careful speech can help improve the standard of your written work. It can be useful, when you are considering the use of a past participle structure, to think of the past tense at the same time so that you can establish clearly in your own mind which is which.

TASK EIGHT

Complete the following table by inserting the present participle, the past tense, and the past participle of each of the verbs shown.

Infinitive	*Present Participle*	*Past Tense*	*Past Participle*
to swim	________	________	________
to buy	________	________	________
to sing	________	________	________
to drive	________	________	________
to go	________	________	________
to light	________	________	________
to think	________	________	________
to bear	________	________	________
to drink	________	________	________
to bring	________	________	________

The three basic methods you have used so far are easily recognisable when used in a sentence. However, the job of linking ideas can be done simply by rearranging and omitting words.

Rearranging and Omitting Words

The two sentences used as an example here contain important statements about money. They can be combined in more than one way by rearranging them (changing the order of the ideas) and leaving out unnecessary words. For example:

Money is essential to an advanced, industrialised society. It is a useful means of valuing goods, services and labour.

(a) *Money,* essential to an advanced industrial society, *is a useful means of valuing goods, services and labour.*

In this version, the main statement of fact is in italics, and would stand on its own as a complete sentence. The other statement is inserted as *additional* information.

(b) *Money,* a useful means of valuing goods, services and labour, *is essential to an advanced industrial society.*

In this second version, the sentence has been rearranged so that the main statement is different. This alters the *emphasis* of the sentence, and enables the writer to indicate which of the two statements he thinks is the most important.

NOTE: You will have noticed in the examples you have been given in this section that sentences need to be *punctuated* properly if they are to be clearly understood when combined into a single sentence. The use of punctuation is explained fully in Unit IV, and you will find further references to sentence linking when you get there. This is because certain punctuation marks can be used as linking devices in more complex sentences.

TASK NINE

Combine the sentences in each section below in two different ways, as you were shown in the last example.

(i) An overdraft is the most flexible way of borrowing money. It is the least costly method of raising small amounts of capital.

Answer: ______________________________

____

Answer: ______________________________

____

(ii) A personal loan is a common form of bank loan. It is given for a specific period.

Answer: ______________________________

____

Answer: ______________________________

____

EXERCISE

Making use of any of the methods we have considered in this section, form a single sentence from each of the following groups. Remember that you are not restricted to using one particular method – any combination of these devices will be acceptable as long as your answers are grammatically correct. It might be helpful to re-read the examples and tasks before you start.

(a) The selling price of goods exceeds the cost price. The gross profit is the amount by which one exceeds the other.

(b) "Turnover" is the name given to the net sales for a particular period. This period can be of any set length such as a month or a year.

(c) A retailer must keep a record of all working expenses. These include such things as rent, rates, taxes, salaries, insurance, advertising, and an allowance for depreciation.

(d) A trader's record of expenses must be accurate. This will enable him to compile a profit and loss account. He will then be able to work out his net profit.

(e) A trader aims to increase his total profits. To do this he tries to increase his rate of turnover. Working expenses would not normally increase in the same proportion as turnover. The business should therefore show an increased net profit.

(f) Some retailers charge low prices which yield only a low profit per article. This might, however, result in increased sales. If sales increase enough, the total profit can still show an increase.

(g) The mail-order trade is transacted mainly through catalogues. These are controlled by part-time agents. The trade has expanded rapidly. The main attractions are free credit and the convenience of home shopping.

(h) Mobile shops serve the customer at home. Some are run as self-contained units. Others are owned by individuals and organisations with fixed-site shops. The main goods sold are groceries, meat and greengroceries.

(i) The door-to-door salesman is often paid on a commission basis. He has to rely on his own ability to sell. He often meets antagonism. His calls are usually unsolicited. He has the double task of overcoming a housewife's irritation, and then making a sale.

(j) Automatic vending is on the increase. The range of goods offered for sale is very wide. The system is convenient for the vendor and the purchaser. Sales and purchases can be made outside normal shop hours.

EXERCISE

Rewrite the following passage, improving the style so that it can be read and understood more easily. You may use any suitable methods of linking sentences and phrases or combining ideas in order to form more fluent sentences.

Hypermarkets

A hypermarket is a retail outlet. This type of outlet is relatively new in this country. It consists of large retail premises. These are very large. They are usually sited in outlying areas. Large car parking facilities are provided. They are sited outside cities to cut costs. Such costs are high rates, rent or purchase price. Hypermarkets cater for the car owning customer. The advantages to the customer are many. There is easy parking. The store offers a wide variety of goods. Goods of every type are on sale. These include groceries, consumer durables, clothing and hardware. Prices are very competitive. A self-service system is operated. Credit card facilities are often available. The hypermarket often opens at off-peak times.

NOTE MAKING

Whatever subjects you have studied in the past you will at some time have had to take down notes on particular aspects of the work. These notes might have been dictated to you; you might have been expected to listen to a talk or lecture and jot down notes as the speaker went along; or you could have been instructed to read a chapter of a book and make your own notes. Whatever the situation, notes are by no means easy to construct or present. In this section we are going to concentrate on making notes from written sources because this is the main area in which the student is often left on his/her own, with little guidance, and is expected to produce a coherent and useful record of information.

The important point you must come to terms with first of all is that "notes" should not be regarded as an easy way of jotting down some facts to save you writing them out "properly". It is true that when you present information in this way you do not have to put every statement of fact into a grammatically correct sentence, but there are other skills which you need to develop in order to make your notes effective. There are also definite functions which your notes must perform. The notes themselves must be compiled and presented as "properly" as any other sort of written work, and are an important form of communication in their own right.

Before we get down to the practical aspects of presenting notes it would be useful to consider *why* we make them. What use are they? What are their functions?

The most obvious use of notes is to provide you with a summary of important information for *revision* purposes. Information on any subject always seems impersonal when it is written in a textbook, but when you make notes the information becomes your own – the notes have your personal "stamp" and style, and this helps you remember them.

The actual process of making notes is in itself an *aid to study*. This is because note making is such a demanding exercise that it forces your mind to concentrate – cutting out distracting noises and diverting activities. This concentration on reducing what you have read to note form implants much of the necessary information in your memory.

Another result of the practice of note making is that it disciplines the mind. Obviously it is difficult to recognise such a benefit in yourself, but if you approach the exercise carefully you will find that it encourages you to *think in an orderly fashion* and *write things down in logical arrangements*. How often have you heard someone say, "I know what I want to say, but I don't know how to say it"? Such a problem is not caused by lack of knowledge, but by a lack of *order* in considering ideas. This is where the discipline and logical thought necessary for making effective notes can stand you in good stead. If you are practised in thinking and presenting information logically and in the correct sequence, you should have little difficulty in expressing yourself clearly and effectively when the situation arises.

The Techniques of Note Making

If the title of this sub-section seems to promise an immediate solution to the problems of making notes, don't be misled. There is no easy way round them. The important thing is that you should identify the necessary requirements/characteristics of this form of communication, and work towards achieving them. There are four things for you to aim at: *clarity, conciseness, accuracy* and *orderliness.*

Clarity

When you have read through your own notes, it is essential that the meaning of everything you have written is perfectly clear. If you are writing notes which might be used by other people, the meaning *must* be clear in order to avoid misinterpretation. Read through your notes as soon as you have completed them and make sure that they are clearly understandable *now*. If not, then you certainly won't understand them in three months' time, so revise your draft immediately.

Conciseness

This, of course, is the most difficult thing to achieve because only you can decide what information is important and what can be left out. You must consider carefully whether or not what you have written expresses in the shortest form the substance of the information you are trying to record. A major problem you will come across when trying to condense information is that your shortened version might not express the sense of the original with accuracy.

Accuracy

It could be disastrous if your notes are constructed in such a way that when you use the information in the future your essays or examination answers are not quite correct because you have misinterpreted the original text. Therefore, read carefully and check your notes thoroughly.

Orderliness

You will probably think this an obvious point to cover, but the aim of bringing it in at this stage is to lead in to a practical scheme of note presentation. In any book you will find there is a system of dividing up the text into sections and sub-sections – these can be *chapters* or *units* or *sections* or *verses*, or they might simply be numbered logically and in sequence. The purpose of this is to enable the reader to find and refer to particular things quickly and easily. Therefore it follows that your own notes will be easier to understand if they are *titled*, *headed*, *sub-headed*, *numbered* and *lettered* accurately. This could be done in a number of ways, but to avoid confusion we will concentrate on *one* method of presentation which can be adapted to most situations.

In order to use this method you will need to understand the terms given below. Fill in the spaces with the correct numbers in the correct form up to twenty.

(a) Upper case roman numerals: e.g. I II III IV ____________________

____

(b) Lower case roman numerals: e.g. i ii iii iv ____________________

____

(c) Arabic numerals: e.g. 1 2 3 4 ____________________

____

(d) Upper case letters of the alphabet (capitals): e.g. A B C D E F

(e) Large capitals: e.g. A B C D E F

(f) Lower case letters of the alphabet: e.g. a b c d e f

These terms are used so that you can easily identify the type of heading required in a particular situation. You can *underline* headings for extra emphasis. The following example will show you how a well-presented set of notes should look. The sequence of headings, numbers and letters will be explained afterwards. Read the original passage carefully, and then analyse the notes seeing what has been included, what has been left out, and how the divisions have been identified. Discuss this with your colleagues and lecturer.

An Example of Note Presentation – 1. The Original Passage

SHARES

When a company wants to raise capital in order to expand its business or buy new machinery it can offer "shares" for sale to the public. People who have some savings to spare can then, if they wish, purchase these shares, thereby investing in a business enterprise with a view to making a profit on their investment. The basic principle of this sort of investment is that the purchaser of the shares is entitled to a "share" in the profits of the company according to the specified terms and amount of his investment.

There are various types of investment in this field which are designed to suit the differing requirements of individual (or group) investors. These types can be divided into three general groups: *ordinary shares, preference shares* and *debentures.* Within the first two of these groups there are further distinctions to be made.

People who want a high return on their capital are often prepared to take calculated risks, and might invest in *ordinary shares.* These are sometimes referred to as *equity shares* because each one earns an "equal" share of profits. It is also fair to say that this type of share carries the most risk and therefore attracts investors who have fairly substantial resources and are looking for big returns. Institutional investors (e.g. pension funds) who are aiming to create a balanced portfolio, and people who are interested in capital gains rather than revenue profits find *ordinary shares* suitable. They can be issued by both private and public companies.

Another type of *ordinary share* is *deferred ordinary shares,* sometimes called *founder's shares.* These are taken by the vendor of a business when it is bought by a larger company, and carry the same sort of risk as *ordinary shares.* The holder of such shares receives his reward as a share of the profits after *ordinary shares* have had some profit. *Deferred ordinary shares* can be issued by a private or public company, but are not very common nowadays.

Under the general heading of *preference shares* there are three different sorts. As the name implies, the holders of straightforward *preference shares* (non-cumulative) usually have a prior right to payment over *ordinary shareholders,* and therefore there is less risk. These shares can be "redeemable" (i.e. "dated") or "irredeemable". There is, however, a definite rate of dividend which is paid only if profits are made, and this rate could be much lower than that achieved by *ordinary shareholders.* Investors seeking security rather than large dividends are normally attracted by this type of share, which can be issued by public or private companies.

Cumulative preference shares have the same characteristics and advantages as *preference shares,* plus a bit more. This is because the dividend is not lost if the company does not make any profits in one year – it accumulates until a profit is made. In the same way, *participating preference shares* are similar to basic *preference shares* except in the reward they yield. In this case the name is again an indication of benefits because, after taking the fixed rate of interest (say 8 per cent), these shares earn extra dividend if the *ordinary shares* get more than a particular rate of dividend. Thus they enable the holder to "participate" in extra profits.

The third group of "shares" are not really shares at all – they are loans to companies and known as *debentures* or *loan stocks.* People who invest in this way are looking for security and minimum risk, and they are therefore happy to accept a fixed rate of interest (usually slightly lower than other types of investment) which is payable whether profits are made or not. Such loan stocks are usually "secured" by the firm's assets, and as the holders are in fact *creditors* not owners of the firm, they therefore rank for payment before holders are of *ordinary* or *preference shares*. Some *loan stocks* are "convertible". This means that they are *loan stocks* for the first few years of their lives, but can be converted to *ordinary shares* after a period of time. This not only gives the holder security and fixed interest whilst the money lent is being put to work, but also gives him the option to take a stake in the equity (and hopefully gain greater rewards) when the company has put the money to good use. Both private and public companies can offer *debentures*, but only if this is permitted in their articles of association.

An Example of Note Presentation – 2. The Notes

SHARES

1. INTRODUCTION

A company offers shares for sale in order to raise capital. This allows members of the public to invest in a business enterprise with a view to making a profit. The shareholder is entitled to a "share" in the profits of the company. The different shares can be classed in groups.

2. ORDINARY SHARES

Under this heading there are two divisions.

(a) Ordinary Shares
- (i) also known as equity shares
- (ii) high return on capital
- (iii) high risk
- (iv) attract wealthy investors seeking big returns (e.g. institutional investors)
- (v) capital gains rather than revenue profits
- (vi) issued by private or public companies.

(b) Deferred Ordinary Shares
- (i) sometimes called founder's shares
- (ii) taken by vendor of business when it is bought by another company
- (iii) high risk – same as ordinary shares
- (iv) dividend paid after ordinary shares have had some profit
- (v) usually by public companies but can be issued by private companies.

3. PREFERENCE SHARES

Under this heading there are three divisions.

(a) Preference Shares
- (i) prior right to payment of dividend
- (ii) less risk than ordinary shares
- (iii) specific rate of dividend payable only if profits are made
- (iv) give security rather than large dividends
- (v) issued by public or private companies
- (vi) can be "redeemable" ("dated") or "irredeemable".

(b) Cumulative Preference Shares
- (i) same characteristics as preference shares except (iii)
- (ii) dividend not lost if company does not make profit in one year – it accumulates until profit is made.

(c) Participating Preference Shares
- (i) same characteristics as preference shares except (iii)
- (ii) extra dividend paid if dividend of ordinary shares goes above certain rate
- (iii) this holder" participates" in extra profits.

4. <u>DEBENTURES</u>

These are not really shares, but loans to companies. Therefore they are sometimes called "loan stocks".

(a) Loan Stocks
- (i) minimum risk
- (ii) fixed rate of interest – usually lower than ordinary shares
- (iii) dividend/return payable whether or not company makes profit
- (iv) holders are creditors not owners, and therefore rank for payment before others
- (v) "secured" by the firm's assets
- (vi) can be offered by private or public companies only if permitted by their articles of association.

(b) Convertible Loan Stocks
- (i) same as basic loan stocks or debentures, plus
- (ii) they can be converted to ordinary shares after a period of time
- (iii) the holder therefore has security and the option to "convert" if he thinks greater rewards can be gained.

5. <u>CONCLUSION</u>

Different types of shares enable companies to meet the different requirements of individual investors or investment groups.

Having read through these notes, your immediate reaction might be that they seem to take up almost as much space as the original passage. However, this is a result of the lay-out and method of presentation which are designed to have a visual impact and establish a "pattern" in your mind. In fact, the original (which is itself a very brief outline of facts) contains more than 725 words, and the notes contain approximately 385 words (including headings). Therefore, if such a reduction can be achieved with a passage which is already written in a concise form, you can imagine how much of a reduction could be achieved if you made notes from a chapter of a textbook.

The Presentation of Notes

A careful study of the notes given as an example would enable you to work out the type and sequence of headings. However, the following checklist will specify these clearly, and remind you of some essential presentation techniques. You should check these against the specimen notes in the text and make sure that you identify and understand the use of each.

Notemaking Checklist

You should use:

1 Large capitals for titles and headings; upper case roman numerals for any necessary numbers (e.g. **UNIT III: SHARES**);
2 arabic numerals and upper case letters for the main section-headings,
3 lower case letters of the alphabet and upper and lower case headings for the smaller sub-headings,
4 lower case Roman numerals and lower case headings for the smallest sections (i.e. the details),
5 a system of progressive indentation (i.e. the "pattern" on the page),
6 underlining for emphasis.

Are your notes *clear? concise? accurate? orderly?*

EXERCISE

Copy the specimen set of notes on shares into your file or exercise book, making sure that you employ the same method of presentation. All headings, number and letter sequences must be exactly the same as in the example, and you should check your work against the note-making checklist. Remember that this is an exercise in *presentation* rather than actual note making. You are given the opportunity to actually construct a set of notes as well as present them in the next exercise.

EXERCISE

The following passage deals with two aspects of "marketing" a product. Construct an accurate set of notes based entirely on the information you are given. Read the *whole* passage before you start so that you have some idea of the overall content. Suggestions for main divisions and sub-headings are given at the end of the passage, but you are not obliged to use these: they are included simply to give you some guidance if you have difficulty in working out suitable ones of your own.

Note Presentation – 1. The Original Passage

ASPECTS OF MARKETING

Any consideration of the chain of distribution – that process by which goods or services are brought from the producer to the consumer – must include a study of the roles played by the main contributors to the process, and these are commonly listed as: the manufacturer, the wholesaler, the retailer and the consumer. However, in a modern industrial society the whole business of getting a product from the producer to its final destination is included under the general term "marketing", and this involves other activities as well as those outlined in the traditional chain of distribution. Two such activities are *market research* and *advertising*.

In today's world, a manufacturer who successfully involves himself in large-scale production expects to reap massive rewards; but failure in such an enterprise results in equally massive losses, and manufacturers certainly can't afford to risk extensive capital investment without being sure of their market. It is quite possible that a number of years and millions of pounds have to be devoted to setting up a production line for a new product, and therefore the manufacturer must be sure that the product is actually acceptable to consumers. It is not always possible to produce a sample product and put it on the market for a time to see how it sells, and so the producer must employ a method of examining and assessing the market before production is considered.

Therefore, market research has become an important preliminary to large-scale production, and it is based upon the assumption that most "new" products are in fact adaptions of, modifications of or improvements on old products. As it is very rare for a completely new product to be put on the market, the job of the market researcher involves studying and investigating public attitudes towards existing products. Through this, the manufacturer can find out what the consumer likes and dislikes, what qualities of a particular product are appreciated most, and what changes are likely to be acceptable.

Another function of market research is to predict increases in market demand. Obviously, it is advantageous to a manufacturer to have some idea of an area in which demand is likely to increase dramatically so that he can adapt, boost or instigate production in order to increase his share of any expanding markets.

Market research is really a development of applied statistics, and the material required by the researcher can be acquired in various ways. Much of it can be found in official publications, or published statistics, or reference libraries, but there is also the need for carefully organised and supervised fieldwork, i.e. meeting and interviewing members of the consumer public, followed by highly specialist (often computerised) analysis and interpretation of the result.

When the market researchers have done their job, the manufacturer has some information on which to base production decisions. However, it would be foolish of him to go into full production and then just hope that the product will sell. The obvious course for him to take is to advertise effectively, thereby hoping to influence consumer attitudes and priorities in favour of his product.

Such advertising has two basic functions: it is an important method of communication through which the consumer is informed of what goods are available; and it is a method of persuasion by which one firm aims to convince the consumer that his product is more desirable than that of a competitor.

The methods of communication used by advertisers are numerous, and include television, the press, radio, the cinema, hoardings, posters, direct mail and "point of sale". A careful study of such media can reveal a great deal about modern marketing techniques and how the advertiser tries to stimulate buying.

Advertising has developed into an immensely useful and profitable industry, and has, like market research, become highly specialised. The firms who concentrate on this sort of work are called agencies, and are paid to produce ideas, to plan, to arrange and co-ordinate the work of the many specialists necessarily involved in a modern, successful advertising compaign.

Note presentation – 2. A Possible Heading Sequence

ASPECTS OF MARKETING

1. INTRODUCTION
2. MARKET RESEARCH
   - (a) Explanation
   - (b) Functions
   - (c) Methods
3. ADVERTISING
   - (a) Aims
   - (b) Functions
   - (c) Media
   - (d) Agencies
4. CONCLUSION

EXERCISE

Using any suitable source available in your college library, make a set of notes which outline the role of *the wholesale trade* in the traditional chain of distribution.

EXERCISE

Using the same source as for the previous exercise, or any other suitable source, make a set of notes of *the retail trade* (including types of retail outlet).

TASK TEN

As you will be using the library for the two preceding exercises, you will have the opportunity of performing this task while you are there. In a previous passage, the section dealing with market research mentioned statistics and the available sources of statistics. These can often be found in the *reference* section of the library. Your task is to browse through the reference section, and give the titles, publishing organisation and frequency of publication of up to five suitable sources devoted mainly to the presentation of statistics.

	Title	Publishing Organisation	Frequency of publication
(i)	______	______	______
	______	______	______
(ii)	______	______	______
	______	______	______
(iii)	______	______	______
	______	______	______
(iv)	______	______	______
	______	______	______
(v)	______	______	______
	______	______	______

STANDARD WORKS OF REFERENCE

The last task involved you in a search amongst the books classified within the *reference* section of your library, so this seems an appropriate point to develop your knowledge of these sources of information a little further. An awareness of the usefulness of standard works of reference is essential to any student – not only those works which relate directly to his/her area of study, but also those which give general information. As you will have noticed, there are numerous reference books available, and they are intended to be used to look up a specific piece of information rather than read from cover to cover.

The following list is by no means comprehensive, but it gives you an introduction to some well-known reference books and their contents.

(a) *Concise Oxford English Dictionary:* alphabetical list of words and their meanings.

(b) *Fowler's Modern English Usage:* correct English style, grammar and usage.

(c) *Roget's Thesaurus:* collection of words connected in meaning, grouped under subject headings.

(d) *A Dictionary of Abbreviations:* as implied by title.

(e) *Dictionary of the Bible* (J. Hastings): a full treatment of facts, concepts and beliefs.

(f) *Oxford Companion to English Literature:* biographies of authors, plots of plays and novels and characters in fiction.

(g) *Everyman's Dictionary of Quotations and Proverbs:* as title.

(h) *United Nations Statistical Yearbook:* statistics relating to various aspects of life in most countries of the world.

(i) *British Standards Yearbook:* details of British Standards applied to all goods.

(j) *Whitaker's Almanac:* reference book for assorted information ranging from population statistics to public schools.

(k) *Who's Who:* biographical dictionary of famous people, published annually.

(l) *Britain: An Official Handbook:* comprehensive coverage of numerous aspects of life in Britain.

(m) *Scientific and Learned Societies of Great Britain:* arranged by subject and then alphabetically by society or institution.

(n) *Telephone Directories:* alphabetical list of names, addresses and numbers.

(o) *Kelly's Directories of Towns:* street directories.

(p) *Keesing's Contemporary Archives:* weekly diary of world events.

(q) *Kemp's Engineer's Yearbook:* published annually, covers all branches of engineering.

(r) *Statesman's Year Book:* general information on most countries.

(s) *Post Office Guide:* information of Post Office services and activities etc.

(t) *Official Rules of Sports and Games:* covers rules of most major sports.

(u) *The Guinness Book of Records:* world records in almost anything recordable.

(v) *Gibbons Stamp Catalogue:* full details of stamps.

(w) *The Highway Code:* rules of the road, information and instruction.

(x) *Collins' Guide to English Parish Churches* (Betjeman): descriptions and illustrations

(y) *Everyman's Own Lawyer:* the layman's guide to the law.

EXERCISE

Answer the following questions in your files and give the title of the book from which you extracted the information. Your answer should be written in the form of a grammatically correct statement, and the source given in brackets. For example:

What is the greatest number of jumps achieved in a given period of time on a pogo stick?
Answer: The greatest number of jumps achieved in two hours on a pogo stick is 14,325 (*Guinness Book of Records*).

(a) What is the meaning of unbroken white lines in the middle of the road?

(b) What is dealt with in British Standard 4224?

(c) What is the population of Hawaii?

(d) In what postal district is the village of Horrabridge in South Devon?

(e) What do the letters L.W.I.V. stand for?

(f) Give a definition of *cordwain.*

(g) In which year was the poet Lord Byron born?

(h) Give one quotation by Oscar Wilde.

(i) What is the British Standards Mark?

(j) Who lives at number 1, Priestwood Close, Henbury, Bristol?

(k) What is the telephone number of your nearest Electricity Board showrooms?

(l) Who was the Poet Laureate in 1973?

(m) What political posts have been held by Mr Edward Heath since 1950?

(n) To what extent has the population of Brazil increased in the last five years?

(o) What aspect of law is dealt with in section 12 of *Everyman's Own Lawyer?*

(p) What is the basic maternity allowance payable in England?

(q) What is the diameter of the moon?

(r) What is the overall stopping distance of a car travelling at 30 mph?

(s) Who was Aaron in the Bible?

(t) Give the face values of the stamps issued to celebrate the independence of the Solomon Islands.

Encyclopaedias

There are two types of encyclopaedia: those which concentrate on specific areas of knowledge, and those more commonly experienced by most students, which are general sources of reference. It is this second type which can usually be found in any library. These general encyclopaedias are extremely useful because they provide information on a vast range of topics within a relatively small set of books.

Most encyclopaedias are arranged alphabetically so that the contents range from topics with the initial letter A in volume one to topics with the initial letter Z in the last volume. The spine of each volume in a set will normally indicate the contents by displaying the relevant key letters of the first and last topic. For example, Volume VII of the Micropaedia of the *Encyclopaedia Britannica* has *Montpel – Piranes;* on the spine, indicating that it contains information of subjects which fall within that alphabetical range. Within a set of encyclopaedias there is usually an *index* volume which lists all the topics covered in the complete set, says which volume each topic can be found in, and gives the page number.

Some popular encyclopaedias which you will probably find in your library are:

The New Caxton Encyclopaedia
The Encyclopaedia Britannica
Chamber's Encyclopaedia
The World Book Encyclopaedia

TASK ELEVEN

Give the names of five sets of encyclopaedias available in the reference section of your library (excluding those listed above), and indicate the number of volumes in each set.

	Title	*Number of Volumes*
(i)	____________________	________
(ii)	____________________	________
(iii)	____________________	________
(iv)	____________________	________
(v)	____________________	________

TASK TWELVE

In which volume or page of the encyclopaedias given do the listed topics appear?

(i) The Encyclopaedia Britannica

Tarim River	________	Police Technology	________
Ropes and Cables	________	Frostbite	________

(ii) The New Book of Knowledge

Ballooning	________	Genetics	________
Soccer	________	Tools	________

(iii) The New Caxton Encyclopaedia

European Unity	________	Trousers	________
Balance of Payments	________	Onion	________

(iv) Chamber's Encyclopaedia

Cinema	________	Gossamer	________
Sharks	________	Brandy	________

(v) The World Book Encyclopaedia

Embalming	________	Jazz	________
Chess	________	Tides	________

(vi) Any other encyclopaedia of your choice ________________

Merchant	________	Record	________
France	________	Biceps	________

EXERCISE

This exercise is in three parts.

(a) There are forty topics listed below. Choose any twenty, and using a suitable encyclopaedia from your college library construct one question for each topic, concentrating on its *origins* or *history*. Do not give the answers, but make a note of them on a separate sheet of paper for later use. You should indicate the topic and the encyclopaedia used, at the end of each question. This specimen question shows how it should be presented:

1. When was the first aircraft carrier put into service? (Aircraft Carriers/New Caxton)

TOPICS

Bookbinding	Bells	Ice cream	Girl guides
Laser	Matches	Printing	Railways
Mines	Submarines	Soccer	Space travel
Trousers	Balloons	Watches	Fingerprints
Embalming	Olympic games	Mirrors	Circuses
Cowboys	Radar	Golf	Guitars
Dominoes	Speedway racing	Titanic	Detectives
Jazz	Television	Cosmetics	Dolls
Rockets	Basketball	Tobacco	Old Bailey
Jousting	Hi-fi	Motor cycles	Gliders

Number your questions 1 to 20 and make sure your name appears on the sheet.

(b) Your twenty questions (without answers) should be handed in to your lecturer/teacher who will redistribute them amongst the members of your group. Your next piece of work is to answer the questions on the sheet you are given, making use of the sources indicated at the end of each question.

(c) When all members of your group have completed *(b)*, you should retrieve your own sheet of questions from the person who has been working with them, together with his/her answers. Check these answers for accuracy, and return them to their owner.

SUPPLEMENTARY EXERCISE

Since the study in Section I relates to a public sector industry which is important to the national and local economy, prepare a case-study on similar lines for an organisation of your choice from the *private sector*.

Aspects of your study will benefit from presentation in suitable diagrammatic forms.

Obviously, your use of language (communication skills) is important, and you should aim to present your information in as clear and concise a manner as possible.

UNIT IV

Achievement Checklist

When you have completed this unit you should be able to:

* State the obligations of the organisation to:
  (*a*) the customer/client,
  (*b*) the employee,
  (*c*) the providers of finance,
  (*d*) the environment;
* Handle and convert British and foreign currencies;
* Use imperial and metric weights and measures;
* Convert units of imperial measures to units of metric measures and vice versa;
* Convert unit costs from one system of weights and measures to the other system;
* Use standard punctuation marks accurately and effectively;
* Adopt a logical approach to traditional comprehension;
* Select relevant information and use it to give clear written answers;
* Understand the uses and functions of the main parts of a business letter;
* Use an acceptable form of presentation for business letters;
* Write and present a simple letter of request.

SECTION I

THE OBLIGATIONS OF THE ORGANISATION

This section deals with the obligations that organisations have towards customers, employees, providers of finance and the environment, i.e. the world about us.

As has already been stated, any organisation (particularly in the private sector) has to cover its costs in order to survive. Indeed one of the main arguments in favour of private enterprise is that it encourages individuals to start businesses in order to make profits. If that is the case then it is reasonable to assume that owners of businesses will usually want to make as big a profit as possible and certainly this has generally been true in the past. This desire for profits encourages organisations to keep their costs as low as possible whilst selling their products on the most favourable terms to themselves as is possible. This is quite legitimate but it has led to situations where, for example, organisations have treated employees simply and solely as a factor of production and not given them very much consideration as human beings. Some organisations have exploited the consumer by misleading advertising or by selling faulty and dangerous goods; others have tried to cheat their suppliers of finance. Until recently there has been little concern shown for the environment although in this case it is fair to say that many people and organisations were often unaware of the damage they caused.

Over a long period of time successive governments have found it necessary to pass laws which insist on certain minimum standards so that consumers, employees, financiers and the environment gain some protection from those who might otherwise try to exploit them. It must be emphasised, however, that in many cases these Acts of Parliament have had to be passed to provide protection against the abuses of a small minority and that many organisations have always acted in a reasonable and honourable manner.

THE ORGANISATION AND THE CONSUMER/CLIENT

In a non-technological society where the bulk of goods and services available are straightforward and uncomplicated and are provided by firms and individuals operating on a small scale, the consumer is usually able to deal directly with the principals of the firms and decide whether the goods and services offered are of the right size and quality required and if the price asked is a fair and reasonable one. For example, even today if you go to a shop or market to buy apples you can often examine them to see if they are of the standard or quality you require. You can look to see if they are firm and ripe and if they are free of blemishes; if so, then you may feel that the price asked is a fair and reasonable one. If not, then you may decide to go to another seller. On the other hand, damaged fruit may be on offer at a special price in which case you may feel that the apples are worth buying at the lower price. You may be able to make similar common-sense decisions about a wide range of goods as long as they are within your range of knowledge and experience. Furthermore in some cases it is possible to discuss price and quality directly with individuals who have the power and authority to make "on the spot" decisions. Such circumstances were, for a long time, the rule rather than the exception, and if disputes or arguments arose between buyer and seller the law adopted the principle of *caveat emptor* which means "let the buyer beware". Basically this meant that providing the seller was not actively dishonest the buyer had to bear any losses he suffered as a result of trading. This system was reasonably fair when both buyer and seller were able to negotiate face to face as equals and the goods or services for sale could be examined by buyers who had a good knowledge of what was required from the seller.

However, in a modern technological society many of the goods we take for granted, such as cars, TVs and refrigerators, are complicated pieces of machinery and few of us have the specialised knowledge needed to assess quality and price realistically. Therefore we must rely on the seller's honesty to provide us with a reasonable quality article at the price asked. Even buying apples may not be the simple task it appears to be if the fruit is pre-packed in polythene bags so that the contents cannot be inspected closely.

Such *pre-packaging* by manufacturers, particularly of food products, still has advantages for both the seller and the consumer. The manufacturer can take advantage of mechanisation and automation to operate on a large scale and reduce unit costs – even allowing for the cost of "extra" packaging. Handling and distribution costs are reduced as are those at the point of sale in the shops. The consumer has the advantage of cheaper goods which will be of a similar taste and quality whenever a particular "brand" is bought together with all the advantages of improved hygiene that such a system provides. Pre-packaging hasn't only revolutionised the food industry. More and more goods are sold in this way and as consumers we have to try to assess suitability, quality and value on very slim evidence.

However, if the consumer is unable to protect his own interests because of the complexity of the product or because it is not easily examined, then he could be prey for the unscrupulous. It is often argued that business organisations which "cheat" their customers or provide inferior goods will be forced out of business by the bad publicity which will result and people will stop buying their products and switch to those of competing firms. Even so, due to the growth of large organisations the range of choice between the suppliers of goods and services is becoming increasingly limited. Banking, insurance, cars, electrical goods, cigarettes and tobacco, soap and detergents, chocolate, bread and milk distribution are U.K. markets dominated by a few giant firms (a situation known as *oligopoly*), not forgetting the goods and services provided by the nationalised industries. There are, therefore, few alternative suppliers of many goods and services and the differences between their products may be so small as to make little difference to the consumer. If a consumer is dissatisfied, however, he can complain to the manufacturer and/or retailer but if they refuse to provide a replacement or to put right some shoddy workmanship then the consumer's only chance of redress is to take the matter to court. If the amount involved is less the £200 then the matter can be taken before the Small Claims Court which has simplified, and therefore quicker and cheaper, procedures than the more traditional courts. In additon, large companies can afford to employ the best lawyers and to make the whole matter as lengthy and complicated as possible, simply to wear down the patience and financial resources of the average individual. Faced with these problems the consumer/client will often shrug his shoulders and change to another brand, unaware that very often he is still a customer of the same organisation as it produces a large number of different brands of the same products. In some cases the "competitor" may be part of a group of companies.

Obviously the vast majority of organisations are going to try to keep their customers happy as too much adverse publicity or too many law suits will eventually affect their sales and therefore their profitability. Even so, profitability is the key to survival for the organisation and if, for example, it has to meet increased costs for raw materials but cannot pass on all the increase directly to the consumer it may "hide" the increase by reducing the quality or quantity of the goods. In advertising its products the organisation will certainly tell consumers of the good points but are unlikely to tell of any of its deficiencies — in fact, they may be tempted to claim more for the product than is really true. In such circumstances the idea of equality between buyer and seller breaks down and it is not sufficient for the principle of "buyer beware" to be the only protection for the consumer. It might be argued that if all organisations acted in a totally honest way at all times then the consumer would have nothing to fear as he could always expect a "fair deal".

There is no universal code of business conduct, and, left to individuals, the "fairness" of any transaction will, to a large extent, depend on the honesty of those involved. Some industries have drawn up "codes of conduct" but they are largely voluntary. (The traditional professions such as law and medicine have strict codes which must be obeyed or offenders can be "struck off" and prevented from practising.) As a result, and usually in response to evidence of deceit and dishonesty, governments have found it necessary to introduce Acts of Parliament to protect the interests of the consumer. The history of consumer protection goes back to the Middle Ages but it is in the last ten years or so that it has become particularly important in response to increasing consumer demand. It is now necessary to consider the various Acts of Parliament which affect the relationship between the organisation and the consumer. There are a number of these, and some are quite complicated so only the main provisions of each are given.

The Law of Contract

In simplified terms a contract is an agreement between (usually) two people which states that one of them will do something in exchange for some form of payment by the other. For example, a contract exists if you offer to buy something in a shop and your offer is accepted. The law relating to contracts is very complicated as it is mostly "judge-made" law, although it is also affected by a wide variety of Acts of Parliament. However, the following conditions must be met for there to be an enforceable contract:

(*a*) the parties involved must be able to make a valid contract (this excludes people under eighteen; the insane; and those under the influence of drink or drugs);

(*b*) one party must *offer* to make the contract and this must be matched by an *acceptance* of the conditions by the other party;

(*c*) there must be some kind of payment involved although it need not always be money. This is known as *consideration*.

If the parties to a contract disagree over its terms either of them can take the matter to the courts which will act as a kind of referee. If one party is found to be at fault they can be ordered to pay damages for any losses suffered by the other party and/or complete the contract whether they like it or not.

As mentioned earlier, the basic principle applied to contracts was that of "let the buyer beware", and anyone could make any kind of contract they wished, whatever the conditions, but this has now been modified by a number of Acts of Parliament.

The Sale of Goods Act 1893

The principle of "buyer beware" is modified. Goods sold by a trader must be suitable for the purpose intended, e.g. a teapot must not leak. The Act did not, however, prevent traders persuading people to make agreements that meant they gave up their basic rights.

The Food and Drugs Act 1955

Standards for the quality and cleanliness of food offered for sale (including the seller's premises) are established. Forbids misleading descriptions and controls labelling and contents of "composite" foods e.g. a "pork" sausage must contain a minimum amount of pork-meat.

The Consumer Protection Act 1961

This Act governs the sale of potentially dangerous goods such as electrical items, oil heaters, poisonous paints on toys and the flame resistance of children's clothes. However regulations are usually only introduced after there has been some damage done – there is no law requiring all goods to be fully examined before they can be offered for sale.

The Weights and Measures Act 1963
The latest in a long series of Acts required that:
(*a*) traders' scales are accurate;
(*b*) pre-packaged goods are marked with their correct quantities;
(*c*) inspectors can have access to business premises at any reasonable time.

The Trading Stamps Act 1964
Prior to this Act it was only possible to exchange trading stamps for goods but now they must be able to be exchanged for cash.

The cash value of stamps is about half the value obtained when exchanging them for goods although such comparisons are usually made with the recommended resale price (R.R.P.) and in reality it may be possible to buy the goods at a far lower price. In such circumstances the difference between exchanging for goods or for cash may not be so great as would appear at first.

Resale Prices Act 1964
Suppliers of goods are forbidden to set the minimum prices to be charged by the retailer although suppliers can advise a recommended resale price (R.R.P.), Certain goods have been exempted from this rule but only after suppliers have obtained approval from the Restrictive Trade Practices Court.

The Trade Descriptions Act 1968
This is a most important Act. False or misleading descriptions of goods offered for sale can result in the seller being heavily fined. Any spoken or written description or advertisement connected with the items offered *must* be accurate. Another important aspect of the Act was to make it illegal to "reduce" prices by crossing out the price on a label and inserting another one to imply a reduction had been made. This is no longer possible unless the goods have been offered for sale at the higher price for at least twenty-eight consecutive days in the previous six months.

The Unsolicited Goods and Services Act 1971
If a firm sends you goods or provides you with a service you have not ordered then you are not obliged to pay. Furthermore if goods are sent to you and are not collected back by the sender within six months they become your property.

The Supply of Goods (Implied Terms) Act 1973
Organisations are not allowed to persuade people to sign agreements which restrict their basic rights under the Sale of Goods Act 1893. The only valid guarantees and agreements now are those which give the consumer rights in additon to those given under the earlier Act.

The Fair Trading Act 1973
Another very important Act in its implications for the business organisation. It established the office of Director-General of Fair Trading who has been given wide powers to keep a watchful eye on the whole field of the sale of goods and supply of services to consumers

to ensure that consumers' commercial interests are not adversely affected and that their health and safety are not put at risk. To try to overcome such difficulties he encourages trade associations to prepare voluntary codes of practice and anyone considered to be guilty of unfair trade practices can be summoned to appear before the Restrictive Trade Practices Court unless they agree to stop. The Director-General is assisted by the Consumer Protection Advisory Committee which is authorised to investigate consumer trade practices relating to:

(a) terms and conditions of sale or supply of services and the method of their communication to the consumer;
(b) promotion techniques and methods of salesmanship;
(c) packaging;
(d) methods of obtaining payment for goods/services.

If the Committee finds that an offence has been committed the offenders can be prosecuted and penalised.

The Consumer Credit Act 1974

This Act was introduced because of the concern that many consumers were being misled by advertisements relating to transactions involving various forms of credit, and by unscrupulous and aggressive salesmen – particularly of the door-to-door variety. The Act controls all forms of lending to consumers including hire purchase, credit sales, credit cards, bank loans and money-lending, although some organisations are allowed to make "exempt agreements". These are:

(a) local authorities;
(b) building societies
(c) insurance companies;
(d) friendly societies;
(e) employers and employees associations;
(f) charities;

Other organisations making loans of less than £5,000 to an individual (not a company) must have a licence to make "regulated agreements" covered by the Act. The Director-General is responsible for licensing and makes sure that applicants are fit to hold such a licence.

The Act also requires that the consumer is fully informed of all relevant facts about an agreement such as the true rate of interest charged and the rights and obligations of each party. The agreement form should be clear and uncomplicated and small print should not be used. The debtor must be provided with a copy of the agreement within seven days of signing it and if it has been arranged partly verbally and away from business premises, e.g. at home, then it may be cancelled within five days of the debtor receiving his copy of the agreement and any monies paid can be recovered.

The consumer also receives protection in cases of default providing he has paid at least one-third of the total amount due. In such cases the creditor must obtain a court order to recover the goods and this will be given only if the debtor has been given every reasonable opportunity to meet his debts (such as reducing the instalments which means that the period of credit is extended).

If the rate of interest charged is too high then the Court can reduce it or order the lender to repay or even cancel the contract.

The Act also makes it possible for the customer/client to obtain details of any information about themselves which has been given to an organisation by a credit reference agency. The organisation would use the information to help it decide whether or not to extend credit.

The Prices Act 1974

This Act empowers the government to subsidise food and regulate its price (and that of other household necessities). Shopkeepers must mark prices on goods and display price lists of their goods so that they can be compared with other shops.

The Restrictive Trade Practices Act 1976

Agreement by groups of suppliers to restrict the supply of *goods* are void unless the parties can prove to the Restrictive Trade Practices Court that the agreement is in the public interest. The Act also allows the Director-General to investigate restrictive practices in connection with *services* under similar circumstances.

It will be apparent that the organisation has many legal responsibilities to the consumer/client and must take great care to make sure that they are observed. It is perhaps a sad thought that it has been necessary to make so many rules and regulations to protect the consumer. Nevertheless it must also be remembered that business organisations have often been the victims of consumers who have tried to take advantage of their ability to embarrass the firm or by trying to cheat the firm by not paying their debts.

The enormous expansion in credit facilities in recent years has led to a corresponding increase in the number of bad debts as people have failed to control their spending properly and have entered into more credit agreements than they can cope with. In some extreme cases irresponsibility of this sort has resulted in total weekly credit instalments exceeding total weekly income! Developments of this kind have led to some organisations establishing credit-rating lists whereby individual consumers are assessed as to their "worth" (this has long been an established *trade* practice). Other lists have been compiled of those people who have failed to keep their side of an agreement and perhaps been taken to court by the lender. Whilst this is understandable from the firm's point of view, these lists have been criticised as being an invasion of privacy.

There have also been cases of people being included on lists because they have been involved in court cases, even though they have been the "innocent" party, or have been listed as a result of mistaken identity. In such circumstances consumers have found it difficult, if not impossible, to obtain credit through no fault of their own, although they now have some measure of protection under the Consumer Credit Act 1974.

It should also be remembered that there are a number of voluntary organisations active in the field of consumer protection. The most important of these is the Consumers Association which examines goods and services offered to the public and publishes the results of their tests in their magazine *Which?* Consumers can become members of the Association although the magazine is available in most public and college libraries. Consumers can also gain advice as to their rights from the Citizens' Advice Bureaux which are sponsored by the local authorities. Newspapers, magazines and television also provide advice and sometimes take action on behalf of their subscribers or viewers. Organisations are not legally obliged to co-operate in any of these activities nor do they *have* to take any notice of their comments or criticisms. However, ignoring them may produce even more adverse publicity and, in practice, most organisations do co-operate. In some cases the organisation can protect itself from a lot of criticism by having its products tested for safety and reliability by the British Standards Institution (B.S.I). If they meet the required standards they can be sold with the "kite" mark which can be a useful guide for the sensible consumer.

THE ORGANISATION AND THE EMPLOYEE

In many respects the obligations that exist between the organisation and the employee have evolved for similar reasons to those that were discussed in the previous section.

As the organisation has tended to be the "strong" party in any dealings with consumers, so it has with employees. Historically, employees have generally been looked on as a factor of production that the organisation should employ or dispense with according to its commercial or economic needs. As a result, hardship has often been experienced by employees in the past when they have suddenly been put out of work, particularly in times of high unemployment when alternative jobs have been scarce. Governmental commitment to full employment, the growth of trade union power and the acceptance of such social objectives as equal opportunities for women have all led to an increasing body of legislation that imposes obligations on the organisation in its dealings with its employees. By and large such legislation has been to the employees' advantage but it should be remembered that many of these developments have added to firms' costs and resulted in increased prices to the consumer. As we saw in Unit I, profitability can be an emotive issue, as are many matters which are implied in any reference to "obligations" between employers and employees. What constitutes "a fair day's pay for a fair day's work" will often depend on which side of the fence you are. An employer might argue that £60 for a 35-hour week is "fair" whilst the employee might demand a "fair" deal which means higher pay for fewer hours work. It is a troublesome question, and whilst we will not consider it in any detail here it should be borne in mind that such differences exist.

Generally speaking, the organisation will have a good idea of the sort of person it wishes to employ for any particular job but even at this stage there are legal obligations to be observed. Changing social conditions and attitudes in recent years have resulted in three Acts of Parliament that affect the selection of an employee.

The Equal Pay Act 1970

This states that where women and men do the same or broadly similar work they must receive equal payment and have the same rights and privileges as men. This Act applies to both full and part-time employment.

The Sex Discrimination Act 1975

The Act states that men and women should have equal opportunity to do the same work although it does allow discrimination where there is a "genuine occupational qualification" (such as coal-mining for men or midwifery for women) which makes it necessary to employ someone of a specific sex. However, it is unusual nowadays to see an advertisement for a "salesgirl" or "salesman"; most would state "salesman/woman" or even "salesperson"!

The Race Relations Act 1976

It is illegal to discriminate against anyone in an employment situation solely because of their race, religion or colour. The Act established the Commission for Racial Equality whose duties include working towards the elimination of discrimination, the promotion of equality of opportunity, race relations and issuing codes of practice for employers.

The organisations' obligations to employees *after* they have been recruited cover a very wide range of circumstances although, in some cases, their importance will depend to some extent on the nature of the organisations' activities. Nevertheless most of the Acts are quite complicated and in general only the main provisions are given. The relevant Acts, again in date order, rather than order of importance are as follows.

The Wages Councils Act 1959

In the U.K., terms and conditions of employment are mostly settled by collective agreements reached by voluntary methods although subject to any overriding government requirements such as an incomes policy. However it has been found that in some trades or industries the organisation is inadequate to ensure satisfactory standards. In such cases the government can establish a wages council to regulate pay and conditions of employment such as holidays.

At present there are forty-four Councils covering industries as diverse as boot and shoe repairing, hairdressing and licensed restaurants.

The Payment of Wages Act 1960

The Act applies to manual workers and their employers. Any employee covered by the Act cannot be made to have his wages paid in any way other than in cash, e.g. direct to a bank, unless they voluntarily agree to the arrangement. Similarly an employer is not bound to agree to a request that wages be paid in any other way than in cash.

The Shops Acts 1950 and 1965

These Acts apply to retail and wholesale premises and were introduced to prevent shop assistants working very long hours, and to make sure that they are allowed adequate rest and leisure breaks. The main regulations relate to the "early-closing" day, compulsory closing times on other days of the week, special rules concerning Sundays, and general provisions regarding conditions of work. It should be noted that the Acts contain a large number of exemptions and alternatives.

The Employers Liability (Compulsory Insurance) Act 1969

All employers must insure against liability for personal injury and disease sustained by their employees. This overcomes the problem of employees being injured at work and not being able to obtain realistic compensation. Some employees do not have to be insured and these include immediate relatives of the employer and domestic servants.

Certain employers are also exempt from the requirements of the Act and these include (amongst others):

(a) any local authority (other than a parish council);
(b) any police authority;
(c) any nationalised industry and its subsidiaries;
(d) employers of ships' crews.

The Contracts of Employment Act 1972
There are two main sets of provisions in the Act.

Firstly, *employers have to give employees written details of their employment.* This information should be given to the employee within thirteen weeks of starting work and should include:

(a) the title or grade of the job;
(b) the date when employment began;
(c) the minimum period of notice to be given by both parties;
(d) the rate of pay and how it is calculated, e.g. overtime, bonuses, etc.;
(e) the interval at which earnings are to be paid, e.g. weekly or monthly;
(f) hours of work and holiday entitlement;
(g) pay and conditions relating to absence due to sickness or injury;
(h) details of any pension scheme and the employee's obligations and rights;
(i) the employee's rights regarding union membership;
(j) details of the organisation's grievance procedures;
(k) disciplinary rules relating to the employee and details of any appeals system.

There is obviously a lot of information to be included in the contract and so many organisations produce a "handbook" detailing conditions of service (particularly for items *(g)* to *(k)* above). If so it is acceptable to refer to the handbook in the contract providing the employee is given ample opportunity to refer to it. Secondly, the Act states *the periods of notice required to end employment.* The employer must give:

(a) one week's notice to a person who has been employed for at least four weeks but less than two years;
(b) one week's notice for each year of continuous employment over two years but less than twelve years;
(c) not less than twelve weeks' notice if the period of continuous employment is twelve years or more.

The employee must give at least one week's notice after four weeks' continuous employment although this does not increase whatever the length of service. Both parties may accept payment in place of notice and in additon have the right to end the contract without giving any notice if they feel that the actions of the other make it necessary, e.g. if one commits a criminal offence against the other.

The Trade Union and Labour Relations Act 1974
The main provisions of the Act are as follows.

(a) An employee has the right *not* to be unfairly dismissed and, if he is, can complain to an industrial tribunal. Dismissal arising out of trade union activity is "unfair". In

other cases the employer has to show that the employee was dismissed because of redundancy, inadequate qualifications, incapability or misconduct for it to be "fair".

(b) An employee may appeal to a tribunal within three months of dismissal if he thinks he has been unfairly treated. If the tribunal agrees with him the employer can be ordered to pay compensation and/or to reinstate the employee.

(c) Both trade unions and employers associations are defined by the Act.

(d) It approves a code of practices for industrial relations which is not legally binding but whether or not it has been followed can be taken into account by an industrial tribunal.

(e) PAYE (pay as you earn) – the employer must deduct income tax and national insurance contributions from employees' pay. He is obliged to give an employee who is leaving a certificate (form P45) showing the total earnings (less any pensions contributions) in the current tax year and the total amount of tax deducted. After 5th April each year the employee must be given an annual certificate of pay and tax deduction (form P60) showing total pay for the year and the total tax deducted. The employee needs to keep the certificate as it may be required when claiming earnings-related social security benefit.

The Health and Safety at Work Act 1974

The aim of this Act is to make firms more health and safety conscious, and as a result imposes a number of obligations to employees on organisations. However, in view of its aims it is explained in detail in Unit X (Book II) which deals with safety at work.

The Employment Protection Act 1975

The Act is intended to improve industrial relations by encouraging the development and strengthening of collective bargaining and to provide employees with new rights and greater job security. The most important parts of the Act deal with trade union membership, and forbid employers to try to prevent employees from joining the union of their choice. Trade union officials must be allowed "reasonable" time off work with pay to carry out their duties and the same applies to employees who hold public offices, e.g. J.P.s, or are members of a local authority. Employers are also required to give trade union representatives information about the organisation so that they are not put at a disadvantage when negotiating pay and conditions. Amongst other matters dealt with by the Act are:

(a) trade union recognition;
(b) guaranteed payment when work is interrupted through no fault of the employee;
(c) maternity rights and pay;
(d) written statement of reasons for dismissal;
(e) remedies for unfair dismissal;
(f) itemised pay statements.

The Act established two important bodies.

(a) The Advisory, Conciliation and Arbitration Services (ACAS) which has powers and duties consistent with its name.

(b) The Employment Appeal Tribunal, consisting of judges and lay members from both sides of industry, which hears appeals on questions of law from the decisions of industrial tribunals on cases arising out of employment legislation.

Preceding legislation outlines the obligations of the organisation to the employee during his or her employment and some of the safeguards which have been erected to prevent unfair dismissal. However, it sometimes happens that an organisation or a part of it has to be closed down because of adverse economic conditions or as a result of a change in trading policy or even because of the death of the owner. In such cases employees would be protected by the Redundancy Payments Act 1968.

The Redundancy Payments Act 1968
If the employee loses his job in any of the circumstances mentioned above he is entitled to payment based on length of service and age as follows:

Age	*Rate per year of employment*
18 - 21	½ week's pay
22 - 40	1 week's pay
41 - 64 men 41 - 59 women	1½ week's pay

NOTES:
(a) Employment before the age of eighteen does not count.
(b) If a "week's pay" exceeds £100, it is to be taken as £100 only.
(c) Only the last twenty years service is taken into account.
(d) Because of items *(a)* to *(c)* the maximum payment is £3,000, i.e. 20 (years) x 1½ (weeks) x £100.

THE ORGANISATION AND THE PROVIDERS OF FINANCE

As the chart on page 150 indicates, finance for the organisation is obtained from two main sources – *owners* and *creditors.* Owners provide funds for use by the organisation as it thinks best and, in return, expect a share of any profit made. If the shareholder in a company no longer wishes to leave his money invested in the company then he can sell his shares to another person. Ordinary shareholders would only be repaid by the organisation in the event of the company being wound up, although preference shares might be redeemed by the company in certain circumstances. Creditors on the other hand usually lend money to the organisation for specific purposes either on a long-term or short-term basis. Creditors are paid interest in exchange for the use of the funds and will be repaid after a stated period of time. Whilst creditors hope the organisation will be profitable, as this will mean greater security for their loan, they are not entirely dependent on high levels of profitability for their return. In general creditors are repaid within relatively short periods of time but in cases where the loan is for a long time, e.g. loan stock, debentures, etc., then it may be possible to sell it to a third party (such circumstances as a rule only arise in connection with limited companies).

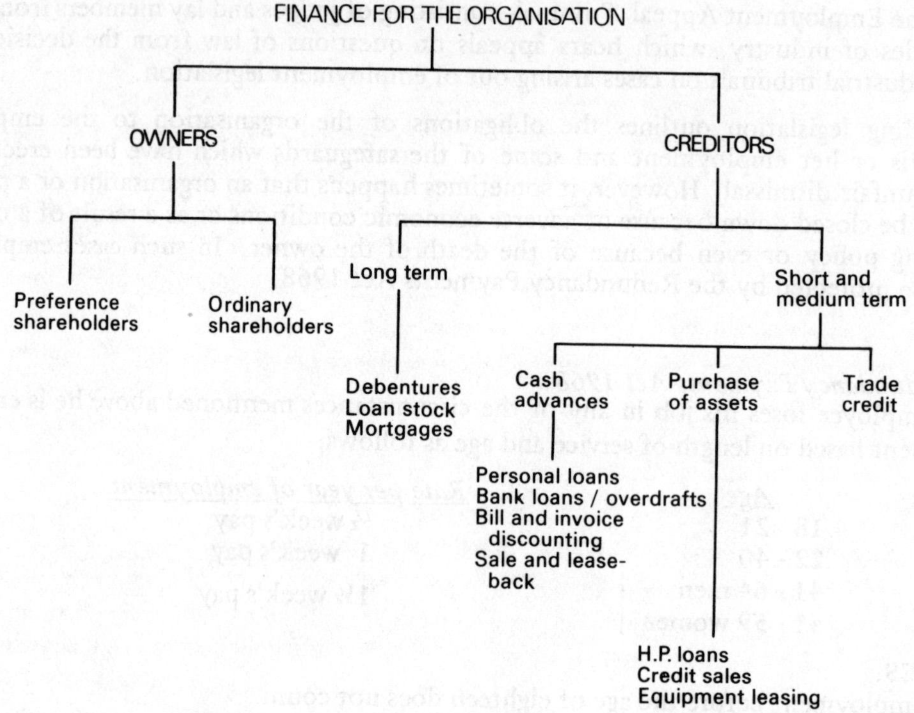

Obligations to owners

The organisation's obligations to its owners will vary according to the type of organisation involved and in the case of sole traders and partnerships will not present any real problems as the owners are in day-to-day contact with the business and are responsible only to themselves for any decisions they make. Nevertheless the Partnership Act 1890 states that all partners must act in the *utmost good faith* towards each other and that all partnership books and records must be kept at the principal place of business and may be inspected by all partners – these rules are no doubt intended to prevent partners "ganging-up" on one another.

As we have seen with the tendency of organisations to grow larger there has been an increasing division between ownership and management, both in terms of aims and day-to-day decision-making. As a result it might be tempting for unscrupulous majority shareholders or managers to withhold information from owners particularly if it meant that disclosure would show them to be inefficient or careless. In the worst cases there might be a positive intention to defraud owners. As stated previously one of the advantages of limited companies is that they can appeal for capital from larger numbers of people but as a result many shareholders will lack any business knowledge and will be easy prey for the unscrupulous company promoter or manager.

You should now return to Unit II, Section I and re-read the part relating to limited companies, which contains a number of items relating to the obligations to owners – particularly when a company is being formed.

So far as limited companies are concerned, therefore, the obligations of the organisation are laid down in the Company Acts and are chiefly concerned with the disclosure of information so that the owner can see the company is being run in a proper and honest manner. The major source of such information for the average shareholder is the *directors' report* which must include, amongst others, the following details:

(a) directors' names and their shareholdings;
(b) company's main activities;
(c) any significant changes in fixed assets;
(d) any amounts raised by share or debenture issues;
(e) contracts in which any director has a material interest and any arrangements for them to acquire shares in the company;
(f) arrangements for the protection of employees' health and safety whilst at work (a requirement of the Health and Safety at Work Act 1974);
(g) average number of employees and their earnings;
(h) any contribution of over £50 for political or charitable purposes.

The report is usually sent to the shareholder with the notice of the company's annual general meeting (A.G.M.). Each company must have an A.G.M. and must give twenty-one days notice of when and where it is to be held. This notice gives the shareholder a reasonable time in which to make arrangements to attend the meeting if he so wishes. (All other meetings are known as extraordinary general meetings and are subject to fourteen days notice.)

It is usual for the annual accounts and balance sheet also to be presented to the shareholders for approval at the A.G.M. (The accounts will include details of any dividends to be paid by the company.) If the holders of a majority of the shares do not agree with the way in which the company is being run by the directors, they can vote them out of office and replace them with their own nominees.

Theoretically at least the nationalised industries are "owned" by the people and their obligations to provide services and/or make profits are included in the various Acts of Parliament which brough them under public control. However, in practice they are very much under the control of the government of the day and the importance attached to their obligations may change if economic circumstances change or if there is a change in government. If such changes do take place they are usually said to be "in the national interest".

Obligations to Creditors

Organisations often borrow money and use their assets as security. They may borrow from banks or specialist financial institutions in different ways and for different purposes but in most cases of short-term (up to two years) and medium-term (up to five years) borrowing the agreement as to the amount, length of repayment period, interest rates, etc., will be governed by a contract between the two parties and the organisation's obligations will be laid down in some detail. If the organisation fails to keep its side of the bargain then the lender can sue them as with any other contract. In such cases it is often one organisation dealing with another and as they are assumed to be "equal" the law leaves them to operate largely on the "buyer beware" principle. Borrowing from individuals, however, is a different matter. Here is another example of the "large and powerful" organisation dealing with the "small and weak" individual and as we saw in the previous two sections laws have been passed to redress the balance between them, particularly when a company issues debentures as this is usually their major source of *loan capital.*

When a limited company issues debentures (or loan stocks) it appoints trustees (often an insurance company) to look after the interests of the debenture-holders. They are obliged to give full details of the issue in any prospectus so that potential lenders can make a properly informed decision as to whether they wish to subscribe for the debenture or not. The document containing particulars of the security for the loan, the methods of repayment and the rights of the debenture holder is known as a trust deed. If the company fails to meet its obligations then the debenture-holders have the right to sue for what is owed them. If the debenture is secured against specific assets they also have the right to sell that asset to obtain payment.

The Company Acts also require a company to:

(a) keep a register of all mortgages and other charges affecting its property which must be available for inspection by creditors (and owners) – these charges must also be registered with the Registrar of Companies;

(b) keep a register of debenture-holders available for inspection by the holders (a register of members must also be kept with similar arrangements).

It should be remembered that any individual or organisation is under a general obligation to be totally truthful and honest in its dealings with the providers of finance (and this particularly applies to creditors), as to give false or misleading information or not giving *relevant* information in reply to any question may make them liable to prosecution under the Theft Act 1968. Furthermore, the borrower should only use the finance obtained for agreed purposes. If a firm borrows money which it says it is going to use to buy a vehicle it would be wrong to use it for, say, paying wages or the electricity bill.

Only a limited company can issue debentures or loan stock to the public but they and other types of organisation can obtain finance from a variety of other sources.

Cash Advances

These usually take the form of a bank loan or overdraft and the bank manager, who is experienced in such matters, will want to know the circumstances that make it necessary for the organisation to borrow money, what it is to be used for, how it is to be repaid and whether any collateral security is available or necessary. Usually no formal, i.e. written, arrangements are necessary when an overdraft is required as it is usually for *relatively* small amounts for *relatively* short periods of time. Even so, overdrafts are expected to be repaid within the agreed time period and if the organisation finds this impossible then it should advise the bank so that alternative arrangements can be made if possible. Interest on overdrafts is calculated daily on the balance outstanding.

With a bank loan a contract may have to be signed which will state how much has to be repaid, i.e. loan plus interest, the period of the loan and the method of repayment, e.g. standing order. For example:

Amount of loan	£2,400.00
Add Total interest	240.00
Total amount to be repaid	£2,640.00

Period of loan = 2 years
Therefore repayments = £2,640 24 months = £110 per month

Private loans will only usually be obtained by small- to medium-sized organisations as the amounts available tend to be rather limited. Also the bigger organisations normally require, and have access to, larger amounts than the individual is likely to have available to lend. In cases where private loans are obtained there is likely to be a close connection between debtor and creditor and often the loan is arranged informally and without the benefit of any written agreement. This can be dangerous for the organisation as whatever the circumstances at the time friends and relatives can fall out and a sudden demand for repayment of a loan might prove disastrous. It is advisable for all conditions relating to the loan to be included in a written agreement (preferably prepared by a solicitor) and signed by both parties.

Bill and invoice discounting are specialised forms of obtaining finance and are actually methods of selling assets, i.e. a bill of exchange or a book debt to another organisation in exchange for a cash payment of less than the face value of the bill or invoice. In such circumstances the seller has an obligation to provide the buyer with all relevant information even if it may reduce the amount he eventually receives. However, in most cases the buyer will be experienced enough to ask all the "right" questions to obtain all the information before agreeing a price.

Purchase of Assets

Organisations need to buy fixed assets from time to time but will not always have the cash readily available to make an outright purchase. Alternatively it may want to spread the cost over a number of years particularly if the use of the asset will make sufficient profit to pay for itself.

The most common methods are by hire purchase or credit sale agreements, both of which have much in common. They both usually involve the payment of a deposit with the remainder of the cost being met by fixed instalments over a stated period of time. The interest paid on credit sales is often lower or non-existent but the length of time to repay the balance may be shorter. However, the main distinction between the two is ownership of the asset. If bought by credit sale then the asset becomes the property of the organisation as soon as the agreement is signed and the deposit paid. If an H.P. loan is obtained then the asset does not become the property of the owner until all the instalments have been paid. Failure to abide by the terms of an H.P. contract can, in certain circumstances, result in the asset being repossessed by the original owner whereas failure to abide by a credit sale contract can only result in the organisation being made liable for the cash balance of the contract. The normal period for both of these methods would not usually exceed five years at most.

There are similarities between these two methods (used for vehicles, machinery and office furniture, etc.) and that used for the purchase of land and buildings known as a mortgage. A deposit is paid and the remainder owed (plus interest) is spread over twenty-five to thirty years. The property to be purchased acts as security for the loan and if the borrower defaults the lender has the right to sell the property to obtain the money due to them.

It is sometimes possible to *lease*, i.e. rent, both property and equipment and whilst the organisation is not receiving a cash payment as such it is obtaining the use of the asset immediately and deferring the use of its own cash resources. Basically the system involves a financial institution buying the asset and then leasing it to the customer organisation for specified equal payments for a stated period of time, e.g. five years. Leases can sometimes be renewed at a revised rental – usually reduced for equipment but increased for land and buildings. The drawbacks to the system are that it is considered to be expensive and the organisation cannot use the asset as if it were its own – permission would have to be obtained from the lessor (the owner) if alterations to buildings were contemplated or if the lessee (the renter) wanted to move equipment from one factory to another.

Sale and lease back is similar to the above but should not be confused with it as in this case the organisation sells its own land and buildings to a specialist property firm that agrees to lease, i.e. rent, the property back to the organisation for a long period of time (commonly forty to fifty years). The organisation pays rent which is reviewed periodically to keep it up to date. The selling organisation can use the cash it obtains for other purposes which it is hoped will be sufficiently profitable to make the transaction worthwhile. This system is only used for land and buildings.

Whatever method is used to buy assets (apart from cash), until they become the property of the organisation it must ensure that they are kept in good order (apart from fair wear and tear) and will usually have to keep them insured against damage or loss. The organisation will also be restricted in its freedom to use the asset as it pleases as it has to conform to any restrictions imposed by the purchaser.

Trade Credit

This term is used to describe the many thousands of business transactions that take place daily whereby a supplier delivers goods to a customer and agrees that payment can be made at some later date – usually within thirty days. As the name implies, these transactions only take place between organisations in the same trade rather than with ordinary consumers (in which case it would be a credit sale).

If the organisation can obtain goods on credit in this way it has thirty days in which to sell them and collect payment before having to pay their own supplier. Alternatively the cash from the sale of the goods may be used for other purposes although obviously the supplier will have to be paid sooner or later. At the very least trade credit may mean that a firm does not have to arrange a loan or bank overdraft to pay its suppliers.

The organisation that obtains credit in this way has an obligation to comply with any conditions made, such as the time allowed for payment. Indeed if payment is made within that time the trader can often obtain a small *cash discount*, e.g. 5 per cent, on the value of the transaction. The supplier hopes to encourage prompt payment by the debtor thereby making the cash quickly available for his own use.

NOTE: *Cash discount* should not be confused with *trade discount* which is the difference between the catalogue price to the consumer and the price paid to the wholesaler or manufacturer by the retailer to enable him to make a profit.

THE ORGANISATION AND THE ENVIRONMENT

The environment is the physical world in which we live – it includes the land, air and water. There is a limited quantity of each of these and their availability and purity are of great importance to us as individuals.

In a simple rural society the amount of land required is limited to that needed for homes, farms and a few simple roads but in our modern technological society the demand for land also covers such things as schools, hospitals, factories, shops, offices, complex transport systems and recreation facilities. Similarly the demands we place on the water supply system are enormous and even in a "wet" country like Britain a few weeks without rain can produce drought conditions. Water is not just needed by people but also by industry and agriculture. Traditionally the water system has been seen as a convenient way of disposing of waste and we have deposited large quantities of effluent in our rivers, lakes and seas. Many of these effluents can be removed by treatment at sewage plants and the water *recycled*, i.e. used again, but there may be some distance from the point the waste is put into the water and the point where it is treated – as a result the stretch of river in between may have been heavily polluted. Last but not least we need air to breathe and even this is in limited supply. Therefore we must treat it with care for if it becomes too contaminated it can be positively harmful, as in the great London "smog" (smoke and fog) of 1952 which was estimated to be responsible for several thousand deaths.

Modern life in an industrialised country is such that apart from the "necessities" needed to sustain us such as food and clothing, etc., we also make use of a wide range of products from cars and washing machines to books and records to give us a "comfortable" standard of living. All these products create waste, either during manufacture or when they are no longer of any use to us and are thrown away. Our waste is extensive and varied and as our standard of living increases it results in an even larger volume of more complicated waste, all of which has to be disposed of. Industrial processes convert raw materials into products and are left with waste (which in some industries like mining may be more than half of the original raw materials). As time passes these processes become more complex and diverse as do the wastes they produce.

In most cases individuals do not query what happens to the waste they produce as long as it is put somewhere where it will not directly affect them. Organisations have very much the same attitude. However in an urban industrial society it is not easy to dispose of wastes so that they do not affect anyone at all. Nevertheless, over the years systems have been developed to deal with sewage and other liquid wastes. Household and industrial rubbish is collected regularly and regulations have been introduced to control the discharge of pollutants into the atmosphere.

In a competitive economic system it is in an organisation's interest to dispose of wastes as cheaply as possible as otherwise its costs (and therefore its prices) will increase and put it at a disadvantage in comparison with its competitors. Of course if *all* producers in a particular industry have to meet these "extra" costs then none of them can gain an advantage. However it must be remembered that many markets are now international and whilst it is relatively easy to impose laws on firms within, say, the U.K. it may be that other countries will not follow suit in respect of their own producers who will thus gain a commercial advantage over the U.K. organisations. Even if international bodies such as the United Nations make "recommendations" they have few powers to enforce compliance, particularly when the "offender" is politically powerful.

Legislation has also been introduced to deal with the need to preserve our surroundings so that they are pleasant and harmonious to the eye. For many years it has not been possible to demolish and/or build permanent structures in the U.K., even on your own land, without first obtaining permission from the local authority. These laws also help to prevent the spread of housing and industry into areas of valuable agricultural land. We also have laws that make it possible to protect and preserve old property of particular architectural or general interest.

It is fair to say that many industrial firms have, whenever possible, used the wastes created in processing their primary product to develop profitable "by-products", e.g. the oil refining industry, but usually this has been done as a matter of self-interest and bigger profits rather than because of any real concern for the environment. However, even where the technology exists to prevent pollution there is often resistance to change. The motor vehicle industry provides an example of this state of affairs. Two of the main pollutants produced by motor vehicles are very fine particules of lead, and carbon monoxide gas. Recent studieš have indicated that accumulation of airborne lead may be responsible for brain damage in young children living in areas with a high traffic density; carbon monoxide is known to aggravate respiratory diseases. The worst effects of these pollutants could be prevented by relatively minor changes to engines although it would add to their cost and reduce their performance. Despite the evidence the motor industry has argued that to put up costs simply means "the public pays" – but the public already "pays" by being adversely affected by pollution. Even so, since pollution of the environment became a matter of popular concern some products have been changed or developed so that they are less harmful to ourselves and our surroundings, e.g. detergents. However, in many cases public authorities are responsible for the disposal through rates and taxes and it is up to the authorities to ensure that their wastes are dealt with properly. However, in many cases public authorities are responsible for the disposal of waste and the organisation might argue that they already pay for disposal through rates and taxes and it is up to the authorities to ensure that their wastes are dealt with properly.

One "pollutant" to which we are subjected is noise. If people are exposed to loud noise over a period of time it can result in them suffering stress and tension – it "gets on their nerves". It is also known that noise damages sensitive parts of the ear resulting in impaired hearing or even total deafness in very severe cases.

Laws have been introduced to deal with the worst effects of pollution and environmental damage but the standards imposed often lead to disagreement – industry often complains that they are too costly or restrictive, whilst environmental pressure groups argue that they are not strict enough.

One thing is certain – we cannot have an industrial society without some degree of damage to the environment and if very strict controls are imposed then it could result in fewer goods being produced at higher prices. Some people argue that this is inevitable anyway as continued economic growth will soon exhaust increasingly scarce resources. One of the major environmental issues at present is whether we should develop nuclear power plants to take over the provision of electricity supply when oil and natural gas run our. Electricity as such is a relatively "clean" product but there is an enormous moral dilemma in developing nuclear energy sources: is it right that we should endanger future generations by producing radioactive wastes that will still be lethal in several thousand years' time and for which there is, at present, no guaranteed safe method of disposal? For example, if such a pollutant is buried deep beneath the earth's surface, it is possible that future geological developments, e.g. rock movements, may disturb the "safe" store of waste and thus allow leakage into the environment.

By far the most important environmental legislation is the Control of Pollution Act 1974 which deals with (*main* provisions only):

- *(i)* waste disposal arrangements;
- *(ii)* licensing of disposal of waste;
- *(iii)* collection and disposal of waste;
- *(iv)* street cleaning and litter;

(*b*) pollution of water, including:
  (*i*) control of pollution of rivers and coastal waters;
  (*ii*) control of discharges of trade and sewage effluent into rivers and costal waters;
  (*iii*) control of discharges of trade effluent into public sewers;

(*c*) noise, including noise:
  (*i*) on construction sites;
  (*ii*) in streets;
  (*iii*) from plant and machinery;
  (*iv*) abatement zones;

(*d*) pollution of the atmosphere, including:
  (*i*) regulations about motor fuel;
  (*ii*) regulations about oil fuel;
  (*iii*) burning of electric cable insulation (to recover metals).

The Act obviously deals with a number of environmental problems and, in general, gives the Secretary of State the power to make regulations covering the detailed technical aspects of control. However, many other statutes also deal with various aspects of environmental protection and some are listed below.

(*a*) The Public Health Acts 1875, 1936, 1961
(*b*) The Alkali and Works Regulations Act 1906
(*c*) The Public Health (Drainage of Trade Premises) Act 1937
(*d*) The Water Act 1945
(*e*) The Civil Aviation Act 1949
(*f*) The Clean Air Acts 1956, 1968
(*g*) The Radioactive Substances Act 1960
(*h*) The Factories Act 1961
(*i*) The Pipe-lines Act 1962
(*j*) The Water Resources Act 1963
(*k*) The Gas Act 1965
(*l*) The Caravan Sites Act 1968
(*m*) The Countryside Act 1968
(*n*) The Town and Country Planning Act 1971
(*o*) The Prevention of Oil Pollution Act 1971
(*p*) The Local Government Acts 1972, 1974
(*q*) The Water Act 1973
(*r*) The Health and Safety at Work Act 1974

This is not a complete list but a quick glance will indicate the wide variety of topics covered as most of the names of the Acts are self-explanatory. It is apparent, however, that any organisation must be very well-informed about the likely legal consequences of any waste it creates or pollutants it discharges and, in general, must take care to ensure that they are kept to a minimum.

TASK ONE

(*i*) Identify the three essential features of a contract. ____________________

____

____

(*ii*) What is meant by the term "let the buyer beware"? ____________________

____

(iii) What are the main provisions of the Trade Descriptions Act 1968? ____________

(iv) Which Act aims to prevent organisations persuading people to give up their basic legal rights as consumers? ____________

(v) State two functions of the Restrictive Trade Practices Court. ____________

(vi) What information must be given to a debtor to comply with the Consumer Credit Act 1974? ____________

(vii) What is the main purpose of the Shops Acts? ____________

(viii) What period of notice should be given to, and by, an employee of five years' standing? ____________

(ix) What documents is the employer obliged to give to the employee under the P.A.Y.E. regulations and what is their purpose? ____________

(x) What redundancy payments would the following employees be entitled to:

(a) Male aged 32, 5 years' service, pay £70 per week ____________

(b) Male aged 20, 4 years' service, pay £50 per week ____________

(c) Female aged 53, 12 years' service, pay £60 per week ____________

(xi) The Partnership Act 1890 states that all partners must act in the "utmost good faith" towards each other. What do you think this term means? ____________

(xii) Refer to Unit II Section I and list the obligations to owners involved when forming a company. ____________________

____

____

(xiii) Distinguish between (a) bank loans and overdrafts (b) cash and trade discount

____

____

____

(xiv) What is the main difference between H.P. loans and credit sales as regards ownership of an item? ____________________

____

____

(xv) In what ways might a typical *commercial* organisation contribute to environmental pollution? ____________________

____

____

SECTION II

CURRENCY

Foreign Currency

Calculations involving money cause, as a rule, few difficulties because people are used to dealing with money in their everyday lives. Thus if someone bought three articles costing £4.25, £2.60 and £1.00 they could quickly find the total cost and the change from £10.00.

TASK ONE

(i) Find the cost of the three articles above and the change obtained from £10.00.
Total cost: ____________ Change: ____________

(ii) Now if these same three articles were bought in the U.S.A. and cost $7.50, $4.55 and $1.75, find the total cost and the change from $15.
Total cost: ____________ Change: ____________

There is no difference in the methods used because both currencies are decimal currencies. This will also be true for the majority of countries, where their currencies are based upon units of 10 and 100.

People who travel widely on business or go on holidays to other countries quickly become used to dealing with the currency of the country they are in because the character of francs and centimes, Deutsche Marks and pfennig, krone and ore, and dollars and cents is exactly the same as pounds and pence.

1 franc (fr) = 100 centimes
1 Deutsche Mark (Dm) = 100 pfennig
1 krone (Kr) = 100 ore
1 dollar ($) = 100 cents.

TASK TWO

(i) Add together

(a) 5 fr 50 centimes, 2 fr 85 centimes and 12 fr 5 centimes

(b) 22.60 Dm, 10.02 Dm and 5.69 Dm

(ii) Subtract

(a) 3.65 Kr from 11.20 Kr

(b) $206.50 from S251.75

(iii) Multiply

(a) 12.52 fr by 6

(b) 212.56 Kr by 20

(iv) Divide

(a) $49.14 by 7

(b) 836.50 Dm by 50

EXERCISE

(a) A customer in a hypermarket near Paris purchased goods to the value of 87.50 fr in the food department, 258 fr in the clothing department and 56.75 fr in the motoring section. How much did the customer spend altogether and what would be left from 500 fr?

(b) A soccer club in Germany wished to buy new playing kit for their senior team. Each player in the squad of sixteen requires a tracksuit costing 62.50 Dm each, a pair of soccer boots costing 37.75 Dm each, two pairs of shorts for each player costing 10.15 Dm each, three pairs of stockings each costing 5 Dm per pair, and two shirts for each out player costing 29.50 Dm each and two goal-keepers' jerseys for each of the two goalkeepers costing 32.25 Dm each. What is the total cost of the playing kit?

(c) A man on holiday in Switzerland estimates that he will spend on accommodation 25.50 fr per night. His meals will cost 15.25 fr per day and excursions a total of 175 fr. If he stays for seven days, sleeping for six nights, in Switzerland how mu ch will his holday cost him?

CURRENCY CONVERSION

With increasing overseas travel and trade it is essential that people not only have a good working knowledge of foreign currencies but that they should be able to convert sums of money from one currency to another. For example, a wine merchant who purchases wine in France and Germany may be required to pay in francs and Deutsche Marks and in order to do that he must know how much is needed in pounds.

This problem is not always an easy one since the relative values of currency change from day to day and even from hour to hour. The rates of exchange vary within fairly narrow limits according to the state of trade between countries. From time to time, however, one country will keep buying more from another country than that country buys from it. If for example the United Kingdom keeps buying more from West Germany than West Germany buys from the United Kingdom there will be more pounds required than there are Deutsche Marks available. People will have to give more pounds for the Deutsche Marks needed leading to a fall in the value of the pound.

This will, if the situation persists, lead to a *devaluation,* which will make exports cheaper and lead to an increase in the quantity exported. At the same time the value of imports will be increased resulting in a decrease in the quantity imported. The reverse situation may apply where a *revaluation* is necessary in order to make the currency dearer than before by increasing the value of exported goods.

The conversion of one currency to another is an exercise which can be carried out in a number of different ways. The method used below appears, initially, to be more involved than it need be but it means only one method needs to be learnt and it will apply not only to converting pounds to foreign currencies and vice versa but also for converting any two foreign currencies.

The method is best seen through a number of examples.

(a) <u>Convert £25 to Dm when £1 = 3.76 Dm.</u>
(This may be achieved by multiplying £25 by 3.76 Dm).

The method of conversion involves asking a number of questions and the written answers form the basis of the method conversion.

Step 1 : Ask the questions and combine these to give the final answer.

Question 1. What do I want to know?
Answer 1. How many Dm = £25 (the unknown value is written first).

Question 2. Using the last quantity (£), what do I know about them?
Answer 2. That £1 = 3.76 Dm.

When the last quantity is the same as the unknown quantity all the necessary questions have been asked.

Now we have

How many Dm = £25
£1 = 3.76 Dm

Step 2 : When the questions and answers have been completed all the quantities on the right hand side (as you look at them) of the " equals sign" are multiplied together, giving 25 x 3.76.

Step 3 : All the quantities on the left hand side are multiplied together (in this case it is just 1).

Step 4 : The answer will be obtained by dividing the right hand side by the left hand side.

$$\text{Thus} \quad \text{Dm} = \frac{25 \times 3.76}{1}$$

Simplify, first making any decimal fractions improper fractions (3.76 becomes $\frac{376}{100}$)

$$\text{Now} \quad \frac{\overset{1}{\cancel{25}} \times \overset{94}{\cancel{376}}}{1 \times \underset{\cancel{4}\ 1}{\cancel{100}}} = 94 \text{ Dm}$$

(b) <u>Change £40 to Italian lira (l) when £1 = 1575 L.</u>

Step 1 : (i) What do I want to know?
(ii) What do I know about £s?

How many lira = £40
£1 = 1575 L

Step 2 : Multiply R.H.S. together giving 40 x 1575
Step 3 : Multiply L.H.S. together giving 1

$$\text{Lira} = \frac{40 \times 1575}{1}$$

Step 4 : Divide R.H.S. by L.H.S. and simplify if necessary.
Thus £40 = 6300 L.

TASK THREE

Convert the following sums of money

(i) £70 to $ when £1 = $1.875

(ii) £25 to Kr. when £1 = 8.56 Kr.

Iii) £300 to Swiss fr when £1 = 3.47 fr.

(iv) £248 to Dm when £1 = 3.75

The same method is applied when changing back from one currency to another. For example:

<u>Convert 255 French francs to pounds when £1 = 8.50 fr.</u>

How many £s = 255 fr
8.50 fr = £1

Step 1 : (i) What do I want to know?
(ii) What do I know about francs?

$£s = \frac{255 \times 1}{8.50}$

Step 2 : Multiply R.H.S. together giving 255 x 1.

Step 3 : Multiply L.H.S. together giving 8.50

$= 3\ \frac{\cancel{51}\ \cancel{255} \times 1 \times 10\cancel{0}}{\cancel{850}\ \ \cancel{17}}$

Step 4 : Divide R.H.S. by L.H.S. and simplify (8.50 becomes $\frac{850}{100}$ but dividing by a fraction, the denominator becomes a multiplier).

= £30

TASK FOUR

Convert the following sums of money.

(i) 496 Dutch guilders to £s when £1 = 4.00 guilders

(ii) 937.50 Dm to £s when £1 = 3.75 Dm

(iii) $1000 to £s when £1 = $1.875
Answer to the nearest 10 pence.

(iv) 500 French fr. to £s when £1. = 855 francs. Answer to the nearest 10 pence.

The value of this method becomes more apparent when two or more values have to be converted.

For example : If £1 = 8.51 fr and $1 = 4.60 fr what will the value of £1 be in dollars?

Step 1 : (i) What do I want to know?
(ii) What do I know about £s?
(iii) What do I know about fr?

How many $ = £1
£1 = 8.51 fr.
4.60 fr = $1

Step 2 : Multiply R.H.S. together giving 1 x 8.51 x 1.

Step 3 : Multiply L.H.S. together giving 1 x 4.60

Step 4 : Divide R.H.S. by L.H.S. and simplify.

$$\frac{1 \times 851 \times 1 \times 1\not{0}\not{0}}{1 \times 1\not{0}\not{0} \times 460}$$

= $1.85

TASK FIVE

(i) If £1 = 8.55 fr express £15 in Dm when 1 Dm = 2.25 fr.

(ii) If £1 = 4.00 guilders and 1 guilder = 2.10 Kr express Kr in £s.

EXERCISE

(a) A businessman visiting France spends £65 on his travelling expenses. In addition he takes £125 to spend and changes this into francs at £1 = 8.55 fr. At the end of his trip he has 213 francs and he changes this back into English currency at a rate of £1 = 8.52 fr.
Calculate:
(i) the number of francs he obtained for his £;
(ii) the value of the 213 francs he had left;
(iii) the total cost in pounds of his trip.

(b) A man, his wife and son go to Spain on holiday. The man changes £250 into pesetas at 145 pesetas to the pound. During their fourteen day holiday each spends, on average, 525 pesetas every day. On return the man changes his remaining pesetas to pounds at a rate of £1 = 142 pesetas. What was the cost of the holiday in pounds?

(c) A man took to Germany 750 Dm which he bought when £1 = 3.75 Dm. On returning home he still had 53.65 Dm which he changed back to pounds at £1 = 3.70 Dm. How much did he spend in pounds?

WEIGHTS AND MEASURES

The system of weights and measures traditionally used in the United Kingdom has always been a difficult mixture to understand fully and use effectively. This has largely been due to the British systems being based upon non-decimal values. If, for example, it was necessary to change 123,456,789 ounces to tons, showing ounces, pounds, stones, hundredweights and tons, four separate division operations would be necessary. First divide 123,456,789 by 16 to give pounds and ounces, since there are 16 ounces in 1 pound. Next divide the resulting pounds by 14 to give stones and pounds, since 14 pounds equal 1 stone; then divide the resulting stones by 8 to give hundredweights and stones, and finally divide the hundredweights by 20 to give tons and hundredweights.

There is no connection between each step in the calculation; the relationship between each has to be committed to memory. The same is true for measures of length, area and volume and for capacity.

Area will appear in a later unit.

Imperial Weights and Measures

Weight		Length		Capacity	
16 ounces	= 1 pound	12 inches	= 1 foot	2 pints	= 1 quart
14 pounds	= 1 stone	3 feet	= 1 yard	4 quarts	= 1 gallon
28 pounds	= 1 quarter (qr)	22 yards	= 1 chain	8 pints	= 1 gallon
4 quarters / 8 stones	= 1 hundred-weight (cwt).	220 yards	= 1 furlong		
20 cwt	= 1 ton	8 furlongs	= 1 mile		
2,240 pounds	= 1 ton	1760 yards	= 1 mile		

The basic operations with these units can be carried out as if dealing with ordinary numbers provided that the particular relationships between each measure is borne in mind. For example:

Add

tons	cwt	qr
8	17	1
17	12	3
12	18	2
39	8	2

Step 1 : Add the quarters giving 6 qr = 1 cwt 2 qr since 1 cwt = 4 qr. Align the 2 qr under the qr and add the 1 to the cwt.

Step 2 : Add the cwt together, including the 1 from Step 1, giving 48 cwt = 2 tons 8 cwt. Align the 8 under the cwt.

Step 3 : Add the tons.

Similar methods are used in subtraction, multiplication and division. In each case one measure is changed to another, as appropriate, during the calculation.

EXERCISE

(a) Add together:

(i) 4 cwt 2 qr 21 lb; 2 cwt 3 qr 19lb; and 1 cwt 1 qr 18lb.
(ii) 7 yd 1 ft 6in; 2 yd 2ft 8in; and 3 yd 4in.
(iii) 19 gall 2 q; 10 gall 2 q 1 pt; and 25 gall 3 q.

(b) Subtract the smaller quantity from the larger:

(i) 34 gall 2 pt; 12 gall 5 pt.
(ii) 18 miles 735 yd; 12 miles 1,058 yd.
(iii) 5 tons 3 cwt 3 qr; 7 tons 13 cwt 2 qr.

(c) Multiply:

(i) 1 cwt 2 qr 18 lb by 6
(ii) 3 gall 1 pt by 14
(iii) 1 yd 2 ft 3 in by 58

(d) Divide:

(i) 12 lb 3 oz by 5.
(ii) 56 miles 125 yd by 27.
(iii) 198 gall by 48.

METRIC SYSTEM OF WEIGHTS AND MEASURES

The imperial (British) system of weights and measures is a difficult system to use because it has no apparent connection with the ordinary system of counting. This leads to problems in any calculation involving weights and measures. This has long been recognised in scientific work where a decimal system of weights and measures has been used. With the entry of the United Kingdom into the European Economic Community it has been decided that in order to trade effectively in Europe, and with the rest of the world, then the goods that the United Kingdom sells abroad should have sizes, weights and other measures specified in a way that is familiar to the customer in all E.E.C. countries.

This has resulted in the gradual introduction of the metric system of weights and measures in the United Kingdom, replacing the imperial measures more and more in everyday situations. It is a decimal system, like counting, and therefore consists of multiples of and sub-divisions of the basic units, obtained from that unit by multiplying or dividing by factors of 10 – *by moving the decimal point.*

The basic metric measures are:

Length	:	the *metre*	(abbreviation m)
Weight	:	the *gramme*	(abbreviation g)
Capacity	:	the *litre*	(abbreviation l)

and all the other measures are either 10 times, 100 times, 1,000 times, etc. bigger than the basic unit or they are one-tenth, one-hundredth, one-thousandth, etc., the size of the basic unit. Each larger or small measure has its own name and these will apply to length, weight and capacity.

Thus measures of length these would be:

10 m = decametre (dam)

100 m = hectometre (hm)

1000 m = kilometre (km)

Metre (m)

$\frac{1}{10}$ m or 0.1 m = decimetre (dm)

$\frac{1}{100}$ m or 0.01 m = centimetre (cm)

$\frac{1}{1000}$ m or 0.001 m = millimetre (mm)

and for measures less than the unit their size can be written as

10 dm = 1 m
100 cm = 1 m
1000 mm = 1 m

With the metric system it is easy to write down the same table for weight and capacity by simply changing gramme or litre for the metre.

For practical use all the measures will not be used by name and it is probable that the following will be in everyday use:

Length

The only value larger than the metre to be used will be the kilometre. Two hundred metres will *not* be called 2 hectometres. For smaller values the centimetre and the millimetre will be used and in precision engineering a thousandth of a millimetre called a micrometre.

Weight

The gram is a relatively small measure and it is unlikely that smaller values will be used in normal situations. The kilogram will be used for most everyday purposes but for very large weights the metric tonne (t), equal to 1000 kg, will be used.

Capacity

The litre will be in common use only, except for smaller quantities, such as for use with medicines, the millilitre will be used.

Since these weights and measures are based upon a decimal system it is easy to change from one to another. Thus 123456789 mm can be quickly expressed in km since we know that 1000 mm = 1 m, and so the 123456789 mm becomes 123456.789 m by dividing the millimetres by 1000 and 123456.789 m becomes 123.456789 km because 1000 m = 1 km and the metres are divided by 1000.

The same number would result if 123456789 mg were changed to kg or if 123456789 ml were changed to kl.

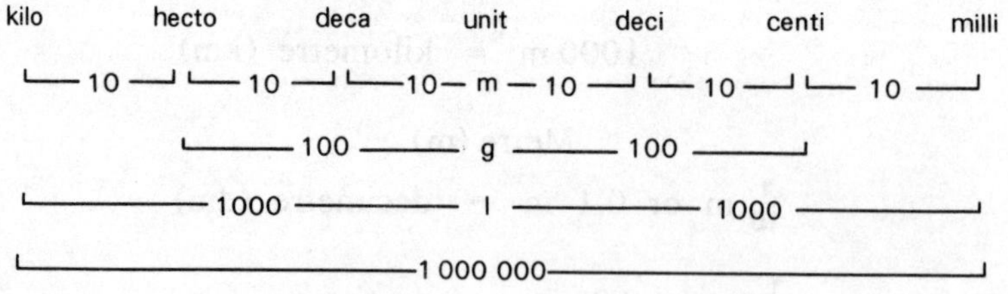

The relationship between each measure can easily be seen from the illustration above. For example:

(a) How many millimetres = 1 decametre?
In the diagram above, from milli to centi is 10, from centi to deci is 10, from deci to metre is 10, and from metre to deca is another 10. This gives 1 decametre = 10000 mm.

(b) How many decigrammes = 7 hectogrammes?
1 hectogramme = 10 by 10 by 10 decigrammes = 1000 dg. Therefore
7 hectogrammes = 7 x 1000 dg = 7000dg.

TASK SIX

Using the table answer the following.

(i)	1 kg = ________ cg	(vi)	9 kl = ________ dal
(ii)	1 dl = ________ ml	(vii)	8 dag = ________ mg
(iii)	1 hm = ________ cm	(viii)	4 dm = ________ mm
(iv)	2 dam = ________ dm	(ix)	6 1 = ________ ml
(v)	4 hg = ________ mg	(x)	15kg = ________ mg

Each question in Task One changes a large measure to a smaller measure, so that the number itself becomes larger. The reverse will happen when a small measure is changed to a larger one. Now instead of multiplying the measure is divided by 10 an appropriate number of times. For example:

Change 8 cm to m. There are 100 cm in 1 metre, so dividing 8 by 100 gives 0.08.

TASK SEVEN

Answer the following.

(i)	1 dg = ________ dag	(vi)	8 cm = ________ ham
(ii)	1 l = ________ kl	(vii)	4 hag = ________ hl
(iii)	5 mg = ________ g	(viii)	7 ml = ________ km
(iv)	4 cl = ________ kl	(ix)	26 m = ________ km
(v)	7 mg = ________ cg	(x)	18mm = ________ km

Just as single values can be changed so mixed values can also be changed. Thus, for example:

(a) If 2 dam 5 m 6 dm is to be expressed in metres, we know that 2 dam = 20 m and that 6 dm = 0.6 m; combining these with the 5 m gives 2 dam 5 m 6 dm = 25.6 m.

(b) Change 2 kg 5 dag 4 g 3 cg to g. Now 2 kg = 2000 g, 5 dag = 50 g and 3 cg = 0.03; combining these with the 4 g gives 2054.03 g.

TASK EIGHT

Change each of the mixed values to the measure shown in the brackets.

(i) 6 hg 5 dag 2 g 7 dg (g) ________________

(ii) 8 dal 6 l 3 dl 5 cl (l) ________________

(iii) 14 kg 3 hg 2 dag 7 g 4 cg (g) ________________

(iv) 2 kg 3 dag 5 g (dag) ____________________

(v) 3 dal 9 l 2 dl 5 cl 2 ml (cl) ____________________

(vi) 10 m 2 cm 5 mm (cm) ____________________

(vii) 5 hl 4 dal 3 dl 6 cl (l) ____________________

(viii) 2 kg 6 hag 3 dg (g) ____________________

(ix) 1 hm 5 mm (m) ____________________

(x) 16 kg 5 hg 1 cg 5 mg (g) ____________________

The basic arithmetic operations with metric weights and measures will be carried out as if dealing with ordinary numbers in decimal form.

For example:

(a) Add together 7 g 5 cg; 9 g 7 dg 5 cg

7.05 9.70 + 0.45 17.20 g	Step 1: Change each value to g. Thus 7 g 5 cg becomes 7.05 g. 9 g 7 dg becomes 9.7 g and 4 dg 5 cg becomes 0.45 g. Step 2: Align each number and add.

It is always best to ensure that the measures are the same before carrying out any operation.

(b) Subtract 2 kg 570 g from 3 kg 8 hg and answer in kg.

3.800 2.570 1.230 kg	Step 1: Change each measure to kg. Thus 2 dg 570 g becomes 2.570 kg and 3 kg 8 hg becomes 3.800 kg. Step 2: Align and subtract.

(c) A builder requires 125 pieces of wood each 4.1 m long.
How many metres of wood is this?

41 x 125 4100 820 205 5125	Step 1: Ignoring the decimal point, multiply 41 by 125. Step 2: Add the results of the multiplication. Step 3: Insert the decimal point. (There is 1 place of decimals)

= 512.5 metres.

(d) 350 kg of flour is put into small bags each containing 1.25 kg of flour. How many bags are needed?

```
        280
125 ) 35000
       250
       1000
       1000
       ----
```

Step 1: Change the divisor to a whole number (1.25 x 100 = 125).

Step 2: Increase the dividend by the same amount (350 x 100 = 35000).

Step 3: Divide 35000 by 125.

TASK NINE

(i) Add together the following and answer in the measure indicated.

(a) 2 km 358 m, 5 km 62 m, and 4 hm 2 dam in metres.

(b) 5 kg 750 g, 1 kg 80 g, and 3 kg 875 g in kg.

(ii) Subtract the second quantity from the first and answer in the measure indicated.

(a) 8 kl 375 l and 6 kl 180 l in l.

(b) 5 hg and 75 g in g

(c) 80 m and 24 m 6 cm in m.

(iii) Multiply

(a) 4 g 5 cg by 34

(b) 3.25 kg by 120

(c) 1.007 m by 700

(iv) Divide

(a) 976.5 m by 9

(b) 5.4 km by 150

(c) 94.5 kg by 1.75 kg

TASK TEN

(i) From a stock of 4500 kg of coffee, the following amounts were sold: 937.5 kg 1375 kg, 250 kg and 312.5 kg. How much remained?

(ii) An electrician has a stock of four 50 metre rolls of electric wire. During the course of the week he uses 20 m on Monday, 17.35 m on Tuesday, 75.80 m on Wednesday, 46.5 m on Thursday and 30 m on Friday. How much has he left?

(iii) Three types of wine are blended to give the required flavour for marketing. The quantities and costs of the wine are:

100 hectolitres at £6.60 per hl
200 hectolitres at £6.63 per hl
300 hectolitres at £6.66 per hl

Find:

(a) The total cost of the mixture.

(b) The selling price of the wine, per litre, to just cover costs.

Conversion of Weights and Measures

As with currency, it is necessary to be able to convert weights and measures. For example, wine may be imported in litres but sold in bottles containing pints and fractions of pints. Thus the importer must have an indication of what he is buying in order to meet his selling requirements.

There are many values available which give the relationship between Imperial and Metric measures, arranged in two ways as a rule, but it would be impossible to commit all of them to memory.

Here are a few *approximate* values:

Weight

1 ton = 1016 kg or 1.016 t
1 lb = 0.454 kg or 454 g
1 oz = 28.3 g
1 kg = 2.2 lb
1 g = 0.036 oz

Length

1 mile = 1.069 km
5 miles = 8 km
1 yard = 0.914 m (exactly)
1 inch = 2.54 cm
1 m = 39.37 in
11 m = 12 yards

Capacity

1 litre = 1.76 pints
1 pint = 568 cl

The methods of conversion are the same as those used in the conversion of currency, based upon a series of questions and answers.

For example:

(a) Convert 11 gallons to litres when 1 litre = 1.76 pints.

How many litres = 11 gall
1 gall = 8 pts
1.76 pts = 1 l

Step 1: (i) What do I want to know?
(ii) What do I know about gallons?
(iii) What do I know about pints?
The last measure is the same as the unknown so all questions have been asked.

Step 2: Multiply R.H.S. together giving 11 x 8 x 1.

Step 3: Multiply L.H.S. together giving 1 x 1.76.

Step 4: Divide R.H.S. by L.H.S. and simplify.

$$\frac{{}^{1}\not{11} \times {}^{1}\not{8} \times 1 \times \overset{50}{\not{100}}}{1 \times \not{176}\ \not{22}\ \not{2}_{1}} \text{ litres}$$

Thus 11 gallons = 50 litres.

(b) Convert 48 miles to kilometres when 5 miles = 8 km.

How many km = 48 miles
5 miles = 8 km

Step 1: (i) What do I want to know?
(ii) What do I know about miles?

Step 2: Multiply R.H.S. together (48 x 5).

Step 3: Multiply L.H.S. together (5).

Step 4: Divide R.H.S. by L.H.S. and simplify.

$$\text{km} = \frac{48 \times 8}{5} = \frac{384}{5}$$

Thus 48 miles = 76.8 km.

(c) Convert 5.5 cwt to kilograms when 1 kg = 2.2 lb.

How many kg = 5.5 cwt
1 cwt = 112 lb
2.2 lb = 1 kg

Step 1: (i) What do I want to know?
(ii) What do I know about cwt?
(iii) What do I know about lb?

Step 2: Multiply R.H.S. (5.5 x 112 x 1).

Step 3: Multiply L.H.S. (1 x 2.2).

Step 4: Divide R.H.S. by L.H.S. and simplify (5.5 becomes $\frac{55}{10}$ and 2.2 becomes $\frac{22}{10}$.

$$\text{kg} = \frac{\overset{5}{\not{55}} \times \overset{56}{\not{112}} \times 1 \times \not{10}}{\not{10} \times 1 \times \not{22}\ \not{2}}$$

Thus 5.5 cwt = 280 kg.

(d) What distance is equivalent to 160 km if 5 miles = 8 km.

How many miles = 160 km
8 km = 5 miles

Step 1: (i) What do I want to know?
(ii) What do I know about km?

Step 2: Multiply R.H.S. (160 x 5).

Step 3: Multiply L.H.S. (8).

Step 4: Divide R.H.S. by L.H.S. and simplify.

$$\text{miles} = \frac{\overset{20}{\not{160}} \times 5}{\not{8}}$$

$$= 100$$

Thus 160 km = 100 miles.

(e) Convert 56 tonnes to tons if 1 kg = 2.2 lb.

How many tons = 56 tonnes
1 t = 1000 kg
1 kg = 2.2 lb
2240 lb = 1 ton

Step 1 : (i) What do I want to know?
(ii) What do I know about tonnes?
(iii) What do I know about kg?
(iv) What do I know about lb?

Step 2 : Multiply R.H.S. together (56 x 1000 x 2.2 x 1).

Step 3 : Multiply L.H.S. together (1 x 1 x 2240).

Step 4 : Divide R.H.S. by L.H.S. and simplify.

$$\text{tons } \frac{\overset{1}{\cancel{56}} \times \overset{5}{\cancel{1000}} \times \overset{11}{\cancel{22}} \times 1}{1 \times 1 \times \underset{\cancel{112}\ \cancel{2}}{\cancel{2240}} \times 10}$$

Thus 56 tonnes = 55 tons.

TASK ELEVEN

Convert the following imperial measures to metric measures.

(i) 165 lb to kg when 1 kg = 2.2 lb.

?kg = 165 lb.
2.2 lb = 1 kg
Kg =

(ii) 39.5 gall to litres when 1 litre - 1.76 pt.

(iii) 1 yard to m when 1 inch = 2.54 cm.

(iv) 5 tons to tonnes when 1 kg = 2.2 lb, correct to 2 decimal places.

(v) 10 gall to litres when 1 litre = 1.76 pt. Answer to the nearest litre.

(vi) 95 miles to km when 5 miles = 8 km

(vii) 20 oz to kg when 1 oz = 28.3 g.

(viii) 1 mile to metres when 5 miles = 8 km.

TASK TWELVE

Convert the following metric measures to imperial measures.

(i) 560 kg to cwt when 1 kg = 2.2 lb

(ii) 50 litres to gallons when 1 litre = 1.76 pints.

(iii) 100 km to miles when 5 miles = 8 km.

(iv) 1 tonne to lb when 1 kg = 2.2 lb.

(v) 2.75 hectolitres to gallons when 1 l = 1.76 pints.

(vi) 200 m to feet when 1 m = 39.37 in. Answer to the nearest whole number.

(vii) 21 m to ft when 1 in = 2.54 cm Answer to 2 decimal places.

(viii) 750 g to oz when 1 kg = 2.2 lb.

EXERCISE

(a) A car's performance is quoted in an advertisement as 32.5 miles per gallon in normal conditions. Find:
  (i) the distance travelled in kilometres on 1 gallon of petrol;
  (ii) the number of litres of petrol consumed for that distance; and
  (iii) the car's performance in kilometres per litre. (5 miles = 8 kilometres and 1.76 pints = 1 litre).

(b) An open-plan office is 45 metres long and is to be carpeted by carpet laid in strips costing £1.50 per foot length. If 4 strips of carpet are required what will be the total cost of carpeting the office? (1 metre = 39.37 inches).

(c) The weight of earth moved by an excavator at one time is 1,080 lb. This is loaded on to a lorry that will carry 5 tonnes. How many complete loads will the lorry safely carry? (1 kilogramme = 2.2 pounds.)

Converting Currency, Weights and Measures

This section looks at ways in which weights and measures and currency are converted together. For example a London merchant may import cloth from Paris. The price he pays may be in francs per metre but in London he sells it in pounds per yard. He therefore has to be able to calculate the price he will sell the cloth for in order to cover his costs.

Suppose he buys the cloth at 11.70 francs per metre. The merchant must find the equivalent price per yard in order to finally arrive at his selling price. The method to be used is like those used in the previous sections. For example: Find the equivalent price in pounds per yard for cloth which costs 11.70 francs per metre when £1 = 8.58 francs and 11 m = 12 yd.

Step 1 : (i) What do I want to know?
(ii) What do I know about yards?
(iii) What do I know about metres?
(iv) What do I know about francs?
Step 2 : Multiply R.H.S. together (1 x 11 x 11.70 x 1)
Step 3 : Multiply L.H.S. together (12 x 1 x 8.58).
Step 4 : Divide R.H.S. by L.H.S. and simplify (11.70 becomes $\frac{1170}{100}$ and $\frac{8.58}{100}$ becomes 858 inverted)

How many £s = 1 yard
12 yd = 11 m
1 m = 11.70 fr
8.58 fr = £1

$$£s = \frac{1 \times 11 \times 1170 \times 1 \times 100}{12 \times 1 \times 100 \times 858}$$

$$= £\,\frac{5}{4} = £1.25$$

Thus 11.70 fr per metre = £1.25 per yard.

The basis of the method is once more asking the questions in sequence commencing with what is required and the final answer must always be in the same unit of money that is unknown at the start of the questioning.

The method will apply when more than the value of a single unit of weight, length or capacity is required.

For example:

(a) The return rail fare on a rail journey in England is £4.32 for a total of 81 miles. What would the equivalent fare be in West Germany for a journey of 100 km if 5 miles = 8 km and £1 = 3.78 Dm.

How many Dm = 100 km
8 km = 5 miles
81 miles = £4.32
£1 = 3.78 Dm

Step 1 : (i) What do I want to know?
(ii) What do I know about km?
(iii) What do I know about miles?
(iv) What do I know about £s?

Step 2 : Multiply R.H.S. together (100 x 5 x 4.41 x 3.78.)

Step 3 : Multiply L.H.S. together (8 x 81 x 1.)

Step 4 : Divide R.H.S. by L.H.S. and simplify.

$$\text{Dm} = \frac{\cancel{100} \times 5 \times \overset{6}{\cancel{\overset{48}{\cancel{432}}}} \times \overset{42}{\cancel{378}}}{\cancel{8} \times \underset{9}{\cancel{81}} \times 1 \times \cancel{100} \times 100}$$

$$= \frac{1260}{100} = 12.60 \text{ Dm}$$

Thus £4.32 for 81 miles is equivalent to 12.60 Dm for 100 km.

(b) Butter costs 40.04 francs per 10 kg in Switzerland. What is the equivalent price in England in pence per kg if 1 kg = 1.1 lb and £1 = 3.50 fr?

How many p = 1 lb
2.2 lb = 1 kg
10 kg = 40.04 fr
3.50 fr = 100 p

Step 1 : (i) What do I want to know?
(ii) What do I know about lb?
(iii) What do I know about kg?
(iv) What do I know about fr?
(Here £1 is changed directly to 100p)

Step 2 : Multiply R.H.S. together.

Step 3 : Multiply L.H.S. together.

Step 4 : Divide R.H.S. by L.H.S. and simplify.

$$\text{p} = \frac{1 \times 1 \times \overset{52}{\cancel{\overset{572}{\cancel{4004}}}} \times \cancel{100} \times \cancel{10} \times \overset{\cancel{20}}{\cancel{100}}}{\cancel{22} \times \cancel{10} \times \cancel{100} \times \underset{\overset{1}{\cancel{7}}}{\cancel{350}}}$$

$$= 52\text{p}$$

Thus 40.04 fr per 10 kg is equivalent to 52p per lb.

(c) Coffee costs £2.80 per lb. Find the cost in Holland for 250 g when 1 kg = 2.2 lb and £1 = 4.00 guilders.
Without writing down the questions, the answers will be:

How many guilders = 250 g
1000 g = 2.2 lb
1 lb = £2.80
£1 = 4 guilders

$$\text{Now guilders} = \frac{\overset{1}{\cancel{250}} \times 22 \times \cancel{280} \times \cancel{4}}{\underset{\overset{10}{\cancel{40}}}{\cancel{1000}} \times 1 \times 1 \times \cancel{10} \times \cancel{100}}$$

$$= \frac{616}{100} = 6.16 \text{ guilders}$$

Thus £2.80 per lb is equivalent to 6.16 guilders per 250 g.

TASK THIRTEEN

Find the equivalent prices in the United Kingdom.

(i) Pence per lb equivalent to 7.48 fr per kg in France when £1 = 8.50 fr and 1 kg = 2.2 lb.

How many p = 1 lb p =

(ii) Pence per pint equivalent to 308 pesetas per litre in Spain when 140 pesetas = £1 and 1.76 pts = 1 litre.

(iii) Pounds per yard equivalent to 1 metre costing 48000 lira in Italy when 11 metres = 12 yds and £1 = 1600 lira.

TASK FOURTEEN

Given the prices in the United Kingdom, find the equivalent prices required.

(i) A journey costs 9.6p per mile. What is the equivalent for 50 km in Sweden when 5 miles = 8 km and £1 = 8.54 kr?

(ii) Francs per tonne equivalent to 6p per lb when 1 kg = 2.2 lb and £1 = 8.25 fr.

(iii) Lira per litre in Italy equivalent to 16p per gall when 1.76 pt = 1 litre and 1575 lira = £1.

EXERCISE

(a) (i) Change a price of 15p per lb to francs per kg when £1 = 8.50 fr and 1 kg = 2.2 lb (answer correct to 2 decimal places).

(ii) If 1 gall of petrol costs 80p, what is the equivalent price per litre in West Germany when £1 = 3.75 Dm and 1.76 pt = 1 litre?

(iii) Carpet costs £7.50 per yard. What is the equivalent cost in Swiss francs when 11 m = 12 yd and £1 = 3.52 fr?

(b) (i) If 10 litres of wine costs 616 escudos what is the cost per pint when 1.76 pt = 1 litre and £1 = 72.5 escudos?
(ii) A journey of 68 km costs 132.30 fr in France. What is the equivalent cost for 136 miles in England when £1 = 8.50 fr and 5 miles = 8 km?
(iii) If 1 kg = 2.2 lb and £1 = 1575 Italian lira, what price per lb is equivalent to 3465 lira per kg?

(c) A wine merchant imports wine from France at an inclusive cost of 3.85 fr per litre. Find:
(i) the cost per gallon of wine when 1 litre = 1.76 pt and £1 = 8.75 fr; and
(ii) the profit from selling 15 dozen bottles of this wine if 1 gallon gives 6 bottles, at £2.75 per dozen.

(d) Cloth is imported from West Germany at 3.67 Dm per metre and sold for £1.05 per yard. If 12yd = 11 m and £1 = 3.74 Dm, find the total profit when 2500 m are imported.

(e) The metric unit of land area is the hectare, and it equals 2.47 acres. Given that $1 = 5.04 French francs, find a price in francs per hectare equivalent to 75000 dollars for 5.4 acres.

SECTION III

PUNCTUATION

The importance of this aspect of written communication has been mentioned in previous units, where it has been relevant to the particular skill being dealt with. However, one of the main problems the student faces when writing a sentence is confusion – he or she knows that punctuation is expected, but is often not sure why it is necessary. This can lead to sentences being crammed with unnecessary commas or incorrectly used semi-colons in the hope that at least some of them will be "right".

The first thing you must accept if you have difficulties with basic punctuation is that it is not a body of knowledge which, once learnt, can be applied uniformly to all situations. Although each punctuation mark has specific functions, there are no set rules to be applied: it is the effectiveness, accuracy and interpretation of individual sentences in which the punctuation is used which proves or disproves its correctness.

Some of the traditional dread can be taken out of the situation by explaining that all punctuation marks should be used according to the requirements of the *writer* i.e. you, with the aim of conveying an exact or particular meaning to the reader. It is up to *you* to choose the punctuation *you* need in order to get your point across, and it can only be regarded as incorrect if it causes:

(a) difficulty in reading because of inappropriate use, too frequent or too infrequent pauses;
(b) ambiguity (double meaning);
(c) confusion;
(d) misunderstanding;
(e) misinterpretation.

Therefore, you should choose and use whatever punctuation you need to communicate your meaning effectively. *You must, however, ensure that any punctuation mark included in your written work is performing one of its accepted functions.* Very often you will find that this is the reason for your punctuation being marked "wrong" by a lecturer or teacher – you have used a particular device in such a way that it is not doing the job it is designed to do. For example, one of the most common mistakes found in written English is the use of a comma when a full stop is required. This gives rise to the following type of structure:

There was a Students' Union meeting yesterday, one of the main topics of discussion was the proposals for the College Rag Week.

There are in fact two separate statements here, which should be presented as two sentences. If they are to stay in their original form, the comma must be replaced by a full stop, and the second statement must begin with a capital letter. (If they were to be joined to form a single sentence, some addition or rearrangement must be made.) Such misuse of basic punctuation can be avoided if you are fully aware of the functions of the various marks, and when they should be used. Remember that the style and quality of your written work will be greatly improved if you *keep any punctuation to the minimum necessary to help the reader understand.* Its main purpose, then, is to help you present your ideas clearly and effectively, and to save the reader the trouble and irritation of having to re-read a passage in order to grasp its meaning. Generally speaking, the better the construction of a sentence, the fewer the signs needed to clarify its meaning. As far as effective communication is concerned, the best type of sentence is one from which all punctuation marks (except the full stop) can be removed without affecting the clearness of what is being said or the ease with which it can be understood.

THE FUNCTIONS AND MAIN USES OF PUNCTUATION MARKS

GROUP ONE: Punctuation marks which denote the length of a pause.

The Full Stop (.)

(a) *General function.* The full stop denotes the longest pause in written communication.

(b) *Uses*

(i) To mark the end of a sentence. (the sentence which follows it should begin with a capital letter). For example:
Thank you for your letter. I am pleased to confirm your order. Delivery will be made on the 28th January.

(ii) To indicate an abbreviation, and where single letters are used to represent a full word. For example:
Berks. (Berkshire); Esq. (Esquire); Co. (Company); B.Sc. (Bachelor of Science); m.p.h. (miles per hour); C.O.D. (cash on delivery).

NOTE: the full stop can be left out if the abbreviation includes the last letter of the complete word. For example: Mrs, Dr, Ltd (Limited).

(c) The full stop is not used after structures which may appear to be, but are not, abbreviations. For example:
1st, 2nd, Fe (and all other chemical symbols).

EXERCISE

Rewrite the following letter, inserting the necessary *full stops* and *capital letters.*

Dear Sir,

We wish to confirm the arrangement made with our representative the removal of your furniture from Chelmsford to Norwich will take place on 28th June our charge for the removal will be £65 (sixty-five pounds) this includes insurance cover we enclose a form of agreement setting out the terms and conditions and shall be glad if you will sign and return it.

Our van will arrive at your house at 7.30 am we should complete the loading in about three hours we therefore expect to deliver to your Norwich address and to complete unloading by about 4.30 pm on the following day

Yours faithfully,

EXERCISE

Copy out the following list of abbreviations commonly used in business, and insert full stops in the appropriate places. Give the meaning of each abbreviation next to it, using your dictionary or any other source to help you. For example:

E.E.C. European Economic Community.

am	Cr	Enc	IOU	pcl
BIF	c/s	est	i/c	pp (per pro)
Beds	CWO	ex div	Kg	pkg
B/L	cwt	FCIS	Ltd	pro tem
Br	dely	fwd	max	qy
BST	Disct	Glos	memo	re
cat	do	GPO	min	recd
c/d	doz	HMSO	mm	ref
cert	ea	Hon	mpg	Rly
c/f	eg	hr	MS(S)	wpm
chq	etc	inc	NB	wt
Co	E & OE	ie	PAYE	yr

The Comma (,)

(a) *General Function.* This punctuation mark denotes the shortest possible pause in a sentence, and is the one which is more frequently misused.

(b) *Uses.*

(i) To separate items in a list. For example:

The price quoted includes purchase price, V.A.T., carriage, and insurance.

NOTE: In the early stages of learning about puncutation you might have been told that "a comma should not be used before the word *and*". This, however is a generalisation which is not accurate. The following points give a more accurate summary of the situation.

(a) *the omission of the comma before "and" is optional in many cases;*

(b) *it should be put in to avoid ambiguity in some cases;*

(c) *it should be left out when only two items are listed;*

(d) *it should be put in when "and" introduces a separate, but related, statement.*

(ii) To enclose an expression which could be left out without altering the main sense of the sentence. For example:

Our company secretary, who has been with us for twenty years, is retiring at the end of July.

(iii) To show the reader that you expect him to pause in order to make sense of the sentence. For example:

Johnson, a part-time student, attends college on Wednesdays.

(iv) To separate introductory words from the rest of the sentence. For example: "Mr. Chairman, I must comment upon the statements made by my colleague."

(v) To introduce or interrupt a quotation. For example:

The Managing Director said, "These are the new safety regulations".

"These", said the Managing Director, "are the new safety regulations".

TASK ONE

Insert the necessary commas into the following sentences.

(i) Miss Warland the Manager's secretary was asked to make the necessary travel arrangements.

(ii) We too are of the opinion that such an investment is inadvisable.

(iii) "I must point out" said the accountant "that such a move will make you liable for capital gains tax."

(iv) Rising to his feet Mr. Jameson called for the resignation of the chairman.

(v) Your letter enclosing an estimate of the cost of further expansion prepared by you at the request of our Board will be considered at our next meeting.

(vi) Having had long experience in work of this kind and controlling as we do large capital resources we can assure you that we are well able to undertake the construction of your proposed hypermarket.

(vii) The order to Office Supplies Ltd included stationery calculators filing cabinets staplers and desk diaries.

(viii) We thank you for your enquiry and have pleasure in enclosing samples of our printing.

(ix) When he phoned he said firmly "I have no intention of paying for the work until it is completed to my satisfaction".

(x) We enclose copies of your order and the delivery note.

NOTE: The comma is an important part of standard letter-presentation, but the modern trend is towards "open" punctuation in business correspondence., This will no doubt be explained to you in detail if your studies include a typewriting option, and will in any case be considered when you reach the section which deals with business correspondence as part of your "people and communications" work. The *traditional* uses of the comma in this context are given below.

Traditional uses of the comma in letters.

(a) Between complete parts of an address. For example:
17 Fife Way, London, S.W.9.

(b) Between the month and year in a date. For example:
28th June, 1978.

(c) After the day of the week, if this is included in a date. For example:
Monday, 28th June, 1978

(d) After the salutation. For example:
Dear Sir,

(e) After the subscription (complimentary close). For example:
Yours faithfully,

The semi-colon (;)

(a) *General function.* If you want to create a pause which is longer than a comma, but shorter than a full stop, use a semi-colon.

(b) *Uses.*

(i) To mark off two or more separate statements which are too intimately connected in meaning to be written as separate sentences. For example:
It is company policy to give all employees under the age of twenty-one years day-release to attend college; however, they must follow a course of study which leads to a qualification approved by the company.

(ii) To separate two statements as in (i) where the second statement needs emphasis and/or contrasts with the first. For example:
On this occasion a discount will be allowed; but in future the full price will be payable.

The colon (:)

(a) *General Function.* A colon is most commonly used in modern English to indicate that something is to follow.

(b) *Uses.*

(i) To split up a sentence where the following part(s) explain or amplify the first statement. For example:

A work-experience programme of this type is advantageous: it not only gives you an insight into the job but also introduces you to possible future employers.

(ii) To introduce a list. For example:
If you join this course you will be expected to study the following subjects: economics, law, personnel management, written communication, and applied office skills.

(iii) To introduce a lengthy quotation. For example:
The Prime Minister said: ....

In Unit III when you were working on fluency of sentences and linking ideas together, we said that certain punctuation marks could be useful in this respect. The semi-colon and the colon are two such marks because, within the range of their own functions, they provide you with further methods of linking statements together and improving the fluency and variety of your sentence structure. Task Two will enable you to recognise and implement the use of the colon and the semi-colon, but it can be demonstrated exactly how they can be used to join a series of short related sentences. For example:

The speaker was not very impressive. His knowledge of the subject was limited. Some of his statements were inaccurate. He was unable to give satisfactory answers to a number of questions arising from the lecture.

As you can see there are four separate sentences in the example. They are all closely concerned with the same subject (the poor quality of the speaker) and the second, third and fourth sentences give us an explanation of the first. Thus you are told that the speaker was not very impressive and then given a number of reasons why this was so. If you glance back over the use of colons and semi-colons, you will see that they can be applied directly to this situation, and the separate sentences could be combined in this way:

The speaker was not very impressive: his knowledge of the subject was limited; some of his statements were inaccurate; he was unable to give satisfactory answers to a number of questions arising from the lecture.

TASK TWO

Insert any necessary colons and/or semi-colons in the following passages.

(i) The good driver knows stopping distances increase with speed and drives accordingly on his engine and not on his brakes knows the braking and acceleration of which his vehicle is capable in an emergency and always adjusts his speed to the prevailing road and traffic conditions.

(ii) There were several reasons for the the unofficial strike at the factory the company did not honour its agreement with the union there was friction between supervisors and other employees the professional officers of the union could not obtain the support of union members and the militant shop stewards were excessively powerful.

(iii) We have today dispatched the following by National Carriers Limited one dozen gooseberry bushes twenty raspberry bushes twenty strawberry plants and three "Victoria" plum trees.

GROUP TWO: Punctuation marks which are used to allow external subject matter or minor digressions to be brought into the basic text.

Brackets ( )

(a) *General function.* To enclose a parenthesis or "aside".

(b) *Uses*

(i) To mark a comment or additional information which is inserted into a sentence as an "aside". For example:
France (a country which I have often visited) is a member of the E.E.C.

(ii) To give clarification or explanations. For example:
Professional sportsmen (those who are *paid* for their involvement in a particular sport) are unable to compete in the Olympic Games.

(iii) To give dates or repeat sums of money. For example:
When the Bank of England received its charter (1694), it was unable to commence business.
We regret to inform you that the purchase price is now £12,000 (twelve thousand pounds).

TASK THREE

Construct sentences on any subject to demonstrate each use of brackets given in this section. Try to avoid imitating the structures used in the examples.

(i) ______________________________

____

(ii) ______________________________

____

(iii) ______________________________

____

The Dash (–)

(a) *General function.* The dash is used for a variety of purposes.

(b) *Uses*

(i) To indicate an abrupt change of thought. For example:
The new production line will increase efficiency and productivity. We might, however, have to reduce the workforce– but that is another question.

(ii) Where a word or phrase is repeated for emphasis. For example:
If we introduce a scheme for voluntary redundancy, there could be serious repercussions – which might affect any future developments.

(iii) As an alternative to brackets to mark a parenthesis. For example:
We have been informed – and have every reason to believe – that the cost of fuel oil is likely to rise in the near future.

TASK FOUR

Construct sentences on any subject to demonstrate the three main uses of the dash.

(i) ____

____

(ii) ____

____

(iii) ____

____

Quotation Marks or Inverted Commas (" " or ' ')

(a) *General function.* These can be used doubly or singly to mark the beginning and end of a quotation. A useful rule is to use single quotation marks if the need arises within a passage already enclosed by double quotation marks.

(b) *Uses.*

(i) Placed around any words actually quoted. For example:
The works manager called the employee into his office and said, "I intend to recommend you for promotion".

(ii) Often used to enclose the names of newspapers, books, etc. For example:
The manager always had a copy of "The Financial Times" delivered to his office.

(iii) To enclose a word or phrase which is isolated for comment, used unusually, or sarcastically (derisively). For example:
The students were taken on an "interesting" visit to an art exhibition.

NOTE: A quotation within a quotation shows the most common use of single inverted commas. For example:

"I was astounded when the manager said, 'I intend to recommend you for promotion' ", said the accounts clerk.

EXERCISE

Rewrite the following dialogue, inserting all the necessary quotation marks/inverted commas. Keep the same paragraph layout as the original. All other punctuation is correct.

As Jayne entered the office she said, Sorry I'm late.

Her supervisor, Miss Tayke, called her over and asked, Have you clocked-in yet? If not, you had better do so right away. Why are you so late, anyway?

There was an accident in the High Street and we had to wait for the damaged vehicles to be removed, explained Jayne..

That's a likely story, laughed Miss Tayke.

At that moment the manager stormed into the office and exclaimed, Some clumsy idiot drove into my car in the High Street and I had to have it towed away before getting a taxi to the office. There was even a reporter from the Chronicle there, taking photographs!

GROUP THREE: Punctuation marks which are put into individual words to clarify their structure or meaning.

The Apostrophe (')

(a) *General function.*

This device is used to indicate possession (ownership) or show that something has been omitted.

(b) *Uses*

(i) To indicate the abbreviation/contraction of a word, where the apostrophe replaces the letter(s) left out. For example:
don't (do not) it's (it is) there's (there is) haven't (have not)

(ii) To show possession (ownership). It is this use of the apostrophe which causes most confusion, as its positioning within the word directly affects the meaning of the sentence. The correct usage of the apostrophe to show possession is set out in the following checklist so that you can find it easily for future reference.

1. If a noun is singular (representing *one* person or thing), possession is shown by adding an *'s.* For example:
The lecturer found *a student's essay* on the floor of his car (i.e. the essay belonging to one student).
2. If a noun is plural *(more than one)* and ends in *s,* possession is shown by putting an apostrophe after the final *s.* For example:
The lecturer found *the students' essays* on the floor of his car (i.e. the essays belonging to a number of students).
3. If a noun is plural and does not end in *s,* possession is shown by adding an *'s.* For example:
The children's playground was flooded (children is plural).
4. When "its" is used to show possession *no apostrophe is needed.* This applies to all possessive pronouns such as: *yours, hers, ours, theirs.* For example:
It's easy to calculate the area of a square: multiply *its* length by *its* breadth.
I'm not sure whether this piece of work is *yours* or *hers.*
5. It is becoming generally accepted nowadays that the apostrophe can be left out of certain structures which (although not really possessive forms) have traditionally used it. It is safe to say that either version is acceptable, but do be consistent. For example:

a day's journey – a days journey
two month's holiday – two months holiday
one month's notice – one months notice

TASK FIVE

Put apostrophes into the following short sentences where they are required:

She was the principals secretary.
Theyre not interested in the firms business.
It isnt yours, its ours.
Hes only got a pounds worth of change.
Shes a childrens nurse.
Ill pretend I was ill.
You neednt have pulled its tail.
The typists chair is in Mr Joness office.
Im taking three weeks holiday.
Pianos are delicate instruments.
The letters havent had stamps put on them yet.
Ive already looked at the boxs label.

TASK SIX

When you have checked the correctness of your answers, make a list of all the words you can find in Task Five which can be classified under the headings given below. The number of spaces does not necessarily indicate the number of possible answers in each column.

Abbreviations/contractions using an apostrophe	*Possessive forms using an apostrophe*	*Possessive pronouns not requiring an apostrophe*

The Hyphen or short dash (-)

(a) *General function.* The hyphen is used to form compound words.

(b) *Uses*

(i) To form compound nouns. For example:
dual-carriageway, brother-in-law, man-servant.

NOTE: There is a trend nowadays to leave the hyphen out of compound words made up of two short words (e.g. today, textbook, boyfriend). This, of course, leads to some confusion, but does mean that the use of the hyphen is *optional* in many cases.

(ii) To form compound adjectives. For example:
a *well-known* product, a *good-natured* person, a *labour-saving* device.

(iii) To separate some prefixes from the word with which they are used, particularly if this is essential to pronunciation. For example:
vice-chairman, post-natal, co-operative, pre-war, re-appear.

(iv) To separate tens and units in written numbers, and written fractions. For example:
twenty-four, three hundred and fifty-one, five-eighths.

GROUP FOUR: Punctuation marks which indicate inflexions of the voice.

The Question Mark (?)

(a) *General function.* The question mark shows that a direct question is being asked.

(b) *Uses*

(i) To replace the full stop in a direct question. For example:
"When will your representative be able to call?"

(ii) The question mark is *not* used when a question is in indirect or reported speech (it is replaced by a verb of "asking"). For example:
The customer asked when their representative would be able to call.

(iii) The question mark is *not* used when a polite request is being made in question form. For example:
Will you please ask your representative to call on Wednesday.

The Exclamation Mark (!)

(a) *General function.* An expression of emotion is usually shown by the use of an exclamation mark.

(b) *Uses*
Inserted after an exclamation or exclamation remark. For example:
"Look out! There's a car coming."
"What dreadful weather we're having!"
"Oh dear! I've lost the file on Mr James Wibb."

EXERCISE

Write out the following passages inserting all necessary punctuation marks.

(a) Citizens of the United Kingdom and the Irish Republic do not require passports or entry visas for travel between their respective countries and Jersey Citizens of Austria Belgium Denmark France the German Federal Republic including West Berlin Holland Italy Liechtenstein Luxembourg Monaco and Switzerland coming to the Island on holiday do not require a passport or an entry visa provided they are in possession of a national identity card.

(States of Jersey Tourism Committee booklet, 1978).

(b) There are over 16,000 acres of land under cultivation in Jersey representing three fifths of the Islands total area with about thirty five per cent of the nine hundred or so holdings being less than ten acres in extent.

(States of Jersey Tourism Committee Information Digest 1978)

(c) Dear Sir,

In reply to your letter of yesterday I express regret that we were not able to allow payment against your cheque No 527610 it appears to have escaped your notice that one of the cheques paid in on 11th August the cheque drawn in your favour by M Tippett & Co was post dated to 25th August and that the amount cannot be credited to your accout before that date to honour your cheque would have created an overdraft of more than £100 one houndred pounds and in the absence of previous arrangement I am afraid we could not grant credit for such a large sum.

I trust this explanation will make matters clear

Yours faithfully

(Adapted from L. Gartside, *Model Business Letters* 2nd edition, Macdonald & Evans, 1974).

CAPITAL LETTERS

So far in Section III of this unit you have covered the basics of punctuation, and should now be aware of many of the problems that can arise. There is, however, a closely related aspect of written English which can cause equal confusion. How often have you wondered, "Should I use a capital letter for this word?" The checklist which follows should give you a useful reference when you are in doubt.

The Main Uses of Initial Capital Letters

(a) *To begin a sentence* (and to begin a direct quotation, even in the middle of a sentence). For example:
The new clerk entered the room. The Manager said, "Please sit down Mrs Williams".

(b) *For proper nouns*, i.e. the names of persons, places, streets, buildings, etc. For example:
We received a letter from Mr Williams at County Hall, Exeter.

(c) *For courtesy titles* (except where the word used does not form part of a title or refer to a particular person). For example:
(i) Mr Jemet; Colonel Wilson; Professor Lee.
(ii) The Principal spoke for a long time.
(*but:* The principal of a college performs many duties.)

(d) *For important words in the titles of organisations and institutions.* For example:
The British Institute of Management; The Houses of Parliament.

(e) *For important words in headings and titles of publications, plays, etc.* For example
(i) I ordered a copy of "Management Today".
(ii) For Proper Nouns (see (b) above).

(f) *For abbreviated titles.* For examples:
M.I.Mech.Eng.; B.A.; A.C.I.S.

(g) *In correspondence.*
(i) For the initial letters of the salutation. For example:
Dear Sir; Dear Madam; Dear Sirs.
(ii) For the initial letter of the first word only in the subscription. For example:
Yours faithfully; Yours sincerely.

(h) *For calendar names,* etc. (except for the names of seasons), *including special days and festivals.* For example:
Monday; February; Easter; Whit Sunday; Remembrance Sunday; Epiphany.
(*but:* The new catalogue will appear in the autumn.)

(i) *For the pronoun "I"* For example:
I'm afraid I will be late tomorrow.

READING AND UNDERSTANDING

One of the main themes of this workbook is communication, so the title of this section could be extended to Reading, Understanding and Communicating. For those of you who have had any experience of written English examinations, this sequence of activities will be recognisable under its traditional name: comprehension. It is frequently used as an examination question because it serves as a thorough test of your ability to perform the three activities which are essential to all aspects of business and social life: you are required *to read carefully;* you must *understand the general theme and specific content of what you have read;* and you are expected *to express yourself accurately* by answering questions based on the information you have been given. Your written answers serve the additional function of enabling an examiner to assess the quality of your *sentence structure, grammar and punctuation,* and, most important of all, *your ability to communicate effectively in writing.*

If you imagine yourself in almost any working situation, you will realise that it will be essential to you at some time to communicate competently with people, and understand documents or instructions. This communication will sometimes be spoken, but much of the time the written word is used to ensure clarity and accuracy. The emphasis in communication is on *people* because it is the understanding of another person (*the receiver* we mentioned in Unit I) that you are aiming to achieve. Every time you write anything down, remember that you are *communicating,* and therefore it must be comprehensible. It is because many prospective employers recognise the importance of this communication that they often look for an applicant who has some proven ability - an examination pass or certificate - in the use of written English.

Comprehension, then, is a task which should be approached with great care, and in a logical manner. A general indication of technique and approach is given in the following outline, and a specimen passage (with questions, answers and comments) comes later in the section in order to demonstrate the points made.

General Approach

Stage 1. Read the passage right through with the aim of grasping its main theme. If you have time, write a sentence on rough paper which summarises this theme. Although not part of the actual comprehension, this will clarify in your own mind what the passage is about.

Stage 2. Read the questions so as to get a general impression of the types of things you are asked to do, and to make sure you understand what is required.

Stage 3. Read through the passage again, this time concentrating on the specific content of each paragraph and identifying information which is directly relevant to the questions. If there is anything you don't understand try to work out what it means by considering the information around it, i.e. in what *context* it is used. A dictionary can be very helpful in this situation, if you are allowed to use it.

Stage 4. Read each question in turn, and construct an answer based on the information in the passage. It is essential that you read the question carefully and give the answer required, because if you misinterpret it in any way you cannot be awarded the marks, no matter how well-written your answer is. *Any answer you give must be written as a complete, grammatically correct sentence or series of sentences, unless you are specifically instructed to do otherwise.*

It is not necessary to rewrite the question before you give the answer - this is a waste of time and energy. However, the answer you give should indicate clearly what you are talking about, and in order to achieve this it might be necessary to repeat a *phrase* from the questions (see specimen comprehension answers, p. 197). You should aim to answer the questions in order. It is not a good policy to jump about and present your answers out of sequence. If you are unable to answer a question, leave the necessary space so that you can return to it if you have time. Another important point is that you should label/number your answers accurately so that they correspond to the question numbers. Incorrect labelling can result in loss of marks. Very often you will find that the number of marks allocated to a question is given on the question sheet. If this is the case, it will help you decide how much time to spend on individual questions; it would be foolish to spend fifteen minutes on a question which is worth only two marks; equally, it would not be advisable to give a single-line answer to a question which merits twenty marks.

If you adopt such an approach to this type of work, it will help you overcome some of the difficulties experienced by many students. More detailed comments and instructions are included with individual questions in the specimen comprehension.

EXERCISE

Revise the section in Unit III on note-making, and then construct and present a concise set of notes on "A General Approach to Comprehension". Base your notes entirely on the information given in this unit, and make sure your method of presentation is correct.

Types of Comprehension Question

It is not easy to classify questions accurately but there are two main types which you can be sure of coming across.

Questions on Content

Although this type of question is fairly straightforward, it does require a thorough understanding of the whole passage. The form of the question can vary. You might be asked to:

(a) identify single facts;
(b) identify a theme, i.e. general idea running through a passage or individual paragraph
(c) summarise certain sections of the passage; or
(d) summarise the ideas/statements related to a particular theme.

Interpretive Questions

These questions will pick out certain words, phrases or sentences and ask you to explain their meaning *as they are used in the context of the passage.* You should bear in mind that many words and phrases can have more than one possible meaning, and it is up to you to interpret the information so that it corresponds to the author's meaning. Very occasionally you will be asked to comment upon or assess the value of some statement an author has made. It is in this type of question only that you are asked to give a personal opinion: you should not assume that you can comment freely upon any question unless you are specifically asked to do so. *Concentrate on what the author is saying,* whether or not you agree with him.

NOTE: There is another type of question which can occasionally come up in a comprehension, and that is one which deals with *style.* The aim here is to test your appreciation of the way the author writes, and the questions can ask you to comment upon his use of figures of speech, e.g. simile and metaphor, irony, humour, etc. You can even be asked about his use of particular punctuation marks, and whether or not they contribute to the effectiveness of his writing. If you do have to answer this type of question you will need to use a combination of personal opinion, accurate knowledge, and careful interpretation.

Specimen Comprehension

The word "pollution" can be associated with such a wide range of activities that it is possible to give only a general definition of what is meant when we consider the topic. We can say that any situation in which man allows any waste matter or surplus energy to escape into the environment, thereby causing any damage to any form of life, can be classed as a polluting situation.

Such pollutants can be identified in a number of forms, including gass, particles in the air, liquids, solid waste, or surplus energy such as radiation, heat, vibration or noise. If we look upon pollution as the end product of a process which begins with the creation of "waste", we can say that almost all human activity is directly contributing to pollution because the production of "waste" in some form is inevitable. However, the term "waste" should not imply "uselessness", because our modern technological society can find many methods of recycling or utilising a wide variety of what are traditionally regarded as waste products.

Even if a prospective pollutant cannot be re-used profitably, there are other methods of pollution limitation such as controlling the expansion of high-waste activities, requiring more effective waste treatment, controlling the manner and location of waste disposal, or suitably protecting vulnerable "victims".

In Britain, control over the disposal of water is the most widely practised method of pollution control. For example, local authority environmental health departments have responsibility for controlling domestic and much industrial air pollution; the regional water authorities exercise control over the disposal of waste into estuaries and inland waterways; the British Waterways Board is concerned with any pollution of canals; and central government has extensive control over the use of radioactive materials.

Despite the fact that these and many other pollution control authorities have wide-ranging powers, there is still much to be done. Because of the lack of uniformity in the implementation of anti-pollution regulations, it is doubtful whether pollution can be reduced to a minimum level within the foreseeable future.

Questions

1. Which authority is concerned with the pollution of canals?

Answer: *The British Waterways Board acts as the anti-pollution authority with respect to canals.*

Comment: This question simply asked you to identify a single fact, and a straightforward statement is quite adequate.

2. What general theme does the author deal with in paragraph three?

Answer: *The author outlines some basic methods of pollution control in paragraph three.*

Comment: As you can see from the question, you are asked to identify a theme and a short, precise answer is the best way of dealing with it.

3. In not more than thirty-five words, summarise what is said in the second paragraph.

Answer: *The author suggests some different forms that pollution can take, and says that much "waste", the origin of most polluting substances, can be recycled and put to good use. (29 words).*

Comment: Again, the type of question is clearly indicated. Remember that a summary should aim to contain the *principal ideas* of a passage, rather than the details. It is a good policy to state the number of words you have used in a summary, and you should always aim to be within the number stipulated. Any additional words will often be penalised.

4. Explain in your own words the meaning of the phrase "prospective pollutant".

Answer: *The phrase "prospective pollutant" is used to describe any kind of waste product which, if it was released into the environment, would cause damage or destruction to some form of living matter.*

Comment: As the question asks you to *explain* the phrase, you should again write a complete sentence which shows clearly what you are talking about. The use of "your own words" is advisable as far as possible in all your answers. However, don't be afraid to use phrases from the original if you can't think of an alternative way of expressing an idea effectively.

5. Give as briefly as possible the meaning of the word "profitably" as used in the passage.

Answer: *profitably - beneficially*

Comment: If you are asked to answer "as briefly as possible", or to "give a word or phrase which means the same as ... ", you can answer in the way shown above, i.e. not writing your answer as a complete sentence. It is essential to remember that the meaning required is "as used in the passage", and therefore in this case the word *profitably* does not necessarily mean *in a financially rewarding way* - it is used more loosely to mean *in a generally beneficial way.* If you are able to provide a single word which gives the same meaning, make sure that your answer is *the same part of speech* as the original word. For example:

profitably (adverb)	*beneficially* (adverb)
frank (adjective)	*outspoken* (adjective)
portion (noun)	*share* (noun)

NOTE: Words which are *similar* in meaning to other words are called *synonyms.* Words which are *opposite* in meaning to other words are called *antonyms.*

6. Explain the use of the semi-colons in paragraph four.

Answer: *The semi-colons are used to link together a series of separate statements which are too intimately related in content to merit being written as separate sentences.*

Comment: The answer to this question is easy, as long as you are sure of the uses of semi-colons! It is a good idea to revise your punctuation regularly so that at least the major uses of punctuation marks become set in your mind.

7. In the last sentence of paragraph one, the word "any" is used four times. Comment upon this.

Answer: *The word "any" is repeated for emphasis. The author is trying to reinforce his statement that any definition of pollution must be very general by emphasising the extent to which pollution and its causes can be found in the activities of man and nature.*

Comment: Question 7 is concerned with style. In this case the basic answer is quite straightforward, but the *explanation* can cause problems. Any stylistic questions will require *explanations,* and will therefore need much careful thought and analysis.

TASK SEVEN

The following questions are based on the passage about pollution. Answer them as far as possible in your own words, following the instructions carefully. Write your answers as complete sentences unless specifically instructed to do otherwise.

(i) What general definition of pollution does the author give?

(ii) What examples of energy pollution are given in the passage?

(iii) Who has responsibility for controlling domestic air pollution?

(iv) What do you understand by the phrase "lack of uniformity in the implementation of anti-pollution regulations"?

(v) Give a single word or phrase to show the meaning of the following words as used in the passage: utilising, location, co-ordinated.

(vi) Explain carefully the use of the hyphen in each of the following words: re-used, wide-ranging.

Before you move on to the following exercises, check your answers to Task Seven carefully, and read through the whole section on comprehension once again. If necessary, revise the uses of various punctuation marks because you will have to answer questions on the subject. You should make full use of your dictionary throughout this part of the workbook.

The two passages used as a basis for the comprehension exercises have been taken directly, or adapted from *Business Communications* by R.T. Chappell and W.L. Read, (4th edition, Macdonald and Evans, 1978). They have been selected because they are conerned with relationships in business – relationships in which we all become involved at some time. Most of you will already have experienced *interview* situations, and the first extract will help you appreciate some of the different purposes for which interviews can be used. You will also be given an insight into how much work the interviewer has to put into the situation. Most of us tend to think of an interview as a one-sided affair, with the interviewer having the easy task. This is not the case. It is much more difficult to be an effective interviewer than to be an interviewee.

The second passage outlines a completely different sort of relationship – that between an organisation and "outsiders". The outsiders can be suppliers, manufacturers, customers consumers, or simply members of the general public, and therefore the relationshop can be formal (subject to some form of legal contract) or informal (such as a consultative arrangement between a local environmental protection group and a large manufacturing organisation). In any of these relationships it is essential to maintain good communications, and it is through a *public relations* department that most large organisations attempt to do this.

EXERCISE

Reading the following extract, and answer the questions at the end.

> Interviews are employed by management for a number of purposes. An outstanding example is selection interviews. Here it is necessary to have full information about the job, and to find out as much relevant information about the applicant as possible. The next step is to match the best applicant against the known demands of the job to ascertain whether he is suitable or whether the post should be readvertised.
>
> There are, however, other valuable applications of interviews. An induction interview is conducted so that the new employee can be eased gently into his new employment and given details of the job and of the proposed training plan. After the interview the newcomer is often shown round the works or department and introduced to his fellow employees.
>
> Progress interviews are conducted so that employees may be given suggestions on how to improve their performance. From time to time employees will have grievances, and the manager will try to remove the causes of the friction and to restore the earlier good relationships.
>
> Another cause for interviewing will be to deliver a reprimand. In this case, too, the manager will try to avoid destructive criticism and to show the employee how he can improve.
>
> But whatever the reason for interview, a systematic approach will ensure that the conclusion reached is the most satisfactory one in the circumstances.

The interviewer should always have a plan. Firstly, he should be clear about the purpose for which the interview is being conducted. Secondly, adequate preparation should be made, so that as much data as possible is available. Often, because the matter is confidential, the interviewer will himself have discreetly to collect this information.

The third stage is vital and deals with the conduct of the interview. Adequate time must be allowed for all the stages of the interview and for each interview. Privacy is usually essential, so that the person being interviewed can be put at ease. The questions or point of view of the interviewer should be put clearly and concisely. The interviewee should be encouraged to speak. Sometimes an irrelevant question can achieve that objective. Attention should be paid to what is said and also what is left unsaid.

Since we also communicate by our attitude, the interviewee should be observed throughout the interview to reinforce impressions made by the spoken word. Notes should be made unobtrusively. Before the interview ends a check should be made to ensure that all the necessary information is avilable. Where it is possible to make a decision there and then, this should, of course, be done. Otherwise the interviewer should explain what is to be the next step and ensure that this takes place. The interview should then be ended.

The fourth step in interviewing procedure is to ensure that the results are checked. For example, an induction interview may follow a selection interview. Opportunity may occur for an informal chat; or a check can be made on the work of somebody who has earlier been reprimanded.

A great deal of the work of the manager is concerned with the conduct of interviews. Thus, it is wise for us to ensure that in this work we do, as far as possible, achieve the object which we set out to attain.

Questions *(Marks)*

1. Give three purposes for which interviews can be used. (3)
2. Explain clearly what you understand by the term "induction interview". (4)
3. Why should an interviewee be observed carefully throughout an interview? (4)
4. Give an example of how the results of a "reprimand interview" can be checked. (3)
5. Give a single word or phrase to express the meaning of each of the following words as used in the passage: grievance, friction, systematic, discreetly, unobtrusively. (5)
6. Explain the use of the commas on either side of the word "too" in paragraph four. What does "too" mean here? (3, 2)
7. What does the author mean in the last sentence of paragraph seven: "attention ... unsaid"? (6)

TASK EIGHT

If you had to interview an applicant for a job, what questions would you ask at the stages indicated below? A maximum number of questions is indicated for each stage, and you are asked to bear in mind that every question should be relevant to the situation in which it is to be used, and should aim to extract useful information from the interviewee wherever possible.

(i) Preliminary "chit-chat" and lead-in to the interview. remember that you should aim to put the interviewee at ease and give him/her a little time to settle down.

(a) ______________________________

(b) ______________________________

(c) ______________________________

(d) ______________________________

(e) ______________________________

(ii) *Previous school/employment record.* The details of any qualifications or examination passes will already be in the letter of application.

(a) ______________________________

(b) ______________________________

(c) ______________________________

(d) ______________________________

(e) ______________________________

(iii) *Family situation.* You do not want to pry into private affairs. Only ask questions which are concerned with the suitability of the applicant or his/her ability to take the job, e.g. accommodation; attitude of close relatives.

(a) ______________________________

(b) ______________________________

(c) ______________________________

(d) ______________________________

(e) ______________________________

(iv) *Conclusion.* Round off the interview and give the opportunity for any further questions.

(a) ______________________________

(b) ______________________________

(c) ______________________________

EXERCISE

When you consider the questions at the end of this extract you should base your answers entirely on the information provided.

Public relations is of increasing importance because more and more information is being demanded by customers, suppliers, the employees, and public, too.

Relationships with customers and propsective customers can be improved by the use of good public relations. All those who have these contacts, either directly, for example, salesmen, or indirectly, for example, correspondents, have the responsibility of promoting the goodwill of the undertaking. Most companies these days insist that their employees should conduct themselves in all their dealings with the public as if they were rendering a service. It is a short-sighted policy to carry on a business with the sole object of making as much money as quickly as possible. The smaller customer should be treated with as much courtesy as those who submit large orders.

We should always remember that to be able to provide an efficient service to customers implies a complete knowledge of the products which the company makes or the services which it provides. All employees should be trained on this principle.

Relationships should also be sound with the suppliers, who will inevitably give the company better service than they will give to those firms who are not so concerned with public relations.

An organisation, too, makes an impact on the market it serves. This impact can result from the advertising material, the quality of its products, its after-sales service, the concern for the amenities of the areas in which its buildings are sited, and the conduct of its employees. We do not exclude international markets. Many of our companies have a profound influence abroad.

As far as relationships with workers are concerned, the modern organisation finds it beneficial to maintain two-way communication by employing such methods as joint-consultation on important issues, by implementing job-evaluation procedures and suggestion schemes, and by issuing regular news-letters or house-magazines. The employee of today wants to know much more than his counterpart in the 1930s about the organisation for which he works.

Public relations work is therefore as necessary for government departments, nationalised industries, and local authorities as it is for businesses large and small. Trade associations and trade unions, too, devote some of their resources to the public relations aspects of their activities. Most organisations will upon request supply details of their products or services.

For example, the Dunlop organisation has published a well-produced booklet copies of which are available for educational purposes. Among the items covered in this publication are the history of the company, its capital structure, the products manufactured, the home factories, raw materials, selling, research, and personnel.

Some large companies charge specialist officers with a great deal of the work of external communications. For example, there may be a public relations or information officer through whom the information about the enterprise's work is co-ordinated. It is obviously wise that all material given to the Press should, where possible, be handled in this way. On the other hand, it is as well to remember that each individual employee is an ambassador of his company. Glossy brochures are not the only or necessarily the best form of external communication.

Questions *(marks)*

1. Give an example of someone who is responsible (i) directly, and (ii) indirectly for promoting the interests of an organisation. (3, 3)
2. Write a single sentence summarising the theme of paragraph two. (5)
3. What is it essential for an employee to have in order to provide an efficient service to customers? (3)
4. Explain carefully how the following words are used in the passage: market, amenities, ambassador. (6)
5. What is the exact function of the hyphen in *short-sighted* (paragraph two), and *co-ordinated* (paragraph nine)? (2)
6. What is the role of a public relations officer? (2)
7. Why do you think it is "obviously wise that all material given to the press" should be the responsibility of a public relations or information officer? (6)

In the last exercise you found out a little about the role of public relations in the world of business, and it was suggested that most organisations would have some formal means of developing and maintaining successful communications with the world outside. The task which follows will give you more practical experience of using the reference facilities of a library, will enable you to find examples of organisations likely to have some form of public relations department, and will provide you with information necessary for completing an exercise at the end of this section.

TASK NINE

Use the reference section of your college library or the nearest public library to find the full name and postal address of one organisation for each of the following groups

NOTE: If there is more than one address, give that of the head office.

(i) Nationalised industries ______________________________

____

(ii) Local authorities ______________________________

____

(iii) National or multi-national companies ______________________________

____

(iv) Insurance companies ______________________________

____

(v) Finance companies ____________________

____

(vi) Banks ____________________

____

(vii) Local companies ____________________

____

(viii) Local or area divisions of nationalised industries ____________________

____

(ix) Trade unions ____________________

____

(x) Trade associations ____________________

____

AN INTRODUCTION TO BUSINESS CORRESPONDENCE

Many of you will already be familiar with the contents of this section, particularly if your complementary studies include office skills. The formal letter is probably one of the most important forms of communication used by any organisation, and because of this it is studied as an integral part of any course concerned with communication in business. This can sometimes lead to a certain amount of confusion and even conflict between traditionally separate subject areas. For example, in "typing" a student might be taught the most modern methods of letter presentation, whereas in "written communications" the tutor might insist upon methods which conform to more established standards.

There should, in fact, be no conflict or confusion, simply *understanding*. We must remember that *effective* communication is the main aim in all circumstances, and work towards this. In this introductory section on business correspondence we hope to bring areas of possible conflict to your attention, and help you understand why such problems arise as well as instructing you in the basic techniques of letter presentation.

The letter is *so* important because it is representative of the person or organisation sending it; it is a reflection of the quality and the efficiency of the sender and therefore acts as a good or a bad advertisement.

The first thing the receiver will notice is the general visual effect of the letter. Is it clear? Is it neat? Is it orderly? Is it accurately addressed? Is the layout consistent? Nowadays there are two principal letter styles, and the following diagrams demonstrate these.

"Fully Blocked" or "Blocked" Style

This means that every line begins at the left-hand margin (excluding the printed letter-head). The diagram on page 206 shows the fully blocked style.

NOTE: If a printed letter-head has a designated space for the date or the references then this must be adhered to. If this is not the case, these these important parts of the letter must be positioned on the left-hand margin as indicated.

Directors. G. B. Davis, R. B. North. M. W. Beevers
W. D. J. Argent. D. A. F. Sutherland

Macdonald & Evans (Publications) Ltd

Estover Road. Plymouth PL6 7PZ
Telephone: Plymouth (0752) 705251
Telegraphic Address MACEVANS Plymouth
Telex: 45635

Reference ____________

Date ____________

____

____

____

____

____

____

____

____

____

____

____

Subscription ____________

____

____

____

Directors: G.B. Davis. R.B. North. M.W. Beevers
W.D.J. Argent. D.A.F. Sutherland

Macdonald & Evans (Publications) Ltd

Estover Road. Plymouth PL6 7PZ
Telephone: Plymouth (0752) 705251
Telegraphic Address: MACEVANS Plymouth
Telex: 45635

Reference ______ **Date** ______

Subscription

"Semi-blocked" Style

This means that the date is put on the right-hand side of the page, opposite the reference; the subscription (complimentary close) is positioned as shown; and the first line of each paragraph is indented. Spacing between paragraphs can be the same as in the "blocked" style. The diagram on page 207 shows the semi-blocked style.

These diagrams give you the visual pattern of different styles of presentation, and, as you will have noticed, a letter is made up of a number of separate and identifiable parts. These are:

(a) the writer's address;
(b) the reference;
(c) the date;
(d) the receiver's address;
(e) the salutation (Dear Sir, Dear Madam, Dear Sirs);
(f) the main body of the letter;
(g) the subscription (complimentary close) – in many business letters this is coupled with another line which indicates that the writer is signing it *on behalf* of the firm;
(h) the signature;
(i) the designation (official position or status of the sender).

NOTE: Other parts can be included if required such as a "subject line" between the salutation and the main body, a "your reference" space either below or in line with the normal reference, and a note at the end of the letter to indicate that there is an enclosure.

We shall be considering the main parts in more detail a little later. First of all there is one problem which must be dealt with.

You can see that both the layout diagrams you have been given assume that the letter is being written on *headed* notepaper, and therefore the sender's address (and possibly some other parts) is already positioned on the page. What would you do, however, if no headed notepaper was available, or if you were writing a business letter in a personal capacity and had to put in your own address? Where would you position it? This is the dilemma that many people find themselves in when they need to write a business letter for their own purposes, or as part of a written communication examination.

There are various solutions – all based on the semi-block presentation – but some explanation is necessary before we look at them. If you are writing a letter which is to be assessed as part of a written communication exercise, rather than purely as a typing exercise, it is obvious that the examiner will put emphasis on your *use of English*, i.e. your ability to write effectively and conform to accepted standards of grammar, punctuation and presentation.

As you will know, the generally accepted method of indicating a new paragraph in normal written work is to *indent* the first line. If this is standard practice in other forms of written work, it is sensible to adopt the same practice in business letters. Thus the semi-blocked presentation is the most suitable because it allows for indentation. (Obviously, you will have to adapt to the requirements of your tutor or examiner when you are *typing* a letter.)

To return to the positioning of the writer's address on unheaded notepaper, two possible presentation methods are indicated by arrows on the diagrams on p. 209.

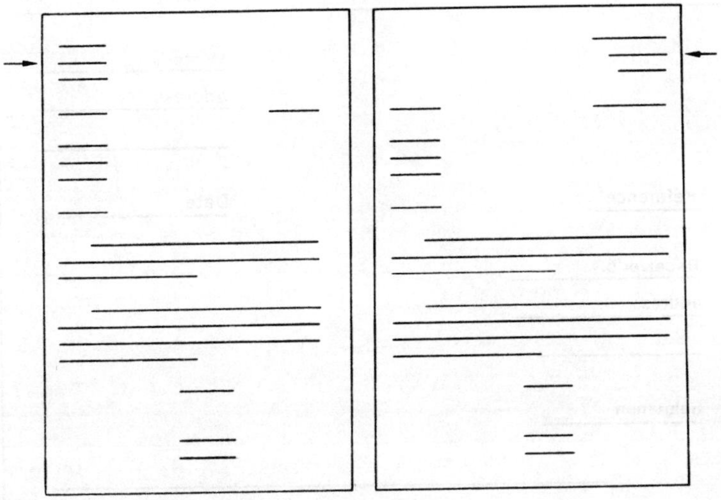

These are both acceptable, but the diagram on p. 210 seems to be a more generally approved method, which could be usefully adopted for all future correspondence work within this book.

You will notice that although the writer's address is on the right-hand side of the page, it is still "blocked", i.e. the beginning of each line is directly below the beginning of the previous line. This matches the receiver's address, and gives the visual impact of the letter a degree of consistency.

Having established the method of presentation you are to use, you can now move on to a more detailed analysis of the main parts of a business letter.

The Writer's Address

(a) It is *not* normal practice for the name of the individual sending the letter to appear at the beginning of this address.

(b) If a house number is used, it is not necessary to put a comma between this and the street name. Avoid abbreviations such as St. (Street), Ave. (Avenue), and Rd. (Road).

(c) There should be a comma at the end of each line, except for the last line *before* the postcode. A full stop is used here.

(d) No punctuation is required in the postcode.

(e) In handwritten letters the address should not be printed completely in capital letters. However, it is acceptable to use printed capitals for the name of the town.

(f) If a house *name* is used instead of, or in addition to a number, this name is written on a separate line.

(g) If there is a recognised abbreviation for the county, this can be used.

Specimens:

17 Watercross Avenue,
BEDDINGFORD,
Surrey.
WL14 3AJ

Morvah,
3 Oakfield Road,
Plymford,
WESTHAVEN,
Staffs.
ST7 6JZ

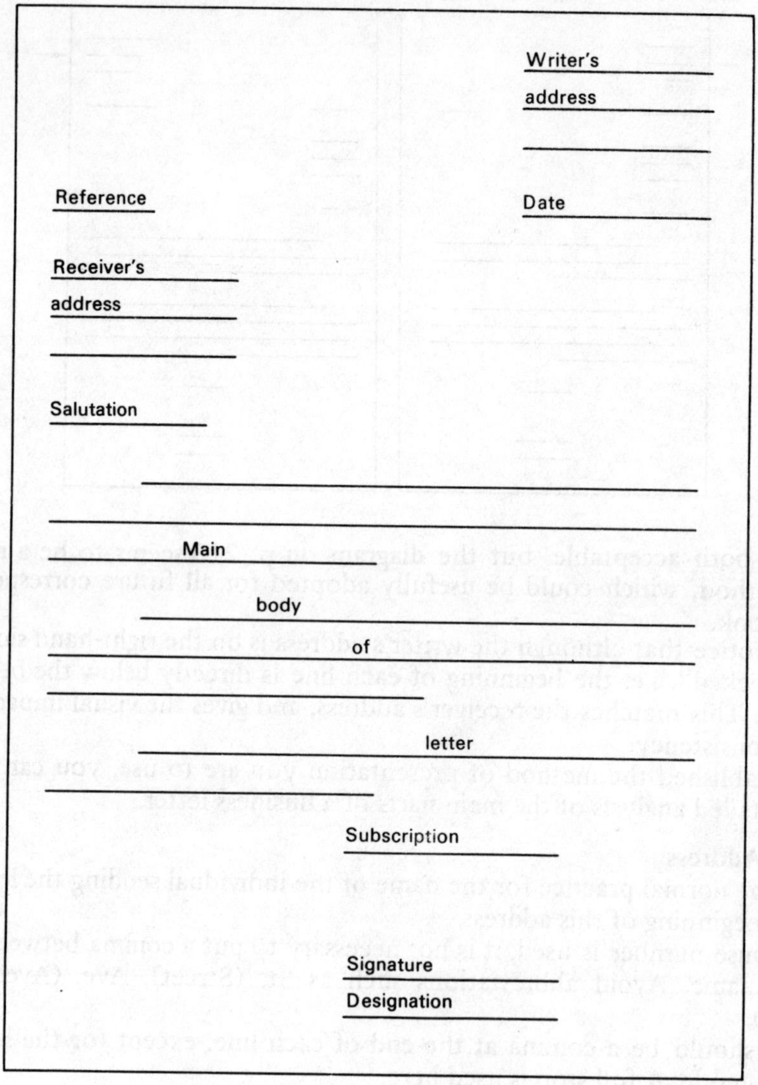

Open Punctuation

One trend in the business world which must be mentioned at this point is the use of *open punctuation.* This means that in a typed letter, the date, the reference, the address, the salutation and the complimentary close (subscription) are presented without any punctuation. The body of the letter is punctuated normally, with certain exceptions.

The main danger for you in using this system is that you might be tempted to carry it over into other work. This is not acceptable, as one of the important objectives of your written communications work is to develop the correct use of standard punctuation. Therefore, if typing is one of your option modules be prepared for the difference in punctuation, and remember that *you must use standard punctuation in all other written communications.*

The Reference

(a) In a typed letter from a firm, this should contain the initials of the person authorising (dictating) the letter and of the typist. Sometimes other symbols are included to help with identification, e.g. branch office number.

(b) In a *handwritten* letter a reference is not normally required unless this is quoted from some previous communication related to the subject of your letter. In this case it should be written as *your ref:* and positioned at the left-hand margin.

(c) Some printed letter heads have spaces for *"our ref"* and *"your ref"*. This is self-explanatory, but the writer's reference should always be placed at the left-hand margin.

Specimens:

Ref: RJW/LSW
Your Ref: ARM/JAY

Our Ref: CMS/SMD/16

The Date

(a) Present the date in the correct order – day, month and year.

(b) The only standard punctuation necessary in the date is a comma after the month.

(c) There is no full stop after endings used with day numbers such as 1st, 2nd, 3rd, 4th, etc.

Specimens:

15th October, 19——

17th June, 19——

The Receiver's Address

(a) The same punctuation rules apply here as for the writer's address.

(b) The name of the person (or his/her official title) should be included.

(c) This name and address is sometimes placed at the foot of the letter – on the left-hand margin – but the most common practice is to position it as indicated in the diagrams.

(d) The punctuation of courtesy titles, qualifications etc. has already been dealt with in the main section on punctuation (see "The Full Stop" on page 181).

Specimens:

The Sales Manager,
Weston Engineering Co. Ltd.,
Broadway,
MALVERN,
Wilts.
WL2 7SN

Miss W. Evans, M.A., B.Ed.,
26 Victoria Street,
WOKING,
Surrey.
ST7 9LD

The Salutation

(a) The standard beginning to a business letter is *Dear Sir*, but others are used in certain circumstances: *Dear Sirs* when the letter is addressed to a partnership; *Dear Madam*, whether a woman is single or married; *Mesdames* when a partnership consists of women only.

(b) The first letter of each word should begin with a capital letter.

(c) The salutation should be followed by a comma.

The Main Body of the Letter

This is the most important part of the letter because it contains the *message*. Bear in mind that effective communication should be as simple as possible. Therefore,

(a) Don't include any unnecessary information.
(b) Express yourself as concisely as possible.
(c) Start a new paragraph for each new point you wish to make.
(d) Conform to all standard punctuation and grammar rules.

NOTE: Many business letters fall easily into the framework of a three paragraph plan which can be generally summarised as:

Paragraph 1 Introduction: this can be on acknowledgement, a reference to previous communication, or any generally informative statement which introduces your main theme.

Paragraph 2. Specific information/facts/reasons.

Paragraph 3. Reference to further action/conclusion.

More detailed analysis of specific types of letters will be given in future sections on correspondence.

The Subscription (Complimentary Close)

(a) In most circumstances *Yours faithfully* should be used.
(b) The first word should begin with a capital letter, but the second should begin with a lower case letter.
(c) The subscription should be followed by a comma.
(d) *Yours sincerely* can be used if the recipient is known to the writer on a personal basis, or if it is desirable to dispense with formality.
(e) The subscription should be started at the middle of the page.

The Signature

(a) This should be the normal signature of the writer, and should not include any courtesy title or otherwise.
(b) A woman can indicate in brackets whether she is married or single e.g. (Miss; Mrs).

The Designation

This simply gives the official status of the writer and, if required, is best printed directly underneath the signature.

TASK TEN

(i) Write your own address in the space opposite, using the correct form, layout and punctuation for a business letter. (If four lines are not enough, draw extra lines above those shown.)	________ ________ ________ ________
(ii) Write today's date as it should be written in a business letter.	________

(iii) Give an example of a reference (you are sending the letter, one of your fellow students is the typist). ______________________

(iv) Give three standard forms of salutation. ______________________
____
____

(v) Write out the two main forms of subscription. ______________________
____

(vi) Give a specimen of how you would sign a business letter. ______________________

The diagram on p. 214 is a specimen of a complete handwritten business letter showing you the positioning of the main parts, and the overall structure. Study it carefully before you attempt the exercises which follow.

You will see that this letter conforms to the general paragraphing plan you were given earlier, and in the exercises which conclude this section you should aim to do the same.

EXERCISE

The following letter is complete except that it is not set out in letter form. All punctuation is correct. A new paragraph is indicated by double oblique lines (//). Rewrite the complete letter, presenting it on plain paper and using the correct layout.

23 Rectory Drive, HENTON, Lancs LE4 12PF 28th June, 19—. The Sales Manager, Northern Carpets Ltd., 174-176 Henshot Lane, BAGGINGTON, Yorks, YK8 9BK Dear Sir,// I have seen your advertisements in "The Sunday Times Magazine" for floor coverings suitable for use on concrete floors, and feel that they could be useful in a workshop/extension I am building on to my property. //It would be helpful if you could send me samples showing your range of suitable coverings and, if one is available, a pattern card of the designs in which they are supplied.//We hope to be ready to lay the covering within a month, and should therefore be grateful to receive the samples and pattern-card as soon as possible. Yours faithfully, William Turson.

EXERCISE

As part of an earlier task you were asked to find the addresses of a number of companies. Write a letter suitable for sending to the public relations officer of one of these companies, asking for any available printed material which gives information about the history and present activities of the organisation. You should explain that you need the information in order to complete an assignment as part of your present course, and point out *tactfully* that you would like to receive any such information as quickly as possible. Use your home address for the heading. Your final letter should be ready for posting.

17, Wolfstan Way,
HENGLEFORD,
Yorkshire.
YK4 6LD

Your ref: DAS/PC/BEC

23rd August, 1979.

The Managing Editor,
Macdonald and Evans Ltd.,
Estover Road,
PLYMOUTH,
Devon.
PL6 7PZ

Dear Sir,

Thank you for your recent letter concerning the proposed extension of the "Human Relations" textbook from twenty to twenty-five chapters.

I can now confirm that the additional manuscript will be submitted before September 30th, and that its length will be approximately fifteen thousand words.

As it will be necessary to make amendments to the original index, I should be grateful for your observations on how this can most easily be done.

Yours faithfully,

C.E. Stafford

EXERCISE

Using any suitable newspaper or magazine, find an advertisement which interests you for goods which can be obtained by mail-order. Write a letter ordering the goods you require and ask for them to be sent C.O.D. Remember that any such order must be accurate and detailed in order to avoid the wrong goods being delivered. Use your own address for the heading. Your letter should be complete and ready to send.

UNIT V

Achievement Checklist
On completion of this unit you should be able to:

- *** Describe the structure of a typical organisation from the public and private sectors:**
- *** Produce an organisation chart for an organisation;**
- *** Appreciate the nature of a percentage and its relationship to fractions and decimals;**
- *** Find one quantity as a percentage of another;**
- *** Find a percentage of a given quantity;**
- *** Express profit or loss as a percentage of cost and selling price;**
- *** Construct a percentage bar chart;**
- *** Appreciate the importance of the essay as a form of communication;**
- *** Use essay plans effectively;**
- *** Construct logical paragraphs;**
- *** Plan, organise and write an essay;**
- *** Use reported speech, and convert direct speech into reported speech;**
- *** Summarise passages effectively;**
- *** Identify and understand common errors;**
- *** Understand basic business terms.**

SECTION I

THE STRUCTURES OF ORGANISATIONS

So far we have examined different kinds of organisations from the point of view of their ownership and objectives. We must now examine how different organisations are structured so that they can achieve those objectives as efficiently as possible.

In a complex modern society people specialise in the kind of work they do and even within some specialist areas the work is broken down into small tasks for individual employees. This division of labour is usually explained by reference to industrial conveyor-belt systems whereby each person is responsible for the completion of a small part of the end-product. It is sometimes mistakenly assumed that the division of labour applies only to productive processes, whereas in fact it applies equally to "non-productive" processes such as the administration of the organisation. Indeed it is generally true to say that the larger the organisation the greater the degree of specialisation.

In a sole proprietorship the bulk of all the work falls on one man and although he may have assistance from employees and employ the services of independent specialists such as accountants, he is ultimately responsible for all the administration and organisation of his business. It is not surprising, therefore, that most organisations of this type operate on a small scale and find such things as V.A.T. particularly difficult to cope with. You learnt in Unit II that one of the reasons for a sole owner to take a partner was to share this burden of responsibility and to allow a degree of specialisation to be undertaken. For example, in a retail outlet one partner might be responsible for ordering and controlling stock whilst the other takes on the job of keeping the accounts.

The *scale* of operations plays an important part of deciding the extent of specialisation that can, and does, take place. A small-scale firm has neither the staff, capital or perhaps the need to share the work to any great extent whereas in a large-scale firm one or two people could not possibly cope with the volume of work let alone be sufficiently expert in all its various aspects. As a result the tendency is to divide the work into units and make them the responsibility of experts. In the case of a large public manufacturing company this division might be as shown in the diagram below.

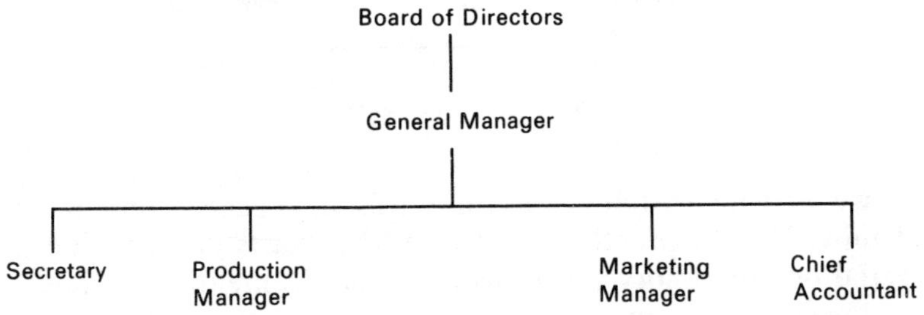

The board of directors is, of course, elected by the owners to represent their interests and in turn the directors have appointed a general manager to ensure that the organisation runs smoothly on a day-to-day basis. This person will almost certainly be well qualified but his main responsibility is to see that the board's policy is put into action. To help him do this, the work of the organisation has been divided into four broad areas (as indicated in the diagram above, and these could be sub-divided yet again to show the different areas of responsibility in more detail (see the diagram below).

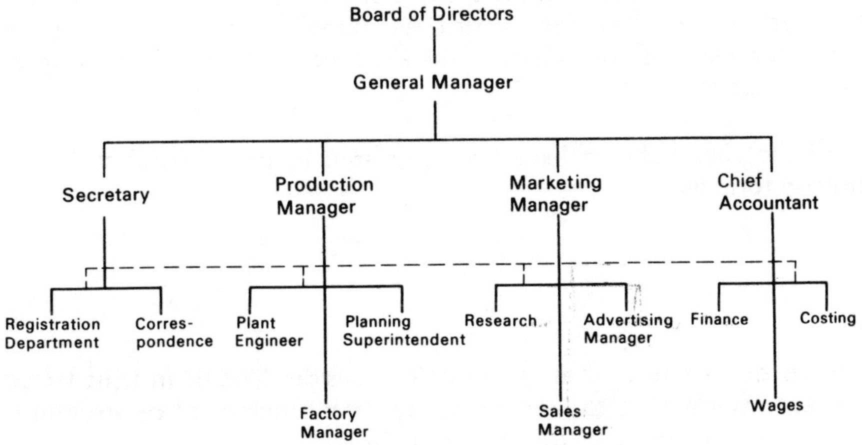

In the chart the broken line illustrates the chief accountant's *functional* responsibility for accounting work in all departments. A *vertical* organisation chart such as this shows the lines of authority within an organisation very well. In the above chart we can see clearly that the sales manager is responsible to the marketing manager who is responsible to the general manager who is responsible to the board.

It would be possible to take each of the sub-divisions within the four major groupings and produce an even more detailed chart of the structure of the organisation. For example, the sales manager might be responsible for four salesmen, two clerks and a typist in which case the manager might draw up a chart for his own department as shown in the diagram below.

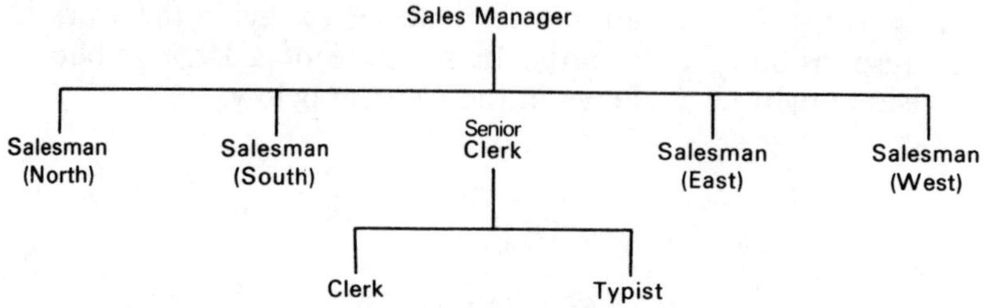

Obviously if we extended each section like this an organisation chart would become very large and unwieldy. In practice, therefore, the charts do not often go beyond the level of managerial or supervisory positions although, as mentioned above, line managers (and those of lower status) may produce charts for their own individual areas of responsibility. In fact such charts can be very useful for showing each member of staff to whom he is responsible and who is responsible to him and are often incorporated in staff handbooks for this very reason.

In many cases the structures of different organisations are similar to one another as whatever their purpose they will have need of administration and accountants; most will be involved in marketing or advertising of some kind; if it is a manufacturing concern it will need production personnel and so on.

So far we have used an imaginery organisation in the charts but if you refer back to Unit III, Section I (p. 90) you will see a chart outlining the structure of a real organisation – the South Western Electricity Board. As you will notice there is quite a similarity between it and our imaginery organisation and similarities of this sort will appear in other charts you encounter.

NOTE: All the charts shown have been prepared in the Vertical style which is the most common form used.

EXERCISE

If you carried out a study of an organisation (besides SWEB) in Unit III you will have sufficient information to prepare an organisation chart of its structure. If so, draw up the chart and add it to your file for Unit III.

TASK ONE

(i) In the space provided underneath the diagram below present the information contained in the horizontal organisation chart in vertical form indicating the functional responsibilities of the chief accountant and the personnel manager.

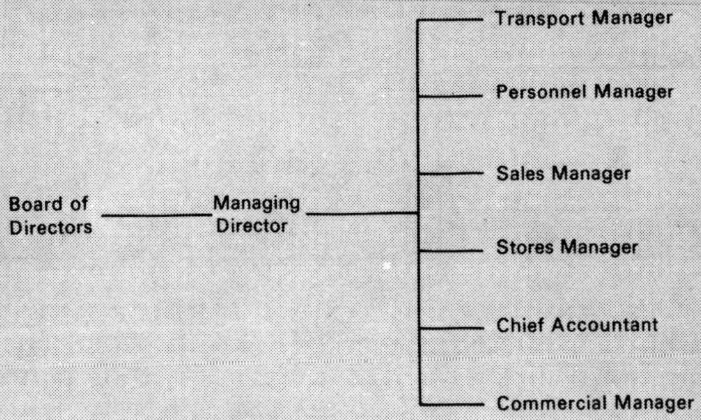

(ii) The people on the chart in the previous Task are listed below. Against each one make notes on what you think are their main duties and responsibilities.

Board of directors ____________________

____

Managing director ____________________

____

Transport manager ____________________

____

Personnel manager____________________

____

Sales manager____________________

____

Stores manager____________________

____

Chief accountant ____________________

____

Commercial manager ____________________

____

(iii) A large manufacturing organisation divides its sales and distribution activities into districts, each under the control of a sales manager. The northern district is typical and is sub-divided into four sales areas each being the responsibility of a representative. They are supported by the district office under the control of an office manager who is directly responsible to the district sales manager. In addition to the manager the office is staffed by an assistant office manager, a ledger clerk, a credit control clerk, an invoice typist and a shorthand typist. The office manager is also responsible for the district warehouse which is staffed by a foreman, an assistant foreman and five warehousemen. Complete the organisation chart in the diagram below for the district.

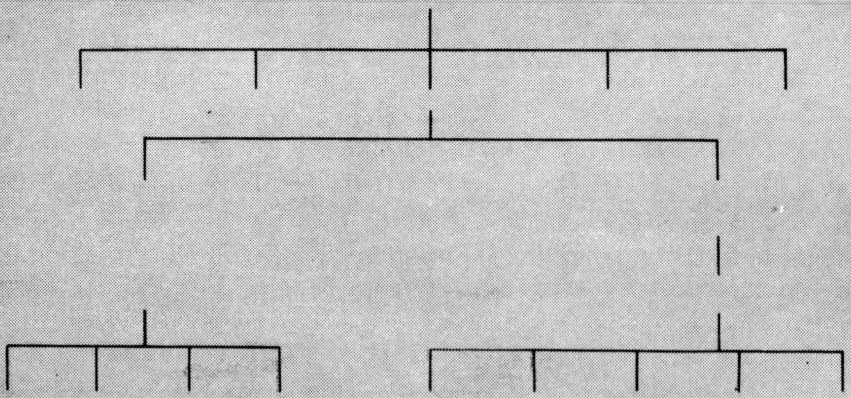

(iv) **Obtain as much information as possible about the structure of your college and present it below as a vertical organisation chart.**

SECTION II

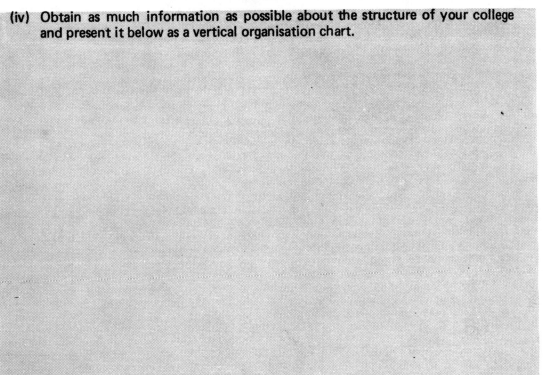

PERCENTAGES : THEIR NATURE

To be able to use *percentages* correctly is important. In business and commerce percentages occur in many different situations and so a thorough understanding is essential.

A percentage is a fraction whose denominator is 100 and has therefore a special relationship with proper fractions and decimal fractions. The fact that a percentage is a fraction of 100 can be easily remembered from the percentage symbol. The sign, %, can be though of as 100 with the zeros placed on each side of the one and twisted slightly. Thus 15% means $\frac{15}{100}$ or is 15 parts out of 100.

Percentages, Fractions and Decimals

The relationship between percentages, fractions and ecimales is an important one. It is useful to be able to change from one form to another in many calculations, the change often making the calculation easier. The process of change is the same as that for changing the denominator in a fraction to 100 and making a change of the same degree in the numerator. Thus ½ becomes $\frac{50}{100}$ 2 is increased 50 times to give 100 and the 1 is increased by the same degree (50). Similarly ¾ becomes $\frac{75}{100}$ when 4 is increased 25 times to give 100 with 3 being increased by the same amount to give 75. This is relatively easy with simple, familiar fractions but with fractions such as $\frac{5}{16}$ the degree to which the denominator and numerator are increased is not immediately apparent. In this situation the fraction is changed to a percentage by multiplying the fraction by 100. For example:

(a) Express $\frac{5}{16}$ as a percentage

$$\frac{5}{{}_4\cancel{16}} \times \frac{\cancel{100}^{25}}{1}$$

Step 1 - Multiply the fraction by $\frac{100}{1}$

Step 2 - Simplify

$$= \frac{125}{4}$$

$$= 31\tfrac{1}{4}\%$$

(b) Express $\frac{2}{3}$ as a percentage

$$\frac{2}{3} \times \frac{100}{1}$$

Step 1 - Multiply the fraction by $\frac{100}{1}$

Step 2 - Simplify

$$= \frac{200}{3}$$

$$= 66\tfrac{2}{3}\%$$

In each example the number of times the denominator is contained in 100 is being found and the numerator is increased by that amount.

TASK ONE

(i) Express the following fractions as percentages

(a) ¼ = 25%

(b) ¾ =

(c) $\frac{1}{5}$ =

(d) $\frac{3}{5}$ =

(e) $\frac{4}{5}$ =

(f) $\frac{1}{10}$ =

(g) $\frac{3}{10}$ =

(h) $\frac{7}{10}$ =

(i) $\frac{9}{10}$ =

(j) $\frac{1}{20}$ =

(k) $\frac{3}{20}$ =

(l) $\frac{19}{20}$ =

(m) $\frac{1}{40}$ =

(n) $\frac{7}{40}$ =

(o) $\frac{11}{40}$ =

(p) $\frac{1}{50}$ =

(q) $\frac{17}{50}$ =

(r) $\frac{49}{50}$ =

(s) $\frac{1}{100}$ =

(t) $\frac{87}{100}$ =

(ii) Express the following fractions as percentages by multiplying by 100 and simplifying.

(a) $\frac{1}{3} \times \frac{100}{1} = \frac{100}{3}$ $= 33\frac{1}{3}\%$	(g) $\frac{7}{8}$	(l) $\frac{7}{12}$
(b) $\frac{1}{6}$	(h) $\frac{1}{16}$	(m) $\frac{11}{12}$
(c) $\frac{5}{6}$	(i) $\frac{3}{16}$	(n) $\frac{5}{9}$
(d) $\frac{1}{8}$	(j) $\frac{13}{16}$	(o) $\frac{6}{11}$
(e) $\frac{5}{8}$	(k) $\frac{1}{12}$	(p) $\frac{5}{32}$

It now follows that if it is necessary to turn a percentage to a fraction then the reverse procedure can be followed. For example:

(a) Express 40% as a fraction

$\frac{40}{100}$ Step 1 - Make the percentage a fraction of 100.

Step 2 - Simplify where possible (20 is common)

$= \frac{2}{5}$

(b) Express 37½% as a fraction

$\frac{37\frac{1}{2}}{100}$ Step 1 - Make the percentage a fraction of 100.

Step 2 - When the numerator is a mixed number change it to an improper fraction ($37\frac{1}{2} = \frac{75}{2}$).

$= \frac{75}{200}$ Step 3 - Multiply the denominator in Step 2 by 100.

$= \frac{3}{8}$ Step 4 - Simplify (25 is common).

TASK TWO

Change the following percentages to fractions, simplifying where possible.

(i) (a) 50% = $\frac{50}{100}$ = ½	(f) 60% =	(k) 12% =
(b) 25% =	(g) 90% =	(l) 52% =
(c) 75% =	(h) 35% =	(m) 84% =
(d) 20% =	(i) 45% =	(n) 38% =
(e) 40% =	(j) 95% =	(o) 97% =

(ii) (a) 12½% = $\frac{25}{200} = \frac{1}{8}$	(f) 2½% =
(b) 62½% =	(g) 82½% =
(c) 33 % =	(h) 22 % =
(d) 16 % =	(i) 6¼% =
(e) 18 % =	(j) 43¾% =

The change from a percentage to a decimal fraction and from a decimal fraction to a percentage are also achieved by multiplication and division. Firstly the decimal fraction is multiplied by 100 to give a percentage: thus 0.37 becomes 0.37 x 100 = 37% (move the decimal point two places from the left to the right). The percentage is divided by 100 to change it to a decimal, 68% becomes 0.68 (the decimal point moves 2 places from the right to the left).

TASK THREE

(i) Change the following percentages to decimals.

(a) 0.55 = 55%	(f) 0.625 =	(k) 0.0825 =
(b) 0.89 =	(g) 0.166 =	(l) 0.2025 =
(c) 0.1 =	(h) 0.105 =	(m) 0.5005 =
(d) 0.4 =	(i) 0.07 =	(n) 0.005 =
(e) 0.375 = 37.5% or 37½%	(j) 0.025 =	(o) 0.0075 =

(ii) Change the following decimals to percentages.

(a) 25%	(f) 76.25% =	(k) 6¼% =
(b) 16% =	(g) 8.75% =	(l) 42½% =
(c) 98% =	(h) 3.05% =	(m) 16⅔% =
(d) 62.5% =	(i) 0.5% =	(n) 8⅙% =
(e) 85.5% =	(j) 0.75% =	(o) ¼% =

OPERATIONS WITH PERCENTAGES

Finding a Percentage of a Given Quantity

When finding a percentage of any quantity the reasoning behind the calculation lies in the division of the quantity into 100 parts and finding the size or value of one part and then collecting together a number of these parts to give the required percentage.

This process is called the *unitary method*, since it revolves around the finding of one of something and then enlarging it. (The method can be applied in many situations without knowing that it is in fact being used.)

For example:

(a) Find 60% of 4 kg

$100\% = 4$ kg — Step 1 - The original quantity is called 100% and written down in that form.

$1\% = \frac{4}{100}$ kg — Step 2 - 1% is found by dividing both sides of the "equal" signs by 100 $\left(\frac{100}{100} = 1\right)$

$60\% = \frac{4 \times 6\not{0}}{10\not{0}}$ kg $= \frac{24}{10}$ — Step 3 - The required percentage is found by multiplying by the appropriate value (1 and $\frac{4}{100}$ by 60)

$= 2.4$ kg — Step 4 - Simplify

Thus 60% of 4 kg is 2.4 kg

This process is time consuming and under normal conditions Step 3 is written down directly and then simplified.

(b) Find 12½% of £160

$12\tfrac{1}{2}\% = \frac{£160}{100} \times 12\tfrac{1}{2}$ — Step 1 - Incorporating Steps 1 – 3 from example (a)

$= \frac{\not{160}^{\,\not{40}\,20}}{\not{100}_{\,4}} \times \frac{\not{25}^{\,1}}{\not{2}_{\,1}}$ — Step 2 - Simplify (12½% becomes $\frac{25}{2}$)

$= £20$

TASK FOUR

Find the values of the following:

(i) 75% of 600

$75\% = \frac{600}{100} \times 75$

=

(ii) 40% of 150

(iii) 20% of 45

(iv) 37½% of 240

$37\tfrac{1}{2}\% = \frac{240}{100} \times \frac{75}{2} \times 2$

=

(v) 33⅓% of 360

(vi) 25% of £36

(vii) 55% of £50

(vii) 6¼% of £96

(ix) 2½% of £20

(x) $16\frac{2}{3}$% of £33

(xi) 75% of 360g

(xii) 4% of 800 litres

(xiii) 87½% of 28 km

(xiv) $8\frac{1}{3}$% of 220 kg

(xv) 66% of 1 tonne (in kg)

TASK FIVE

The questions in this Task are similar to those in Task One.

(i) 20% of the work-force are clerical workers in a firm employing 620 people. How many is this?

(ii) 62½% of the orders received by a mail order company are processed and the goods dispatched within one week of receipt. If on one day 4,960 orders are received how many are dispatched in a week?

____

____

____

____

(iii) The cost of making a machine is £500. Of this 60% is labour, 25% materials and 15% overheads. Find the value of each element of the cost.

____

____

____

____

Expressing one value as a percentage of another

This aspect of work with percentages is of great importance since it enables comparisons to be made between two or more similar pieces of numerical information. For example, if two firms, making a similar product, have 60 and 400 people respectively working for them and the smaller employs 6 extra people and the larger employs 36 extra people, it is easy to say the larger has increased in size most. But this answer will be true if considered in *absolute* numbers. If, however, both firms had originally employed 100 people they would not increase their work-force by the same number if the same rates of recruïtment were used. These *relative* increases can be found by looking at the increases in percentage terms by expressing the extra workers as a percentage of the original number.

Using the unitary method the original number is expressed as 100% and the increase is found as follows:

$60 = 100\%$	Step 1	- Express 60 employees as equal to 100%
$1 = \frac{100}{60}\%$	Step 2	- Express 1 employee as a percentage by dividing both sides by 60
$6 = \frac{10\not{0}}{\not{6}\not{0}} \times \not{6}$	Step 3	- 6 employees is required as a percentage so multiply each side by 6.
Thus 6 employees = 10%	Step 4	- Simplify.

Once again this take a long time and can be easily shortened.

Using a 36 increase on 400 employees the percentage increase would be:

$\frac{36}{400}$ Step 1 - Make the number required as a percentage a fraction of the original number.

$9 \quad \frac{\cancel{36}}{\cancel{400}} \times 1\cancel{00}$ Step 2 - Multiply by 100 and simplify.

Thus 36 employees = 9%

Now it can be seen that the small firm has increased its work-force by a greater percentage than the large firm.

TASK SIX

Express the first quantity as a percentage of the second quantity.

(i) 25 and 50	(vi) 3p and 15p	(xi) £14.40 and £16.00
(ii) 5 and 20	(vii) £6 and £10	(xii) £7.20 and £9.00
(iii) 25 and 150	(viii) £10 and £16	(xiii) 55 cl and 250l
(iv) 12 and 32	(ix) £21 and £175	(xiv) 96 cm and 2m
(v) 24 and 144	(x) £12.50 and £50	(xv) 150 kg and 1 tonne

(NOTE: for (x) to (xiii) change both values to pence and for (xiv) to (xv) change the larger quantity to the same units as the smaller).

TASK SEVEN

(i) 700 men and 410 women were interviewed in a survey. What percentage of the total interviewed were men and what percentage were women?

(ii) A conference centre can accommodate 750 people; during three separate conferences 30 places were unused at one cenference, 54 at another and 39 at a third. What percentages were unused at each conference?

(iii) In a certain year an employer paid £16,000 in wages and £34,000 in other expenses. What percentage of *total* expenditure was in wages?

Percentage Changes

In the previous section one value has been expressed as a percentage of another. This is very important when considering a change in the value or size of a quantity. The change is often given in percentage form, as an increase or decrease on the original value. For example:

(a) The cost of manufacturing an article increases from £64 to £72. Find the change in cost as a percentage of the original manufacturing cost. The problem falls into parts: what is the actual increase and what would this have been if the original price were £100?

$$\begin{array}{r} £ \\ 72 \\ -\underline{64} \\ \underline{8} \end{array}$$

Step 1 - Find the increase (or decrease) in value (£72 - £64).

$$\frac{8 \times 100}{64}$$

Step 2 - Express the increase (£8) as a percentage of the original price (£64) and simplify.

$$\frac{100}{8} = 12\tfrac{1}{2}\%$$

(b) The same procedures are followed when there is a decrease. Thus, if the value of orders exported falls from £28,800 to £24,000, the percentage decrease will be:

£	
28,800	
- 24,000	Step 1 - Find the actual decrease (£28,800 - £24,000).
4,800	Step 2 - Express the decrease as a percentage of the original value and simplify.

$\frac{\not{4}\ \ 48\not{0}\not{0}}{\not{2}\not{8}8\not{0}\not{0}} \times 100$
$\not{2}\not{4}$
6

$= \frac{100}{6} = 16\frac{2}{3}\%$

TASK EIGHT

Find the percentage increase or decrease when:

(i) £108 becomes £135

£
135
-108
£27

$\frac{\not{3}\ \ \not{2}\not{7}}{\not{1}\not{0}\not{8}} \times 100$
$\not{1}\not{2}$ 4

$= \frac{100}{4} = 25\%$

(ii) 160m becomes 216m

(iii) 60 g becomes 57 g

(iv) 75m becomes 72m

(v) £3.20 increases to £3.40

(vi) £7.50 is reduced to £6.50

TASK NINE

(i) An assembly line worker increased his production from 48 units per day to 54 units per day. What percentage increase is this?

(ii) The revenue from selling 1 tonne of metal alloy falls from £2,500 to £2,400. What is the percentage decrease in revenue?

(iii) The wages paid by a company to its clerical workers is increased from £3,500 per week to £3,780 per week after a pay award. What percentage increase resulted from the pay award?

Changes in value may occur where the percentage change and the amount of change is known. From these the original value can be found, again using unitary method. For example:

(a) A salesman increases his sales by 5%. If this increase amounts to £1,040, what is value of his sales?

$5\% = £1{,}040$	Step 1 - Equate 5% to the sum given.
$1\% = \frac{£1{,}040}{5}$	Step 2 - Find the value of 1% (divide both sides by 5).
$100\% = \frac{£1040 \times \cancel{100}\ 20}{\cancel{5}\ 1}$	Step 3 - Multiply both sides by 100 and simplify.
$= £20{,}800$	

This can be shortened with ease, reducing the steps followed.

(b) 8% of a transport container contains 560 kg of a commodity. What is the total weight that may be carried.

The question is asking for 100% to be found when 8% is known.

$$\frac{\overset{70}{\cancel{560}} \times 100}{\cancel{8}} \text{ kg}$$ Step 1 - Divide the known quantity by the given percentage and multiply by 100

= 7,000 kg Step 2 - Simplify.

TASK TEN

Find the full value or quantity of which:

(i) 25% is 35

(ii) 75% is 60

(iii) 20% is 19 metres

(iv) 55% is 165 litres

(v) 39% is 468 kg

(vi) 84% is £420

Take special care with the fractions in the following.

(vii) 37½% is 48

(vii) $5\frac{5}{11}$% is £240

(ix) 6¼% is £25.50

(x) $66\frac{2}{3}$% is £39.80

(xi) $2\frac{1}{2}$% is 5.5 km

(xii) $16\frac{2}{3}$% is 48.6 kg

TASK ELEVEN

(i) 32% more employees are needed by a manufacturer to meet a large number of urgent orders. If 96 more people are employed what was the original number of employees?

(ii) A $6\frac{1}{4}$% increase in price adds £7.20 to the cost of an article. What did it cost before the increase?

(iii) The cost of manufacturing a product is reduced by 16% as the result of improved methods. If this represents a saving of £25 on one article, what did each previously cost?

Finally, percentage changes may occur where the size is known after the percentage change has taken place but not the original value. The solution to this sort of problem often causes difficulty because the relationship between the size after the change is not considered correctly in percentage form.

Suppose, say, the price of an article after a 20% increase is £15, and the original price is required.

The price before the increase is *always* 100% so the new price is 100% plus the percentage increase and is therefore 100% + 20% = 120%. It is this concept that causes problems: having a percentage greater than 100. But percentages are only another type of fraction and they can be greater than one when mixed numbers are used.

(a) The price of an article is £15 after a 20% increase. Find the original value.

Using the unitary method, the original price can be found as follows.

$120\% = £15$

Step 1 - The new value expressed as a percentage (120%) is made equal to the value.

$1\% = \frac{15}{120}$

Step 2 - 1 % is found by dividing each side by 120.

$100\% = £\frac{\cancel{15}^{5} \times \cancel{100}^{5}}{\cancel{120}_{\cancel{4}\,2}}$

Step 3 - The original value, 100%, is found by multiplying and simplifying.

$= \frac{£25}{2} = £12.50$

(b) A 12% increase in weight gives a total weight of 448 kg. What is the original weight?

Following the shortened method:

$112\% = 448$ kg

Step 1 - The new weight is expressed as a percentage (100 + 12).

$100\% = \frac{\cancel{448}^{4}}{1\cancel{12}} \times 100$ kg

Step 2 - Find 1% by dividing by 112 and then 100% by multiplying.

$= 400$ kg

Step 3 - Simplify.

Similar procedures are adopted when there is a decrease in size. Now the new percentage will be less than 100%.

(c) 10% is deducted from the price of goods in a sale. What is the original price of goods sold for £27?

$90\% = £27$

Step 1 - The new price is expressed as a percentage (100 *minus* 10 = 90%).

$100\% = \frac{\cancel{27}^{3}}{\cancel{90}} \times 10\cancel{0}$

Step 2 - Find 1% by dividing by 90 and then 100% by multiplying. Simplify.

$= £30$

TASK TWELVE

Find the original values if

(i) 25% increase gives 375 g

(ii) 20% decrease gives 40 litres

(iii) 5% decrease gives 19 km

(iv) 15% increase gives £10.35

(v) 30% decrease gives £3.15

(vi) 37½% increase gives £550.

(vii) $33\frac{1}{3}$% increase give £26.40

(viii) 6¼% decrease gives £7.50

(ix) 2½% decrease gives 97½p

(x) 11¼% decrease gives £44.50

TASK THIRTEEN

(i) The market value of a factory site increases by 21% to £3,025,000. What was its value before the increase?

(ii) After an advertising campaign a company increased its orders over the previous month by 14% to 1,026. How many orders were there in the previous month?

(iii) In a sale the price of an article is reduced by 30% to £3.15. How much was it reduced?

EXERCISE

(a) A company's sales fell by £2,250 from £14,600 between one month and the next. What was the percentage decrease?

(b) The operatives in a factory receive an increase of 7½% on their hourly rate of £1.40. What is the new rate of pay?

(c) 27½% of the cost of new machinery has to be paid by the purchaser before it can be installed. If the manufacturer received £2,200, how much does the machinery cost?

(d) The capital of a partnership is £87,500 and increased by 16%. What is the new capital?

(e) The fixed assets of R.U. Busy increase from £8,800 to £9,350 and the current assets increase from £2,300 to £3,415. Find the percentage increase in fixed assets and the percentage increase in total assets.

COST PRICE AND SELLING PRICE

Gross Profit and Gross Loss

This aspect of percentages is largely concerned with the *cost price* and the *selling price* of goods. In Unit I the difference between the cost price and the selling price was defined as the *gross profit* when the selling price exceeds the cost price and *gross loss* when the cost price is the greater.

The profit can easily be expressed in percentage form, based upon both the cost price and the selling price. Traditionally percentage profit (or loss) is calculated on the cost price rather than selling price because logically an article is bought and profit added before it is sold. However, in business the gross profit is related to selling price since it is easier to estimate gross profits over any length of time, on the basis of sales, that is on *turnover.*

In the following examples, profit or loss is based upon the cost price and the methods employed are the same as those in previous sections of this Unit. Only the applications are different. For example:

(a) An article costs £30 and is sold for £34.50. Find the percentage profit.

£
34.50
\- 30.00
4.50

Step 1 - Find the gross profit (selling price less cost price).

% profit $\frac{4.50}{30.00} \times 100$

Step 2 Express the profit as a percentage of the cost price by making it a fraction of cost price and multiplying by 100.

$15\ \frac{\cancel{450}}{\cancel{3000}} \times \cancel{100}$

= 15%

Step 3 - Simplify (remove the decimal point by multiplying denominator and numerator by 100).

(b) A chair cost £50 and is sold at a profit of 26%. Find the selling price.

Profit = £ $\frac{\cancel{50}}{\cancel{100}_{\ \cancel{2}}} \times \cancel{26}^{13}$

= £13

Step 1 - Given the cost price is equal to 100% find profit by dividing cost by 100 and multiplying by the required percentage. Simplify.

Selling price = £50 + £13
= £63

Step 2 - Add the profit to the cost price.

(c) A retailer makes a 40% profit when he sells a commodity for £21 per tonne. What was the cost price per tonne?

Step 1 - The selling price is 140% (cost price + profit in percentage form) and is made equal to the selling price.

Cost price = £ $\frac{\cancel{21}^{\,3}}{\cancel{140}_{\ \cancel{2}}} \times \cancel{100}^{5}$

= £15

Step 2 - Find the cost price (100%) when 140% is given by dividing selling price by 140 and multiplying by 100.

TASK FOURTEEN

Find the profit or loss per cent when

	(i) Cost price £45, selling price £54	(ii) Cost price £1.00 loss 20p
	__________	__________
profit =	__________	__________
% profit =	__________	__________
	__________	__________

(iii) Cost price £4.50, selling price £4.00

(iv) Cost price £800, selling price £920

(v) Cost price 10p, profit 2½p

(vi) Selling price 75p, gain 25p

TASK FIFTEEN

Find the selling price when

(i) Cost price £20, profit 15%

profit = $\frac{£20}{100}$ x 15

=

selling price =

(ii) Cost price £64, loss 25%

(iii) Cost price £6.25, profit 20%

(iv) Cost price £840, profit 45%

(v) Cost price £9.60, less $8\frac{1}{3}$%

(vi) Cost price £4.60, loss $33\frac{1}{3}$%

TASK SIXTEEN

Find the cost price if

(i) Selling price is £26

profit is 3.50

cost price = £ ____

(ii) Selling price is £18.55

loss is 3.45

cost price = £ ____

(iii) Selling price £160, loss 20%

cost price = $£\frac{160}{80} \times 100$

=

(iv) Selling price £56, profit 12%

cost price = $£\frac{56}{112} \times 100$

=

(v) Selling price £81, loss 10%

(vi) Selling price £1.05, profit 40%

(vii) Selling price £52, profit $8\frac{1}{3}$%

(viii) Selling price £9.75, loss 2½%

EXERCISE

(a) Find the percentage profit when
- (i) Selling price = £330 and profit is £45
- (ii) Cost price is £2.25 and selling price is £2.75
- (iii) Cost price is 37½p and selling price is 42½p
- (iv) Cost price is £15.75 and profit is £2.25

(b) Find the selling price when
- (i) Cost price is £175, profit of 15%
- (ii) Cost price is £18.75, loss of 12½%
- (iii) Cost price is £9.81, profit of 11¼%
- (iv) Cost price is £6.50, profit of 16¼%

(c) Find the cost price when
- (i) Selling price is £365, loss of 27%
- (ii) Selling price is £312, profit of 4%
- (iii) Selling price is £15.80, profit of 5 %
- (iv) Selling price is 82½p, loss of 12%

(d) (i) A retailer buys an article for £3.50 and sells it for £4.20. What percentage is added to the cost? Find the profit as a percentage of selling price.
(ii) Men's shirts are bought for £8.00 and sold for £9.80. Find the profit as a percentage of the cost and of the selling price.

(e) (i) The price of a car is increased by a distributor by 7½% from £2,960 to give its selling price. Find the cost to the customer.
(ii) A camera costs £18 and is sold for a profit of 30% on the cost price. Find the selling price.

(f) (i) An article is sold for £52.50 at a profit of 5%. How much did it cost?
(ii) A plot of building land is sold for £1,152, which represents a 20% profit on its cost. What was the cost price?

Selling Price and Net Profit

The previous section dealt with gross profit (or gross loss) but in any selling operation expenses must be taken into account and these when removed from gross profit will give *net profit* (or net loss).

Once more the calculations involve an application of a basic percentage operation. Net profit, in percentage form, is always based upon selling and thus gives an immediate indication of profits being earned. For example:

An article costs £20 and the expenses involved in selling it at a net profit of 12½% are £8. Find the selling price.

Cost + expenses = 100 − 12½
= 87½%

Step 1 - If selling price is 100% and net profit is 12½%, express the cost price plus expenses as a percentage.

(£20 + £8)
87½% = £28

Step 2 - Add the cost to expenses and make equal to the percentage from Step 1.

$$\text{Selling price} = £\frac{28}{87\frac{1}{2}} \times 100$$

Step 3 - Find the selling price (100%).

$$= \frac{{}^{4}\cancel{28} \times {}^{4}\cancel{100} \times 2}{\cancel{175}\,\cancel{7}_{\,1}}$$

Step 4 - Simplify.

= £32

TASK SEVENTEEN

Calculate the selling price when
(i) Cost price is £32, operating expenses £13, net profit 10%

Selling price = (100 − 10)%
= 90%

Cost price + expenses
= £32 + £13
= £45

$$\text{Selling price} = \frac{£45}{90} \times 100$$

= £

(ii) Cost price is £120, operating expenses £70, net profit = 5%

(iii) Cost price is £135, operating expenses £90, net profit = $16\frac{2}{3}$%

(iv) Cost price is £1.92, operating expenses £1.08, net profit = 20%

(v) Cost price is £2.50, operating expenses £0.50, net profit = 33 %

EXERCISE

(a) Merchandise is sold at a net profit of 12½%. If it costs £630 and selling expenses amount to £140, what will be the selling price?

(b) A retailer bought 500 articles for 34p and his selling expenses amount to £60 for the consignment. At what price does he sell each article to give a net profit of 8%?

(c) Goods cost a wholesaler £180. His operating expenses are 30% of the selling price and his net profit is 10% of the selling price. What is the selling price of the goods purchased by the wholesaler?

(d) A retailer buys pens for £8.40 per dozen and sells them at a net profit of 18%. If his selling expenses are 12% of the selling price how much does he charge for each pen?

SUPPLEMENTARY WORK

Unit III dealt with diagrammatic presentation and the bar charts illustrated are not suitable for making meaningful comparisons since the totals and components making up the totals cannot be easily related. However, percentages enable comparisons to be made very easily, thus if totals can be reduced to percentages then comparisons between totals can be made usually using a *percentage bar chart.* This chart is drawn in the same way as the component bar chart. The whole rectangle represents the total and it is sub-divided to show the components in the same proportions as the components making up the total. The whole rectangle now represents 100% and each component is percentage of the whole. For example:

The information contained in the table appears in Unit III as a component bar chart. The sales recorded in the three departments of a shop selling shoes are drawn below as a percentage bar chart:

Sales in £000s

Year	*Women's*	*Men's*	*Children's*	*Total*
1975	32	26	21	79
1975	41	34	29	104
1977	55	40	36	131

Step 1: The sales in each department are found as a percentage of total sales for the year. Thus in 1975 Women's accounted for $\frac{32}{79} \times 100 = 40.5\%$

Men's accounted for $\frac{26}{79} \times 100 = 32.9\%$

and Children's accounted for $\frac{21}{79} \times 100 = 26.6\%$

The table now appears as:

Percentage of Sales

Year	*Women's*	*Men's*	*Children's*
1975	40.5	32.9	26.6
1976	39.4	32.7	27.9
1977	42.0	30.5	27.5

Step 2: The total sales for each year are represented first by drawing rectangles whose height represents 100%.

Step 3: Each rectangle is sub-divided to illustrate each component.

Step 4: The axes are labelled, a title given and a key to the components added (see the diagram on page 243.

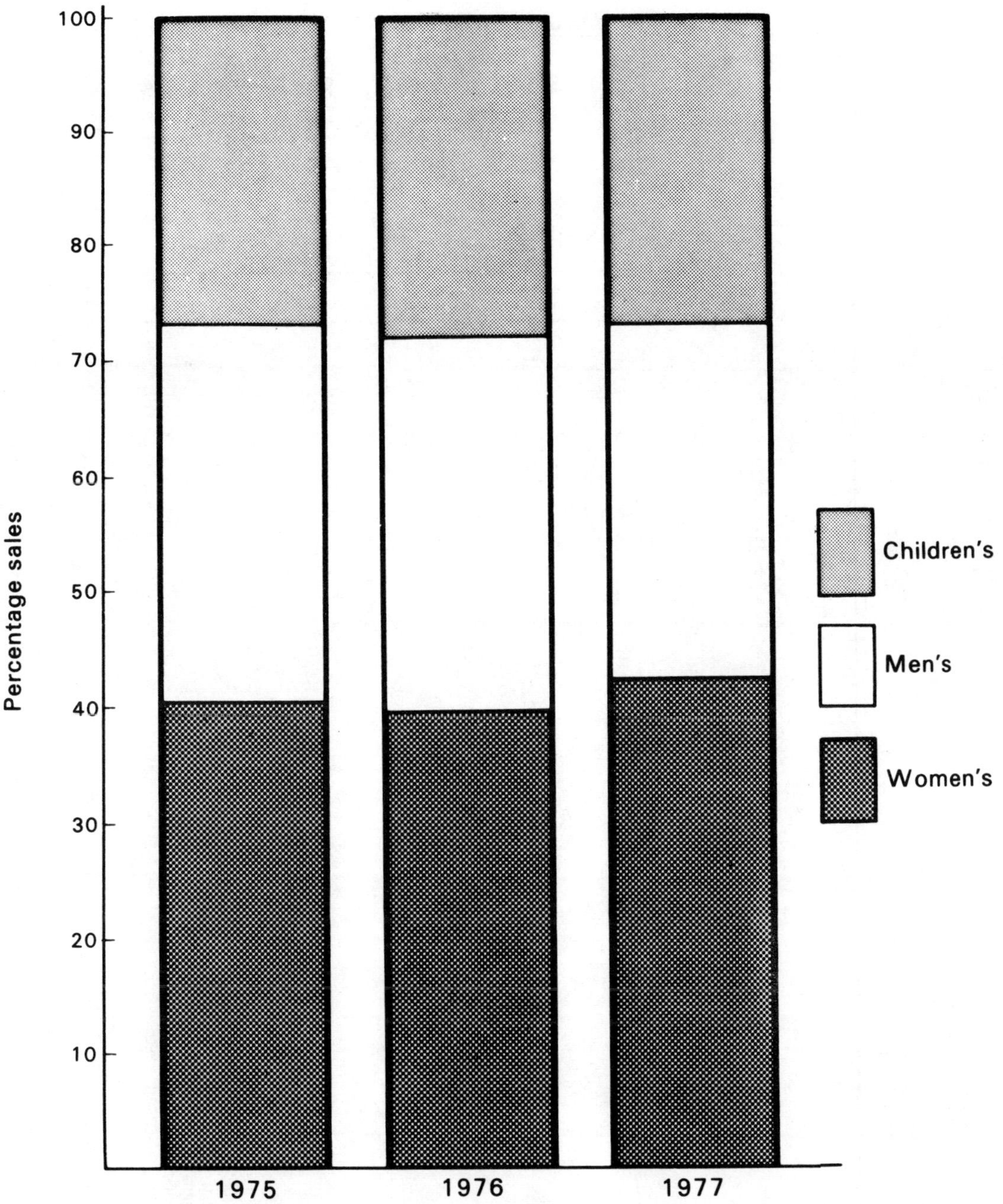

TASK EIGHTEEN

(i) Draw a percentage bar chart to illustrate the sales of three companies comprising a group producing electrical components, during three consecutive months.

Production (000s)

Company	*May* No	%	*June* No	%	*July* No	%
X	15		18		17	
Y	18		18		24	
Z	20		28		32	

(ii) Compare the costs of production and revenue from selling 1 tonne of steel in the years shown below.

	This year £	%	*Last year* £	%
Revenue per tonne	5,000	100	5,200	100
Costs:				
Materials	1,500		1,200	
Overheads	1,000		1,100	
Labour	2,200		2,800	
Profit	300		100	

EXERCISE

(a) Use a percentage bar chart to show the value of sales of computer equipment in three major sales areas in each quarter of the year shown.

	Sales in £000s			
	1st Qtr.	*2nd Qtr.*	*3rd Qtr.*	*4th Qtr.*
Home sales	39.0	30.0	57.5	40.5
North American sales	14.5	13.5	16.0	15.0
European sales	17.5	16.0	19.0	17.5

(b) Compare the authorised share capital for the Talk and Chalk Co. Ltd. with the issued share capital by means of a percentage bar chart.

Authorised capital:
From Ordinary shares £80,000
From Preference shares £20,000

Issued capital:
Ordinary Shares £65,000
Preference shares £15,000

Pie charts may also be constructed using percentages in the calculation. Each component is first expressed as a percentage of the total and that percentage of 360° is found (1% = 3.6°). For example:

The manufacturing expenses of the Rochub Fishing Tackle Company have shown that for every £1 their costs are:

Labour 64p
Rent 10p
Power 8p
Insurance and Tax 8p
Depreciation 10p

Step 1: Express each component as a percentage

Labour $\frac{64}{100} \times 100 = 64\%$

Rent $\frac{10}{100} \times 100 = 10\%$

Power = 8%

Insurance and Tax = 8%

Depreciation = 10%

Step 2: Find the given percentage for each component of 360°

Labour $\frac{64}{100} \times 360 = 230.4^{\circ}$

Rent $\frac{10}{100} \times 360 = 36^{\circ}$

Power = 28.8°

Insurance and Tax = 28.8°

Depreciation = 36°

Step 3: Draw the pie chart (see diagram on page 247).

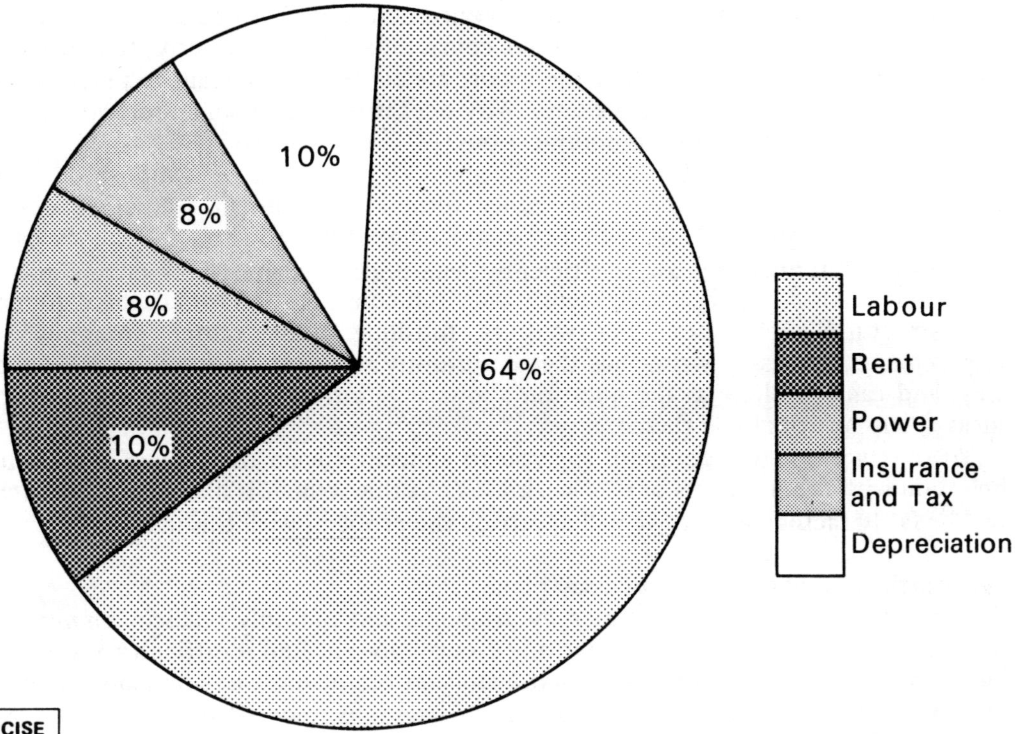

EXERCISE

(a) The net sales of a manufacturer are made up of 60% for cost of materials, 30% expenses and 10% profit. Illustrate using a pie chart.

(b) The expenses likely in the planning stages for marketing a new product are estimated by a manufacturer to be

Wages £2,000 Materials £4,000 Overheads £1,200

Express each of these as a percentage and then represent the expenses as a pie chart.

(c) (i) Using the balance sheet for Slow and Easy (see p. 113) illustrate the fixed and current assets by means of percentage bar charts.
(ii) Compare the current assets of Slow and Easy (see p. 113) with the current assets of Chalk and Talk (see p. 115) using pie charts.

SECTION III

WHY ESSAYS?

Many students regard essay writing as a necessary evil which teachers and lecturers impose upon them in order to make life more difficult. It is not until you understand *why* the essay is such a popular form of written communication that you will be able to approach the task with confidence. As a student concerned with "business" themes you might wonder what place the essay has in your course of studies. Obviously, the business letter the memorandum, the notice and the report are all directly relevant to practical working situations – but what use is the essay? Why does it form such an important part of most examinations in English and Communications?

The answer is simple: the essay is the most *flexible* type of composition in written English. This is because it can be either formal or informal, factual or descriptive, informative or emotive. This flexibility enables the writer to show that he/she can select information carefully and use it efficiently; can organise material effectively into related parts; and can use language competently with full consideration for accepted grammatical and structural techniques. As well as fulfilling these rather pompous-sounding requirements, the essay writer has the opportunity to be interesting in a varied and lively way, and can – as long as the question allows it – introduce personal opinions and new ideas to support the basic theme.

To start with, it will be useful for you to concentrate on the type of essay which can help you with other aspects of this workbook. At this stage it is likely that any such essay will be fairly factual, and so we will approach the problem with this in mind.

Is it worth wasting time with an essay plan?

This question is raised many times by students, and the only realistic answer is that it depends on how good you are at writing essays! Do you find it difficult to start? Do you have difficulty in controlling the length? Do you often miss out some important points? Do you find it difficult to know how many paragraphs to use? Do you "dry up" halfway through? Do you repeat yourself? Do you run out of time? Do you find it difficult to write a conclusion?

All these "Do you...?" problems can be solved if you have a logical and clear essay *plan* on which to base your final piece of work. The time you need to devote to this plan, and the detail in which it must be written, will decrease as you become more used to keeping your essays under control. The first thing to understand is that any essay will conform to a standard "shape" or structure. This means that it will have

(a) an *introduction,*
(b) a *main body* or *development* section, and
(c) a *conclusion.*

If you think back to Unit III you will remember that you spent some time studying the techniques of note making, and concentrated on a particular method of presentation. It is now time for you to extend the use of this knowledge and apply it to a new situation. It is this sort of *adaptability* which could be very useful to you in a working situation, and will show your employer that you are not limited in the type of problems you can cope with.

TASK ONE

Glance back over the section in Unit III on note making, and refresh your memory on the method of presentation, the layout and the visual pattern on the page. Then compare it with this simple outline for an essay plan.

TITLE

1. INTRODUCTION
2. MAIN BODY
   (a) Paragraph
   (b) Paragraph
   (c) Paragraph
3. CONCLUSION

As you will have seen, the two layouts are identical except that the essay plan has *general* sub-headings rather than specific ones.

To show you how this type of essay plan works, the following specimen deals with an essay based on one aspect of the retail trade — hire purchase. The actual essay question is:

"What are the advantages of hire purchase as a form of consumer credit?"

Plan

THE ADVANTAGES OF HIRE PURCHASE

1. INTRODUCTION
   Hire purchase: popular form of consumer credit; not only advantageous to the consumer — also to other commercial agencies.

2. MAIN BODY
   (a) The Consumer
      (i) can possess goods before owning them
      (ii) spreads payments over period
      (iii) regular payments can be monthly or weekly
      (v) can improve a family's standard of living
   (b) The Retailer
      (i) increases turnover
      (ii) can increase profits
      (iii) helps him to compete with opposition
   (c) The Manufacturer
      (i) sales of products rise
      (ii) this can lead to increased production, and
      (iii) better production systems, therefore
      (iv) lower units-costs
   (d) The Financier
      (i) very rewarding
      (ii) the repayments system effectively increases the nominal interest rate, therefore more profits
   (e) The General Community
      (i) keeps demand high, which sustains high employment
      (ii) this leads to increased prosperity
      (iii) consequent increased production, decreased unit costs and competition between retailers *can* lead to reduced prices

3. CONCLUSION

Not true to claim that there are no disadvantages to H.P. but over-all benefits make it important part of advanced economy.

This particular plan shows one way of approaching such an essay. The introductory section indicates the type of approach the writer is going to use, by bringing in the idea that hire purchase can be advantageous to a number of separate interest groups. The main body of the essay is divided up into a logical consideration of these separate interests, and each paragraph is given a specific title in order to identify the theme. The conclusion rounds off the essay by emphasising that the writer has concentrated on one aspect of the subject (the advantages), and putting hire purchase into its true context as part of a complex economic system.

NOTE: Although an essay *plan* can be arranged under definite sub-headings, *these should not appear in the final essay.*

A carefully constructed essay plan can, then, help you decide on the following things:

(a) the scope of the essay (i.e. the *limit* of the information you include, which is often made clear in the question);
(b) the length of the essay;
(c) the structure of the essay;
(d) the general subject of each paragraph;
(e) the specific content of each paragraph;

It will also help you to avoid running out of time, "drying up" halfway through, missing out important points and repeating yourself.

EXERCISE

Draw up a suitable essay plan for this title:

"What kinds of organisation exist in the private sector of the economy, and what are their chief characteristics?"

You should base you plan entirely on the information you have dealt with in previous units, and present it in the correct form.

What is a paragraph?

Another question you might ask is "When do I start a new paragraph?" Both these questions are really concerned with the same problem. It is essential for you to understand the basic function and purpose of paragraphs before you can use them properly. You have done much work in previous units on sentence structure, and this will help you with your paragraph structure. For our purposes, the most useful definition of a paragraph is:

A paragraph is the full and logical development of a single idea.

Although this indicates the simplest use of a paragraph, it is the most practical point from which we can start. Assuming, then, that you wish to write a paragraph on one aspect of a general theme, you must have some statement within that paragraph which explains clearly what you are talking about. Such a statement is often referred to as the *topic sentence.* For example, look at this short paragraph:

> Everard Wilson attends the College of Further Education on Thursdays. He is studying for the Business Education Council General Certificate. The course includes such areas of study as People and Communications, Calculations, The World of Work, Elements of Data Processing and Retailing. If he completes the course successfully, he hopes to enrol for a National Certificate course.

The first sentence gives an indication of the general theme. This is the topic sentence. The subsequent sentences give more specific information about the situation. You should be aware of how the paragraph is arranged because it is important that ideas should be presented in logical order. For example, it would be much more difficult to grasp the meaning if the paragraph was arranged like this:

> The course includes such areas of study as People and Communications, Calculations, The World of Work, Elements of Data Processing and Retailing. He is studying for the Business Education Council General Certificate. Everard Wilson attends the College of Further Education on Thursdays. If he completes the course, he hopes to enrol for a National Certificate Course.

Anyone reading the first sentence of this paragraph would have no idea about which course or whom the writer was talking. This is why you should aim at a *logical development of ideas* i.e. they should follow each other in natural sequence, and be easily understood in the context of the paragraph. It is useful if the first sentence gives the reader some idea of what the paragraph is about, and because of this it is quite common to find the topic sentence at the beginning.

TASK TWO

Rewrite these short paragraphs, so that the ideas are presented in logical order, with the topic sentence at the beginning.

(i) They are often treated carelessly. Careful attention means fewer major overhauls. A typewriter is an expensive and complicated piece of equipment. Many people take them for granted and regard them as being expendable.

____

____

____

____

____

(ii) A dust cover should be put over the machine whenever it is not in use. This basket should be cleaned, together with the type faces. If any erasures have been made, it is obviously better if the rubber dust is prevented from falling into the basket. The chrome parts of the typewriter can be polished. Dust can be removed with a soft cloth or a long-handled brush. There are simple rules for daily care and maintenance.

(iii) The bearings on which the type bars run should be lubricated less frequently. As well as dusting, the typewriter needs oiling from time to time. The amount of oil used should be kept to a minimum. All joints and points of friction should be given attention. The oil used should be very fine and can be applied with a special brush or a needle.

(iv) If the typewriter develops any mechanical trouble, this should be dealt with by a specialist mechanic. An inexperienced hand could damage the machine even further. Such an expert will be able to identify the trouble quickly.

(v) However, even this sort of care is wasted if the typist does not treat her machine with care. This must be done by experts used to servicing such equipment. After a few years a machine needs to be stripped and cleaned. Regular overhauls mean less trouble.

In talking about paragraphs, as with most aspects of written communication, we must stress the importance of correct grammatical structures. *Always make sure that your sentences are complete, accurate and punctuated properly.* In the exercise below you are given some "jottings" on particular topics. There is no attempt to write sentences – only to give you an indication of the required content.

EXERCISE

Each of the following blocks of information should be expanded to form a coherent paragraph. You must write grammatically correct sentences, but the length of these sentences is left to your discretion. You should insert all the necessary words to create suitable grammatical structures, together with all punctuation. You can rearrange the material if you wish, as long as your final paragraph is logical and easy to understand.

(a) Savings banks: enable people to deposit relatively small sums for saving; modest rate of interest; withdrawn at short notice; some savings banks "secured" by the State, – e.g. Post Office Savings Bank, Trustee Savings Bank.

(b) Merchant banks: important business organisation; many started as merchants or traders; gradually moved to financing trade rather than actually trading themselves; many have long experience in trade and finance – some 150 years

(c) Functions of Merchant Banks – varied; one main one – accepting Bills of Exchange; also used to launch new issues of shares; other activities – foreign exchange business, loans for industry, acting as trustees, advising on investment. Some involved in London's gold market.

(d) Joint Stock Banks: aim – make profit for shareholders by performing banking services for customers; post-war – great increase in services offered; many have tried to increase customers by changing staid image; extensive advertising – press and television; hope to appeal to young people starting work as well as those with established incomes.

(e) Joint Stock Banks also serve industry and business; advances/loans, not long-term capital for plant or other assets; temporary provision of additional working capital; bank also can act as registrar for companies/local authorities who issue securities; handle formalities necessary for new issue, registration of transfers, payment of dividend and interest warrants.

You might have found the previous paragraph-writing difficult because much of the basic information was unfamiliar to you. Whether or not this is the case, the exercise will certainly have tested your ability to work out the general meaning of some fairly complex ideas, and organise information into cohesive and sensibly structured sentences. It is very different problem, of course, when you actually have to *write* a paragraph yourself on a particular topic. Not only do you have to be concerned with sentence structures, organisation and sequence, but you also have to think of what to write.!

EXERCISE

In this exercise you are given a number of topic sentences. The theme of each is debilerately general so that you can expand it in whatever way you find most interesting or suitable. There are no restrictions on the ideas you can introduce. You should choose any *three* of these topic sentences, and use them to introduce a short paragraph (60 - 100 words) of your own invention.

Obviously you should remember all the desirable qualities of a paragraph we have considered so far, e.g. correct sentence construction, accurate punctuation, logical development. The topic sentence must be an integral part of your paragraph.

(a) The customer is always right.
(b) The atmosphere in the lift was very tense.
(c) Education should be a process of preparation.
(d) His curiosity eventually got the better of him.
(e) Tact is an essential quality of business communications.

Having practised re-arranging and writing paragraphs, you are now ready to attempt some work on a complete essay. Before you write one yourself, you can spend a little time on *reading* a short composition which deals generally with a topic you will have become familiar with in Section I of this unit – Organisation Charts. You will be asked to complete an exercise based on this essay.

Organisation Charts

An organisation chart showing lines of authority and responsibility in a company can be of great assistance to management in improving the communications system and organising delegation of work. Many companies issue such a chart as part of their public relations or staff relations activities, in order to show clearly who is in charge of what aspects of the business.

The task of preparing a chart makes it possible for every section of an organisation to be brought under review, and the relationships of the sections to one another can be analysed and assessed. As well as this, the management are forced into considering the position of individual employees, and deciding exactly what authority should be delegated to each person in order to enable him to carry out his responsibilities. Each man should know his job, and the scope of all new jobs should be laid down.

As the size or activity of an organisation increases, it is essential that the senior people are relieved of many day-to-day responsibilities in order to concentrate on more important work. It is also necessary for the more junior employees to take on these responsibilities in order to gain some experience which will prepare them for the future. Such delegation is made easier if there is a recognised organisational structure, and the creation of an organisation chart is a major step towards analysing the organisation and establishing such a structure.

Organisation charts are thus an aid in many aspects of management. Where they do not exist, they should be prepared as soon as possible. It must be emphasised, however, that it is necessary for the organisation structure to be flexible enough to allow adjustment when the basic circumstances change.

Organisation charts are useful tools in management, and can be applied successfully, not only to the large organisation, but also to the small one.

(Adapted from *Business Communications*, Chapell and Read, Macdonald and Evans)

EXERCISE

Re-read the composition on "Organisation Charts" carefully, and produce a *plan* from which it could have been written.

EXERCISE

Construct a suitable plan and write an essay on each of the following subjects. You can use this workbook as your main source, or find other suitable sources in your college or public library. Your tutor will probably want to check each plan before your write the essay.

(a) Discuss the advantages and disadvantages of the economies of scale.
(b) What reasons might a government have for nationalising an industry?
(c) Compare and contrast the organisation of a partnership with that of a public limited company.
(d) Outline the obligations of the organisation to its employees.
(e) In what ways can an organisation obtain short to medium term finance in cash?

SUMMARISING INFORMATION

You have already had some experience of this type of work in Unit III, where your exercises in note making required you to *shorten* or *condense* blocks of information, and present them in a particular form. This gave you personal notes which are useful for reference and revision.

Then, in Unit IV you were given guidance on how to approach traditional comprehesion work, and some of the questions there asked you to *summarise* the author's ideas or themes. If you think carefully about this, you will realise that what you have been asked to do is *report* what the author said about a particular topic, *condense* or *shorten* it, and write it as far as possible *in your own words.* These activities, when put together, embody the main principles of summary (You might have heard the term *precis* used to describe the same sort of work).

Your ability to summarise information is one of the most important you can develop, because in business you must be able to pass on, briefly but accurately, information you have received. In its most simple form, you are making a summary when you tell somebody what you watched on the television last night, or what you have read in the newspapers, – you are reporting the essential facts. In a more formal situation you might be asked to summarise what happens at a meeting, what is contained in a series of letters, or what can be found in a particular report.

The word *report* has been used numerous times already in this part of Section III, and when talking about summary we should realise that it is one of the vital keys to success, because any summary you give will be in *reported speech.* This needs some explanation, so let us consider "speech" first of all.

When you actually say something to somebody you are using "direct speech". For example, you might say to a fellow student, *"I am going to the refectory at lunch-time."* As you can see, the actual words spoken are enclosed within inverted commas, which are used in written English to indicate a direct quotation. Now, if your fellow student wanted to tell somebody else what you had said to him, he could do it in two ways. He could either quote the exact words you used, or he could *report* what you said in this way:

He said that he was going to the refectory at lunch-time.

This is certainly not a direct quote, but it conveys exactly the same meaning. As we pointed out before, this method of reporting what has been said is essential if you are to summarise information competently.

TASK THREE

Imagine that you have overheard the following simple statements being spoken by one of your fiends. What would you say if you wanted to explain to another person what your friend had said? Do not use direct quotes, Start your answer by using the words given.

(i) "I was late on Tuesday."
Reported Speech: He said that ______________________________

____

(ii) "Where are you going this evening?"
Reported Speech: She asked him ______________________________

____

(iii) "It's nearly time to go home."
Reported Speech: He told her ______________________________

____

You probably found this task extremely easy. This is because it is designed to demonstrate a straightforward and commonly used process which most of us can complete quite naturally, and with little thought. There are, however, a number of identifiable techniques being used here, and it would be useful for you to have a working knowledge of them.

To transfer from direct to reported speech (sometimes referred to as *indirect speech*) you should bear in mind the following procedures:

(a) *Introduce the reported information with a verb of "saying"*

e.g. *Direct Speech:* "It's not my car."
Reported Speech: He *said* / He *claimed* / He *swore* } that it was not his car.

NOTE: Any suitable verb of "saying" can be used.

(b) *Verbs should be moved into the past tense, or one stage further into the past*

e.g. (i) *Direct Speech:* "I *have* lost my keys."
Reported Speech: She explained that she *had* lost her keys.
(i) Direct Speech: "I *watched* the concert on television."
Reported Speech: He said that he *had watched* the concert on television.

Sometimes a statement is made which cannot be moved into the past because it is regarded as always being true. In this case, the present tense can be retained.

e.g. *Direct Speech:* "The world *is* round."
Reported Speech: He explained that the world *is* round.

NOTE: It can be difficult to decide what part of the verb is required, and one of the main problem areas is with the use of the future tense. Normally you can assume that the words *shall* and *will* are changed into *would* in reported speech.

e.g. *(i) Direct Speech:* "I *shall* be catching the bus home tonight."
Reported Speech: *He said he would* be catching the bus home that night.
(ii) Direct Speech: "You *will* fall if you are not careful."
Reported Speech: She told him that he *would* fall if he was not careful.

(If you are not sure of the use of *shall* and *will,* you will find a full explanation in the last part of this section which deals with a number of common problem areas.)

(c) Pronouns should be changed in this way

I → he or she — we → they
you (singular) → he or she — you (plural) → they
The same applies to possessive pronouns:
mine → his or hers — ours → theirs
yours (singular) → his or hers — yours (plural) → theirs

e.g. *(i) Direct Speech:* "It is my duty to arrest *you*," said the detective.
Reported Speech: The detective said it was his duty to arrest *her*.
(ii) Direct Speech: "That wallet is *mine*," claimed the customer.
Reported Speech: The customer claimed that the wallet was *his.*

(d) When an adjective or adverb shows nearness of time or place it should be changed to show remoteness

today → that day — here → there
yesterday → the day before — this → that
now → then — tomorrow → (the next day) (the day after)

e.g. *Direct Speech:* "I'll meet you *here tomorrow.*"
Reported Speech: He told her he would meet here *there the next day.*

As you have probably noticed, it is not necessary to use a question mark when you transfer a direct question into reported speech. This is because the question mark is usually replaced by a verb of "asking".

e.g. *(i) Direct Speech:* "Where are you going?"
Reported Speech: I *asked* him where he was going.
(ii) Direct Speech: "How much is this watch?"
Reported Speech: He *enquired* how much that watch was.

TASK FOUR

Revise the procedures above carefully, and then rewrite the following short passages in reported speech. The name or designation of the person(s) speaking and spoken to is given in brackets at the end of each question.

(i) "I was admitted to hospital yesterday for an emergency operation, and shall be be unable to travel for another three weeks. Will it be possible for my flight reservation to be transferred to a later date?" (Mr. Gervaise on the telephone to a booking/travel agent.)

(ii) "The re-organisation of our offices has been the subject of an investigation by a firm of management consultants. They have made a number of recommendations that will result in a decrease in staff. I very much regret this, but it seems unavoidable in the present economic situation." (Manager speaking to trade union representative.)

(iii) "If we hope to be successful in the overseas market, we must bear in mind one further point. Any quotations we give in sterling will create serious problems because movements in the rate of exchange make it impossible to work out prices correctly. However, many of the foreign buyers will choose to deal with us in preference to other firms if we quote our prices in the local currency. Therefore I recommend that our catalogues and price lists should be printed in the language and currency of the area in which we hope to sell. I am confident that this would greatly strengthen our competitive position." (Sales manager to board of directors.)

The tasks involving the use of reported speech have been included to help you get used to some basic skills essential to good summary. We must now return to the main theme. As with other formal exercises in communication it is useful to adopt a logical approach to summary of any kind. Remember, you are expected to demonstrate that you *understand*, that you can *be selective*, that you can *use language competently*, and that you can *report accurately* what has been said or written without letting your personal attitudes or opinions creep in to the finished work.

General Approach

Stage 1: Read the complete original from beginning to end. This will enable you to grasp the overall theme so that you know what the author is talking about. If the original is difficult to understand read it again.

Stage 2: Identify your task. If you are attempting an examination question, read the question carefully; if you are carrying out a work-related procedure, make sure you know exactly what is required.

Stage 3: Read the original once more, and jot down any important points which are directly related to the question or job you are working on. At this stage you are being very selective, so you should

(a) Leave out
- (i) any supporting information which is not absolutely essential to an understanding of a main idea;
- (ii) any information which is not directly related to the main points you are trying to summarise;
- (iii) all comparisons;
- (iv) all repetitions;
- (v) all examples;
- (vi) inessential details;
- (vii) any descriptive passages; and

(b) Shorten: If there are any phrases in the passage which are important, but could be reduced to a single word, this should be done.

e.g. (i) The problems of the farms were bound to be worsened by such a *serious and widespread shortage of water.*

(ii) The problems of the farmers were bound to be worsened by such a *drought.*

TASK FIVE

Provide a *single word* which expresses the meaning of the phrases given below.

(i) fit to eat ____________________

(ii) unable to be seen ______________________

(iii) a case in which a knife is kept ______________________

(iv) a person who always sees the good side of things ______________________

(v) unable to be understood ______________________

(vi) alike in every detail ______________________

(vii) a fungous growth on a damp surface ______________________

(viii) pull or twist out of shape ______________________

(xi) unable to read ______________________

(x) a projecting tube or lip through which liquid is poured ______________________

TASK SIX

Shorten the following sentences by replacing a suitable part of them with a single word. In the original sentence underline the phrase you are replacing, and in your answer under the single word you have inserted.

(i) The students were told that they would have to produce a series of questions for obtaining information on special points as part of their assignment.

____

____

(ii) When he expressed doubts about the new profit the sales manager was told he was a person who always took a hopeless view of everything.

____

____

(iii) Mr Wilson decided to leave the country and settle overseas when he was told he was being made redundant.

____

____

(iv) The representative was told that he would receive a certain percentage of the total value of sales as well as his basic salary.

____

____

(v) The board decided that it was necessary to have a person appointed to act on their behalf in Hamburg.

____

____

Stage 4: Using your jottings from Stage 3 as a guide, write a rough draft of your final summary, aiming to stay within the specified number of words. Do not count your words individually at this stage -- you can estimate how many you have written by assessing how many words you put on an average line, and multiply this by the number of lines.

When you have completed this rough draft it must be checked thoroughly to make sure you have not added any information, altered the meaning of anything, or put in your own opinions. It is also important to ensure that your main points are presented in logical order and that there is a clear development of the theme.

NOTE: You will often find that if you can identify the topic sentence of a paragraph. this will summarise the theme. Glance back through your work on paragraphs to see if this is true.

Stage 5: Write out your final version neatly and clearly, paying particular attention to sentence structure, grammar, punctuation, fluency and paragraphing.

To help you remember the essential points a summary is given in the checklist below:

Do

(1) make sure you *know what is required*
(2) make sure you *understand the theme*
(3) select *essential points only*
(4) *arrange your ideas logically* so they make sense
(5) *leave out digressions, examples, comparisons, repetitions*
(6) *write in reported speech*
(7) *keep within the stipulated number of words*
(8) *use language which is* straightforward and *as simple as possible*
(9) *write in your own words* as far as possible
(10) *check your grammar, punctuation and spelling*

Do not

(1) add any information
(2) alter the meaning or emphasis of anything
(3) simply list a number of points
(4) give your own opinions

It is a fairly common thing in textbooks for the student to be asked to read a passage, and then read a specimen summary of that passage in the hope that he or she will identify understand, absorb and remember the techniques used in producing it. This, we feel, is a vain hope! There is only one way to master such techniques, and that is to *use* them. Although the next part of this section is entitled "Specimen", you are expected to be *involved.* If you read carefully you should be able to understand what is being done at each stage. The actual writing of the final summary is left entirely up to you. First of all, read the passage which considers one aspect of communication and human relations within the structure of an organisation.

Specimen

Within any business organisation there are established procedures to assist communication between management and staff. These procedures are usually systematic, which means that a certain sequence of activities is necessary in order to complete the communication process. However, such formal systems can never compare in value with informal contacts whereby a casual -- even unplanned – conversation can often solve a problem quickly and easily. The modern trend towards open-plan offices has certainly made a contribution to improving access to management, but this is not enough. The manager must make a deliberate attempt to encourage staff to discuss problems and difficulties with him, and must prove that he is really interested in them and their work.

The apparently insurmountable barrier between staff and management is one of the greatest causes of poor labour relations. The bigger the organisation, the more complex its structure, and the more difficult it is for this barrier to be overcome. It becomes necessary in some situations – such as multi-national companies – for a liaison officer to be appointed, with the sole task of improving or aiding communication. However, his job can be made extremely difficult when other employees know he hasn't got the authority of managers and tend to regard him as yet another obstacle to direct communication.

Personal contact between those who give the orders and those who take them is essential if friction is to be avoided. People like to think their employers are interested in them and care about their problems, and a genuinely sympathetic approach can stimulate a positive and beneficial response.

(approx. 260 words)

You have now completed *Stage 1* of the summarising process, and *Stage 2* is to identify your task. This is:

Summarise the main ideas of the passage in not more than 130 words.

As you move on to *Stage 3*, the task becomes more difficult because you have to start being selective. As with all note making, a recognisable system of presentation can be useful, so you should stick as closely to previous presentation methods as you can. Study the following notes carefully in conjunction with the original passage, paying particular attention to the way in which only the main points have been selected. For convenience, these notes are divided up to correspond to the paragraphing in the original.

PARAGRAPH I

(a) Formal Communications Procedures
- (i) present in any organisation
- (ii) designed to aid communication between management and workers

(b) Informal Communications Procedures
- (i) better – can solve immediate problems quickly and easily
- (ii) modern management should deliberately encourage such direct access, to show interest in employees.

PARAGRAPH II

(a) Barriers
- (i) formal procedures often regarded simply as barriers to communication
- (ii) the bigger the company, the bigger the problem

(b) Liaison Officers
- (i) some big companies try to solve problems by appointing liaison officers
- (ii) however, they are often regarded as yet another barrier by employees.

PARAGRAPH III

(a) Personal Contact

(i) essential to avoid friction

(ii) employees like to think managers *care* about their problems

(iii) a sympathetic personal approach can ensure good staff/management relations

EXERCISE

When you have studied these notes carefully, proceed to *Stage 4*, which requires you to write a rough draft of the final summary, basing it on the notes in Stage 3. This should be done on rough paper so that you can *make all the checks and adjustments necessary to fulfil the requirements of the task.* Make sure you write grammatically correct sentences, and stay within the specified number of words. When you have done this, and had your work checked by your tutor so that any last minute changes can be made, move on to Task Seven.

TASK SEVEN

Write you completed summary in the space below. You are allowed only fifteen lines, so you must write neatly and carefully, making sure you get eight or nine words on every line.

EXERCISE

Reduce each of the following short passages to approximately half their present length. Both passages have been adapted from *Modern Business Correspondence* by L. Gartside (Macdonald and Evans 1976).

(a) In any form of written composition the first paragraph should be in the form of an introduction, which must be interesting and indicate clearly what the subject of the composition is. It must be interesting because the aim of the writer is to capture the attention of the reader; and it must indicate the subject so that he knows what to expect. It is advisable to keep this introductory section as short as possible so that the reader does not feel his time is being wasted – if it is too long-winded he will quickly lose any initial interest he might have had. (102 words).

(b) The closing paragraph is just as important as the opening one. It can serve the function of summarising the preceding information and drawing any necessary conclusions. Like the first paragraph, it should not be too long, and the writers' aim should be to leave his reader with an impression of completeness and finality. He should be in no doubt that he has come to the end. Whether it is desirable to give a brief summing-up, an apt quotation, or a quick look into the future, doesn't matter – as long as the composition is brought to a suitable finish. (98 words)

EXERCISE

You will almost certainly find this piece of work difficult, and therefore it is arranged in a slightly different way. As you can see, there is a space on the right in which you can write brief explanatory notes. You should read the passage carefully and then make sure you understand it by asking your tutor to explain any difficult words, phrases or ideas. If necessary you can ask for each paragraph to be explained so that you can clearly grasp its meaning. Make any necessary notes in the space provided to help you remember what any particularly difficult sections mean. Your task is to *summarise the passage in not more than 200 words.*

NOTES

During this century much work has been done by study groups and research organisations on behaviour at work. In the beginning, much of the emphasis was put on the conditions in which employees had to perform their tasks, and many studies showed that improved conditions and machinery could lead to greater output per man-hour. There was little concern among most study groups – many of which were sponsored by industrial and commercial concerns – about the work itself. Social scientists were more concerned about whether the work was satisfying, meaningful and worthwhile.

Since the 1930s however there has been a gradual development of different attitudes and approaches, and more interest in what the man at the machine *thinks* about his job or what the worker on the assembly line *feels* about the work he is doing. As more and more information was collected and studied the evidence showed that there was a growing awareness amongst the work-force of the need for individuals to be interested in what they were doing. It was recognised that if a person was interested in and enjoyed the job he was doing, he would put more effort into performing it efficiently.

A lot of research and effort nowadays is devoted to examining and analysing work situations to see how they can be made more interesting for the worker. The aim is to *motivate* a person to work more efficiently by making sure the job being done provides a degree of satisfaction and a sense of fulfilment. Research has shown that in western industrial society one of the main reasons for dissatisfaction for the average worker is concern about promotion prospects, closely linked to a desire to achieve personal growth and development. The traditional belief that pay was all that mattered has given way to the pressures exerted by a restless workforce prepared to show its dissatisfaction. Motivation is now the key word.

In an ideal situation, motivated work is work that is *meaningful,* has obvious and recognisable benefits for society, is satisfying in its work content, and provides an individual with opportunities for planning, judgment and decision-making thus giving variety and leading the development of an active and well-balanced individual.

One of the problems for industry is that no matter how much effort is put into rearranging or redesigning jobs in order to provide a motivating work situation, the benefits are seldom apparent in the short-term. Company profits do not often immediately reflect the greater satisfaction of the work-force. However this is a course which must be followed with perseverence if stable industrial relations are to be a feature of a future economy. Industry and commerce must realise that, in the long term, any improvement in morale is likely to lead to greater keenness and interest in the job, less absenteeism and internal conflict, and, almost certainly, greater output. It is in the interest of all to "humanise" work.

WHAT'S WRONG WITH IT?

How often have you had to ask the question given in the title to this part of Section III? The time will come when you find you have made a simple mistake in grammatical construction or used a particular word incorrectly, and then have to ask, "What's wrong with it?" The purpose of the notes, explanations and examples which follow is to help you understand a few of the most common problem areas in written English.

TASK EIGHT

First of all, you are given some basic words which can cause confusion. A brief explanation of each is provided and then a space is left for you to insert an example showing how it should be used. However, *check the correctness of your example with your tutor before you write it in,* and make sure it is carefully presented because this part of the workbook will be useful as a reference section if you are ever in doubt.

Word	*Meaning*	*Example*
there:	(i) in that place	
	(ii) to that point	
they're:	contraction of "they are"	
their:	belonging to them	
where:	(i) at what place	
	(ii) to the place in which	
we're:	contraction of "we are"	
were:	past tense of the verb "to be"	
wear:	(i) to carry on the body, e.g. clothes	
	(ii) to become impaired by use	
weir:	a dam across a river	
to:	in the direction of, towards	

too:	(i) in additon	____________
	(ii) in excess	____________
two:	the number 2	____________
want:	present tense of the verb "to want" – to desire	____________
wont:	custom or habit	____________
won't:	*short for "will not"*	____________

EXERCISE

Write the following sentences, correcting them where necessary.

(a) "Wear are you going?" I asked.

(b) They spent most of they're time talking about computers.

(c) He decided to where a life-jacket while he was out in the boat.

(d) Their is a good deal of controversy about how to train systems analysts.

(e) The referee threatened too abandon the match because their was to much fouling.

(f) Their going to see too football matches on the same day.

(g) They went they're to see their relatives.

(h) "Two be, or not two be, that is the question."

(i) The police failed too arrest the two criminals.

(j) Six hundred workers were banned from doing overtime.

(k) "Where did I leave the car?"

(l) Their are two letters for you too read.

(m) Come to the South West weir the sun always shines.

(n) When the river was in flood, the water rushed over the were.

(o) We wear going swimming but it started two rain.

(p) The task was to difficult too be attempted by two people.

(q) It was so cold that they decided two where there overcoats.

(r) I think there going to look at the weir.

(s) They're were sixteen pupils in the class.

(t) Disc-brakes where very well as long as their put in correctly.

Some Basic Words and Phrases which cause Confusion

(a) *Due to:* This can be used after any part of the verb "to be".
e.g. His lateness *was due to* the fog.
Owing to: This can be used in all other cases.
e.g. *Owing to* the fog, he was late.

(b) *Between:* Used when talking of two subjects only.
e.g. The ball went *between* the posts for a goal.
Among: Used when talking of more than two subjects.
e.g. There was a fight *among* the supporters.

(c) *Each other* Used when referring to two things or people.
e.g. The two students complimented *each other* on their success.
One another: Used to refer to more than two things.
e.g. The members of the board discussed the proposal with *one another.*

(d) *Either:* This means any one of two.
e.g. I can kick the ball with *either* foot.
Any: This means any one of three or more.
e.g. I can meet you *any* day next week.

Shall and Will

The first thing you must realise when considering these two words is that the *future* tense can be split into two types:
(i) the simple future, i.e. a simple forecast of what is going to happen; and
(ii) the future with determination, i.e. implying that somebody will *make* something happen, no matter who tries to prevent it.
e.g. I *shall* be late tomorrow. (Simple forecast.)
I *will* go to the cinema tonight. (Determination, i.e. I *will* go whether or not you try to stop me!)

The reference frames below show how the use of "shall" and "will" changes, depending on which person the verb is associated with.

Simple Future

	Singular	*Plural*
1st	I shall	we shall
2nd	you will	you will
3rd	he / she / it } will	they will

Future with Determination

	Singular	*Plural*
1st	I will	we will
2nd	you shall	you shall
3rd	he / she / it } shall	they shall

Therefore, when you are trying to work out which of these two words you should use, you must decide first of all which of the future meanings you need– the simple future or the future with determination – and then whether you intend to write in the 1st, 2nd or 3rd person.

NOTE: The use of the words "should" and "would" is the same as for "shall" and "will": "should" corresponds to "shall" and "would" to "will".

TASK NINE

In the sentences below, the words *shall* and *will* are used correctly. Discuss with your tutor why that particular form of the future tense is required in each sentence, and then write a brief explanation in the space provided.

e.g. I *shall* telephone Walker and Co. tomorrow morning.

Explanation: A simple forecast of what is going to happen is being made by the speaker. The use of "I" shows that it is written in the first person.

(a) I *will* go to the meeting tomorrow even though it is being held during working hours.

Explanation: ________________________

(b) They *will* reconsider the case tomorrow.

Explanation: ________________________

(c) I *shall* be pleased to receive the stationery on Thursday.

Explanation: ________________________

(d) My mind is made up – he *shall* go.

Explanation: ________________________

(e) He claims that you *will* support his evidence.

Explanation: ________________________

Further and farther

A general distinction can be made between these two words by always using *farther* when speaking of distance.

e.g. (a) The representative had to travel much *farther* each day when his sales area was extended.

(b) Before the meeting closes I would like to raise a *further* point.

Agreement of the "relative"

A relative pronoun and its associated verb must *agree* with the word to which it is related. For example:

"He is one of those people who *is* always getting into trouble."

In this sentence the relative pronoun "who" is directly linked to "people" which is plural. Therefore, if its antecedent is plural, "who" must be plural, the thus the associated verb must be plural. The plural form of the verb "to be" in the present tense is "are" and therefore the original sentence should read:

He is one of those people who *are* always getting into trouble.

plural

Lay and lie

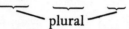

If you find these words confusing, remember that they are two completely different verbs

(a) "To lay" *is the type of verb which requires an object (i.e. you always lay something)*. It means: *deposit, set, cause to lie.* For example:

He laid *the document* on the table.

The verb is declined like this in its present and past tenses;

<u>*To Lay*</u>

Present tense		*Past tense*	
I lay	we lay	I laid	we laid
you lay	you lay	you laid	you laid
he / she / it } lays	they lay	he / she / it } laid	they laid

(b) *"To lie"* does not have to be followed by an object. It can mean: *recline, be horizontal, at rest;* or *make false statement.*

e.g. I *lie* in the sun as often as I can.

I wonder if he will *lie* in court.

The verb is declined like this in its present and past tenses:

<u>*To Lie*</u>

Present tense		*Past tense*	
I lie	we lie	I/we	lay (if you mean *reclined*)
you lie	you lie	you/you	
he / she / it } lies	they lie	he / she / it } /they	lied (if you mean *told an untruth*)

TASK TEN

This task is essentially a dictionary exercise, but with some of the terms you might find it more satisfactory to use other sources in your college library. The purpose of the task is that you should provide yourself with a glossary of common business terms for reference purposes. Give as full an explanation as you can for each term. It would be a good idea to write your answers in pencil in the first instance, so that you can alter your explanation if it is not accurate enough.

Advice note ____

____

Affidavit ____

____

Agenda ____

____

Agent ____

____

Arbitration ____

____

Articles of association ____

____

Assets ____

____

Auditor ____

____

Balance of payments ____

____

Balance of trade ____

____

Balance sheet ____

____

Banker's draft ____

____

Bonded goods ____

____

Broker ______________________________

____

Cartel ______________________________

____

Catalogue ______________________________

____

Chamber of Commerce ______________________________

____

Cheque ______________________________

____

Commission ______________________________

____

Consignment note ______________________________

____

Contract ______________________________

____

Cover(ing) note ______________________________

____

Credit note ______________________________

____

Current account ______________________________

____

Debit note ______________________________

____

Delivery note ______________________________

____

Del credere agent ______________________________

____

Deposit account ______________________________

____

Depreciation ______________________________

____

Discount ______________________________

____

Dividend ______________________________

____

Endorsement ______________________________

____

Freight ______________________________

____

Goodwill ______________________________

____

Inflation ______________________________

____

Insolvency ______________________________

____

Insurance ______________________________

____

Interest ______________________________

____

Inventory ______________________________

____

Invoice ______________________________

____

Jobber ______________________________

____

Lease ______________________________

____

Liabilities ______________________________

____

Limited liability ______________________________

____

Liquidator ______________________________

You will be given the opportunity to expand this glossary of business terms in Book Two.

SUPPLEMENTARY EXERCISES

(a) Revise your previous work on prepositions, and then write sentences using the following phrases:

superior to	responsible for	a substitute for
deficient in	responsible to	in deference to
coincide with	correspond to	correspond with

(b) This is an exercise in combining sentences and improving written style. The following letter should be rewritten in a suitable style. Use any methods you think are appropriate to turn this into a presentable and efficient piece of business communication.

Dear Sir,

Thank you. We have receive your letter. We have also received the consignment of goods. These were the goods you despatched to us. They arrived on the 14th.

We have to make a report. We regret this. Certain of the items were damaged. The damaged items were three rugs. They were damaged in transit. They had come by rail. There were other rugs. There were also rolls of carpeting. These other goods had been subjected to ill-treatment. They were dirty. Some were dirtier than others.

We are concerned about the three rugs. These are our main concern. They are seriously damaged. They are damaged to such an extent as to make them unsaleable. Other items are not so badly damaged. These could be cleaned. This should not affect their value. This involves expenditure. We have a feeling. Such expenditure should be your responsibility.

This has proved inconvenient. Much time has been wasted. We have customers. These customers have been waiting for some rugs. They have been waiting a long time. We hope you will replace the damaged rugs. This should be as soon as possible. We look forward to hearing from you. Please inform us of the action you intend to take. Yours faithfully,

(c) Change the following direct questions into indirect speech.
It might be useful for you to read through the previous work you have done on this.

(i) "Where are you going?" we asked them.
(ii) I said to him, "How much did you pay for your car?"
(iii) "What is the price of this book?" he said to the assistant.
(iv) "Do you want tea or coffee?"
(v) "Did you ring the bell?"

(d) Form nouns from the following words, and then include each of your answers in a sentence to show that you understand its correct use.

able deceive know renew clean

(e) Form adjectives from the following words, and then include each of your answers in a sentence to show that you understand its correct use.

adventure value trouble anxiety sympathy

(f) Form verbs from the following words. Give the infinitive of the verb, and then use any part of that verb in a sentence of your own to show you understand its meaning.

circulation solution proof critic friend

CROSS MODULAR EXERCISE

(A) Read the following extract which has been adapted from the third edition of *Business Administration* (Macdonald and Evans 1979) by L. Hall. The extract explains the internal structure of one type of organisation.

FORMULATION OF POLICY

Definition. The policy of a business undertaking is a statement of its primary objective, accompanied by a directive indicating the general pattern to be followed to secure its implementation.

Sectional policies. The policy of top management is communicated to the lower levels of management only in general terms. At that point it branches off into the separate secional policies of the respective managers, by whatever name they are called. Although these "managers" must work together as a team to implement the general policy, each of them is individually responsible for his own sectional policies. In a large manufacturing company, the most important of these sectional policies (considered separately below) are: *(a)* financial, *(b)* marketing, *(c)* production, *(d)* personnel.

Financial policy. In formulating financial policy, consideration must be given to the following:

(a) *Capital.* Initially, a decision must be made concerning capital requirements, and in what form and from what sources capital is to be obtained. If we take a public limited company by way of example, the promoters must decide:

(i) what the company's authorised (or nominal) capital shall be (this must be stated in the company's memorandum of association);

(ii) how much of that authorised capital it will be necessary to issue initially;

(iii) if the shares are to be offered to the public, by what method – by prospectus, offer for sale or "placing";

(iv) what classes of shares are to be offered, if it is decided to offer more than one class;

(v) what other forms of finance it is int

(v) what *other* forms of finance it is intended to employ (e.g. debentures, loan stock, etc.) originally or at a later date.

(b) *Working capital.* At all times care must be taken to ensure adequacy of working capital. This will permit the company to meet its everyday commitments and work to optimum capacity.

(c) *Capital expenditure.* Prior to a company's incorporation, the calculation of its capital requirements must, obviously, take into consideration fixed assets. If, for example, the company has been formed to acquire an existing business, the purchase price of that business must be included.

(d) *Revenue expenditure.* Requirements to meet expenditure on materials, labour and all other forms of revenue expenditure must also be calculated.

(e) *Credit.* Capital requirements may be influenced very considerably by decisions affecting the giving and receiving of credit; for example, the wholesaler in most trades would be expected to afford comparatively long-term credit facilities, whereas the retailer in the same trade may, himself, sell only on a cash basis. If credit *is* given and received, there must be adequate control and to that end, the following are subsidiary to the financial policy:

(i) The setting up of a credit control system, to reduce bad debts and standardise the system for debt collection, etc.

(ii) The earning of all cash discounts, by prompt payment of accounts.

Marketing policy.

(a) *The broad policy* of any manufacturing business will state in general terms what it intends to produce and hopes to sell. It will, for example, make it clear that it is intended to produce machine tools and not electrical components. If, however, the policy is to succeed, considerable thought must be given, and many decisions taken, by the marketing director (or manager) and others responsible for its implementation.

(b) *The main considerations* upon which a working marketing policy may be based include:

(i) Profit planning. Where a budgetary control system is employed, the whole structure of the budget and, therefore, of the policy may be based upon a planned profit.

(ii) Sales volume. In order to achieve that profit, the volume of sales must be estimated. This may introduce many problems which, in a large organisation will require considerable market research.

(iii) Market research. A thorough study of the market will provide answers to most of the problems. Properly conducted, the research will reveal the present and future trends of the market.

(iv) Sales promotion. Having ascertained the market potential, planning must be then directed towards promoting sales to the level necessary to earn the planned profit. In order to acheive this objective, advertising, public relations and perhaps other subsidiary policies will be formulated and treated as the separate responsibilities of managers within the marketing group.

(v) Sales. The selling and distribution of the goods produced are usually treated as a separate department; that is, they are usually separated from the public relations and sales promotion (or advertising) departments. They are, nevertheless, an essential part of the marketing team, and will probably be responsible to a marketing manager or marketing director.

Production policy. The planning of production is based upon the facts of the market research and the figures of the sales budget; therefore, the broad policy of the production department is to keep pace with the requirements of the sales organisation. To meet these requirements, production must be carefully planned and controlled. How this is achieved depends upon the size of the organisation, the processes employed and the end product; in general, however, some or all of the following are taken into consideration in formulating a production policy.

(a) *Volume of production* required, stated in specific terms and/or as a percentage of possible production capacity.

(b) *Design.* The design of the product is probably influenced by the results of market research.

(c) *Production planning of:*

(i) material requirements;
(ii) labour requirements;
(iii) machines, tools and other equipment required.

(d) *Production control.* Various control arrangements may be planned as part of the overall production policy, including:

(i) control of labour efficiency;
(ii) quality control;
(iii) control of the progress of orders.

Personnel policy

(a) This section of the overall policy is closely allied to one of the primary functions of management namely *motivation.*

(b) *The aims* of a sound personnel policy are:

(i) to maintain an effective, contented and adequate working force at all levels, capable of implementing the other sections of the overall policy;
(ii) to close the gap between management and employees by providing adequate means of communication, so as to ensure that employees are made aware of policy decisions promptly;
(iii) to provide conditions of employment calculated to increase efficiency, give encouragement towards maximum effort, and minimise friction.

(c) Responsibility for interpreting the personnel policy is usually in the hands of the personnel officer or personnel manager.

(d) Content. In formulating a personnel policy, provision must be made for the following:

(i) *Recruitment;* that is, using the appropriate sources of recruitment for particular jobs.
(ii) *Selection and placement* of employees, an aspect of personnel policy which is now being considered more carefully and handled more scientifically by enlightened employers.
(iii) *Training.* The personnel policy might well include training, as many employers are now providing their own training schemes, or permitting employees to undertake external day-release or "sandwich" courses.
(iv) *Wages.* No personnel policy would be complete without a wages policy. It will deal with the general wage structure for the production departments and the salary structure for the administrative staff.
(v) *Promotion.* If the training policy is to succeed, opportunities for promotion must be offered. In conjunction with any promotion scheme, a system of merit rating may be introduced.
(vi) *Welfare.* The management must decide what welfare facilities it is prepared to provide. Nowadays, most employers are expected to provide these and various "fringe benefits" on a generous scale. They are, in any case, now required by the Employers' Liability (Compulsory Insurance) Act 1969, to insure employees for bodily injury or disease sustained during, or arising out of, employment.
(vii) *Health and Safety.* Apart from any voluntary efforts on the part of the employers to maintain reasonable health and safety standards, they must conform to the provisions of the current Factory Act, the Offices, Shops and Railways Premises Act 1963, and the Health and Safety at Work Act, 1974.
(viii) *Redundancy.* Recent legislation has compelled employers to include this as part of their personnel policy although it must be acknowledged that many employers were already making provision for redundancy of employees before it became mandatory in the industries affected.
(x) *Joint consultation.* The personnel policy may also provide machinery for joint consultation, as this provides a very useful means of management-employee communication.

(B) Use your dictionary, and provide appropriate definitions of the following terms: (a) Prospectus; (b) Budgetary; (c) Subsidiary; (d) Implementation; (e) Formulate; (f) Personnel; (g) Motivation; (h) Minimise; (i) Enlightened; (j) Mandatory.

(C) Using the information in the original extract, relate the responsibilities of the personnel manager and the chief accountant in a manufacturing organisation to their counterparts in the department store. You should aim to write a paragraph of not more than ten lines to explain the responsibilities of each of the above in the department store organisation.

(D) The incomplete table below shows the turnover in this department store during one year.

Annual Turnover		
	Turnover	*Total*
Mens wear: Men's Boys'	 800,000 400,000	*
Ladies' fashions: Women's Girls' Children's	 1,600,000 600,000 200,000	*
Household: Furniture Floor covering Hardware	 400,000 275,000 225,000	*
Electrical: Radio and T.V. Appliances	 200,000 400,000	*
Haberdashery		150,000
Household textiles		300,000
Footwear		150,000

You are required to:

(*a*) complete the sub-totals marked by an asterisk;
(*b*) find the total turnover for the year;
(*c*) express each sub-total as a percentage of the total turnover;
(*d*) construct a pie chart to show the turnover for the store and the seven departments.
(*e*) The store is subsequently taken over by a group who set new sales targets for the seven departments. If for each of these the turnover is increased by

Mens wear	7½%	Haberdashery	2½%
Ladies' fashions	5%	Household textiles	3%
Household	3%	Footwear	6%
Electrical	8%		

calculate the new turnover for each department and for the store as a whole.

Index